THE POLITICS OF THE VISIBLE IN
ASIAN NORTH AMERICAN NARRATIVES

Examining nine Asian Canadian and Asian American narratives, Eleanor Ty explores how authors empower themselves, represent differences, and re-script their identities as 'visible minorities' within the ideological, imaginative, and discursive space given to them by the dominant culture. In various ways, Asian North Americans negotiate daily with 'birthmarks,' their shared physical features marking them legally, socially, and culturally as visible outsiders and, paradoxically, as invisible to mainstream history and culture.

Ty argues that writers such as Denise Chong, Shirley Geok-lin Lim, and Wayson Choy recast the marks of their bodies and challenge common perceptions of difference based on the sights, smells, dress, and other characteristics of their hyphenated lives. Others, like filmmaker Mina Shum and writers Bienvenido Santos and Hiromi Goto, challenge the means by which Asian North American subjects are represented and constructed in the media and in everyday language. Through close readings grounded in the socio-historical context of each work, Ty studies how authors and filmmakers meet the gaze of the dominant culture and respond to the assumptions and meanings commonly associated with Orientalized, visible bodies.

ELEANOR TY is a professor in the Department of English and Film Studies at Wilfrid Laurier University.

The Politics of the Visible in Asian North American Narratives

ELEANOR TY

鄭綺寧

UNIVERSITY OF TORONTO PRESS
Toronto Buffalo London

ISBN 0-8020-8831-7 (cloth)
ISBN 0-8020-8604-7 (paper)

Printed on acid-free paper

National Library of Canada Cataloguing in Publication

Ty, Eleanor, 1958–
The politics of the visible in Asian North American narratives / Eleanor Ty.

Includes bibliographical references and index.
ISBN 0-8020-8831-7 (bound)   ISBN 0-8020-8604-7 (pbk.)

1. Canadian prose literature (English) – Asian Canadian authors –
History and criticism.   2. American prose literature – Asian American
authors – History and criticism.   3. Asian Canadians in literature.
4. Asian Americans in literature.   5. Chinese Canadians in motion
pictures.   I. Title.

PS8089.5A8T9 2004   C818'.540809895   C2003-905794-1

University of Toronto Press acknowledges the financial assistance to
its publishing program of the Canada Council for the Arts and the
Ontario Arts Council.

This book has been published with the help of a grant from the Canadian
Federation for the Humanities and Social Sciences, through the Aid to
Scholarly Publications Programme, using funds provided by the
Social Sciences and Humanities Research Council of Canada.

University of Toronto Press acknowledges the financial support for
its publishing activities of the Government of Canada through the
Book Publishing Industry Development Program (BPIDP).

Contents

Acknowledgments

For enlightening conversation, encouragement, and friendship, I am indebted to Patricia Chu, Rocío Davis, Donald Goellnicht, Roy Miki, Marie Lo, Karlyn Koh, Sarita See, and Rhacel Parreñas. Authors Wayson Choy, Hiromi Goto, Shirley Lim, and Cecilia Brainard were kind enough to share ideas and partake of food with me at some point during the writing of this book. Denise Chong graciously allowed me to use her photographs in chapter 1. They are reproduced by permission of Denise Chong.

The work was greatly facilitated by a Research Grant from the Social Sciences and Humanities Research Council of Canada. Wilfrid Laurier University gave me financial support in the form of Initiatory Grants, Travel Grants, Book Preparation Grants, and Short Term Research Grants. I have used the libraries and media collection at the University of Toronto, the University of California, Berkeley, and the University of California, Los Angeles. I am grateful to these institutions and their efficient librarians and staff.

At the University of the Philippines, Diliman, I had useful discussions with Lily Rose Tope, Cristina Hidalgo, and other members of the Department of English and Comparative Literature. I enjoyed the hospitality of Benjamin Lim and William and Helen Sia in Manila. In Vancouver, my aunt, Lily Lim Yap, gave me immeasurable support.

Parts of this book have appeared in print before. Chapter 1 was published in *English Studies in Canada* (2002) 28.2. Chapter 2 was published in a special issue of *Lit: Literature Interpretation Theory* (2001) 12.3 on Asian American Literature and Culture, Part II, edited by Karen

Chow. Copyright (2001) from 'A Filipino Prufrock in an Alien Land: Bienvenido Santos's *The Man Who (Thought He) Looked Like Robert Taylor*' by Eleanor Ty. Reproduced by permission of Taylor and Francis, Inc. <http://www.routledge-ny.com>.

The book has benefited from suggestions made by anonymous readers from SSHRC, the University of Toronto Press, the Aid to Scholarly Publications Program, and particularly from rigorous comments made by my editor at University of Toronto Press, Siobhan McMenemy.

I owe much to my colleagues in English, Film Studies, and Women's Studies at Wilfrid Laurier University for making my daily life such a pleasure. Special thanks go to my commuting friends Lynn Shakinovsky and Maria Dicenzo for lively discussions on the 401. I learned much from my graduate students in my course on Asian Writers in the Diaspora taught in the fall terms of 1999, 2000, and 2002. Finally, my gratitude to my mother, Vicenta Ty, and my loving and supportive crew at home – David, Jason, Jeremy, and Miranda Hunter.

Preface

I begin this book with a recollection of an amusing, though somewhat disconcerting, experience, familiar, I think, to many Asian American and Asian Canadian academics. It has occurred a number of times when I happen to mention my occupation to those whom I encounter for the first time. This little narrative about my fields of specialization reveals much about contemporary cultural assumptions regarding race and location. When I tell people that I work at a university as a professor, they are always rather astonished that I am in the English department (rather than in math or business, I suppose). Although we like to believe that in today's progressive society there is no longer this kind of 'prejudice' or stereotype about Asians, these reoccurrences reveal the presence of deep-seated and unarticulated social stigmas about the place of racialized subjects. Asian Americans and Asian Canadians have come to be associated with certain areas (engineering, computers) but not traditionally with others (English, history, or European languages). Those of us who are in the latter areas encounter various reactions – wonder, disbelief, discomfiture, sometimes awe – and still have to work harder than unracialized subjects to prove ourselves to our colleagues, our students, and the larger community. Current academic discourses about employment equity and minority recruitment have improved conditions somewhat, but wearing the mantle of the other in the academic world is not without its encumbrances. In the early years of my career, when I told people that I worked in late-eighteenth-century literature, I often got a surprised and puzzled reaction: 'Oh ...' and then a short silence. It got to the point that I unconsciously began avoiding discussion and disclosure about my occupation and area of specialization, especially in the company of strangers. Often, the initial silence is followed by curiosity: 'Who are the writers? Are they British?' Or worse, 'Is the eighteenth century during Shakespeare's time?' or 'Do you work on *Jane Eyre*?' Fortunately, now when I tell them I work on Asian Canadian and Asian American writers, I do not get the same surprised reaction. People still ask silly questions, like, 'Do they write in English?' But the difference is that most people nod understandingly when I speak of Chinese Canadian authors or give such names as Amy Tan or Denise Chong.

The point that I am raising with this anecdote is related to what I call 'the politics of the visible.' As I am Asian, and look Asian, people expect me to work on and teach in certain areas. The most familiar images are the Asian computer wizards and math geniuses. And if one is not in computers or math, the next possibility is ethnic specialization, work in minority culture, and the like. Just as my position as a racialized subject was somewhat confusing to others when I was working in eighteenth-century literature, ironically, I am now in a privileged position of being perceived as the 'native informant' in Asian Canadian and Asian American literature. It is rather ironic, because although being Asian Canadian, and having spent the first fifteen years of my life in Asia, does put me in a position of some knowledge, giving me an edge over the non-Asian, the field of Asian American studies has grown so much in the last twenty years that being 'native' has only really put me in the starting gate. There is now a considerable history of Asians in North America along with cultural, national, and religious particularities of countries with vastly different histories, such as Japan, mainland China versus Taiwan, British-colonized Hong Kong, North and South Korea, the Philippines, India, Pakistan, Sri Lanka, and Vietnam, which do not come 'naturally' to any native. One has to immerse oneself in these histories in much the same way as one has to do research about Georgian England.

In critical terms, what does it mean to shift locations, to move from doing work on late-eighteenth-century British women writers to contemporary Asian North Americans? For me, in spite of obvious differences in the two fields, I think my earlier background in reading eighteenth-century literature has provided me with a very good set of theoretical tools and paradigms with which to approach contemporary Asian North American writers. One could say that I have simply relocated sensibilities. That eighteenth-century notion of 'sensibility,' which

Johnson defined as a 'quickness of perception of sensation, and delicacy,' was prized not only by eighteenth-century women, but is present
in many Asians. Taiwanese American filmmaker Ang Lee, director of
films such as *Crouching Tiger, Hidden Dragon* and *Eat Drink Man Woman*,
had never read Jane Austen before he directed *Sense and Sensibility*. But
when asked in an interview about how comfortable he was with late-
eighteenth-century British culture he simply said, 'Jane Austen is very
Chinese.' There's a certain amount of truth in this.

My first two books were on how women novelists of the 1790s
negotiated with the period's prevailing notions of gender, identity, and
female selfhood. In *Unsex'd Revolutionaries: Five Women Novelists of the
1790s* (1993), I studied the novels of radical thinkers Mary Wollstonecraft,
Mary Hays, Helen Maria Williams, Elizabeth Inchbald, and Charlotte
Smith. These novels challenged Edmund Burke and other conserva-
tives' notion of the benevolent patriarch, and questioned existing ideas
about female education, the rights and 'wrongs' of woman, and the
duties of a wife. In *Empowering the Feminine: The Narratives of Mary
Robinson, Jane West, and Amelia Opie, 1796–1812* (1998), I discussed the
ways in which three women of different ideological and social backgrounds empowered themselves and politicized the sentimental novel
without necessarily breaking with cultural definitions of the feminine.
They redefined female subjectivity by demonstrating how qualities of
the feminine, such as sensibility, propriety, chastity, and feeling, could
have potency and pleasure, and could effect social change. In both
books, my readings, though grounded in the historical, social, and
literary contexts of the late eighteenth century, were informed by post-
structuralist and feminist theories about the construction and formation of the subject.

Though contemporary Asian American and Asian Canadian writers
seem very distant from the world of eighteenth-century British women,
there are some interesting parallels between them. Mary Wollstonecraft,
Mary Hays, and Charlotte Smith often made comparisons between the
subjugation of women and that of racial others, such as Turkish women
and African slaves. My point is that, like eighteenth-century women,
Asians in North America have historically been feminized and
marginalized, by governmental policies, by exclusion laws, by immigration quotas. In late-nineteenth-century and early-twentieth-century
America, Asian men had to take on domestic duties because of the lack
of women in the country. 'China men' suffered 'legalized humiliation
and degradation ... at the hands of the dominant race' (Goellnicht 193).

Male and female Asian bodies were seen to be 'feminine,' often sexualized and exoticized. Lisa Lowe has argued that since the mid-nine-
teenth century, for the European, the Oriental woman 'generates sexual
pleasure, yet she is impassive, undemanding, and insensate herself; her
oriental mystery never fails to charm' (*Critical Terrains* 76). Today, Asian
men and women make up a large proportion of service and domestic
labourers – nurses, orderlies, nannies, busboys, and waiters on cruise
ships. In addition, the growth of the sex trade industry in developing
countries such as Thailand and the Philippines is bolstered by this
perception of the willing and hypersexualized Asian body.

Femininity, docility, passivity, mystery, delicacy, dangerous sexuality
– these qualities, which were ascribed to women in the eighteenth
century, have now been mapped onto Asian identities and Asian bodies. Women and Asians/Orientals function as the other, whom the
dominant androcentric Anglo-European culture uses to construct its
own subjectivity. In his work on the Near East, Edward Said notes that
'orientalism' is 'not so much a way of receiving new information as it is
a method of controlling what seems to be a threat to some established
view of things' (*Orientalism* 59). Feminist theorists, who have explored
positions of the subject in the psychosymbolic order to the greatest
degree, point out that such processes of projection and exclusion have
been integral to the formation of the subject. Postcolonial theories have
similarly developed notions of otherness, mimicry, the performativity
of ethnic identity, and abjection. Culturally, women and racialized others both function as the threatening other. Judith Butler has argued that
'the exclusionary matrix by which subjects are formed thus requires the
simultaneous production of a domain of abject beings, those who are
not yet "subjects," but who form the constitutive outside to the domain
of the subject' (*Bodies* 3). Butler's observations about gendered identity
apply equally well to racialized subjectivity, as race and gender and
other categories operate simultaneously. Robert Lee points out that 'the
Oriental as a racial category is produced, not only in popular discourse
about race *per se* but also in discourses having to do with class, gender
and sexuality, family, and nation' (7).

To complicate matters, Chinese and Filipinos have culturally specific
traditions that contribute to their complicity in their figuration as an
'Oriental' and feminized other. Asian 'deferential' reflexes are a product of 'repression as well as of custom' (Woodside 47). Confucian teaching emphasizes unquestioned obedience to parents, elders, and other
figures of authority, which lends credence to the stereotype of passivity

and docility, while Chinese culture's valorization of delicacy and little-ness in women add confusion to the image of dangerous Asian femi-ninity. Filipinos, who experienced centuries of Spanish colonial rule followed by a half-century of American imperialism, have internalized a sense of their own inferiority, what Nilda Rimonte calls 'that burden of persistent self-hate' which 'produces an acute, destabilizing, discom-fiting self-awareness, akin to that situation in which one feels ashamed, *nahihiya*' (41–2). As well, extreme impoverished conditions, unemploy-ment, and the lack of a stable national government have contributed to the fantasy of the power of Euro-Americans and other foreign cultures. Filipinos and Filipinas working as agricultural and service labourers in Asia, the Middle East, and America have had to adopt servile, eager-to-please attitudes in order to survive. As E. San Juan, Jr, puts it, Filipinos have been transformed into the 'ideal self-regulated subjects' not just because of 'their Americanization through language, but with it their internalizing of a decorum of submission – an imaginary relation to the real conditions of existence – which at the minimum guaranteed sur-vival' (*Philippine Temptation* 37). That is why Leny Mendoza Strobel insists on the return of Filipino Americans to 'indigenous conscious-ness,' to a 'reconstructed identity' that 'replaces the obsequious, infe-rior identity which before had no conscious access to its own strength and integrity' ('Born-Again Filipino' 125, 126).

Though these areas are centuries and worlds apart, and entail contextualization and historicizing, in both fields I ask many of the same questions. What happens when the marginalized or the subaltern tries to speak? In eighteenth-century novels, heroines who possessed sensibility were more sensitive to the plights of those in distress and those in need, were more attuned to the beauties of nature, and so forth. Writers were able to harness this quality and use it to bring attention to the marginalized or dispossessed. For their part, Asian North American writers not only have to contend with the stereotypes prevalent in Euro-American culture, but also have to deal with 'the more subtle ways that a dominant culture presents the minority Self with a wide range of seemingly positive modes of inclusion into its body of repre-sentations while simultaneously subordinating the minority subject to the logic of the Other's Symbolic' (Palumbo-Liu, 'Minority Self' 76). David Palumbo-Liu argues that the 'political unconscious of minority subjects' includes 'the cultural authority of the Other' ('Minority Self' 79). Culturally constructed notions of race, ethnicity, and gender be-come 'embodied knowledges' that operate 'largely below the level of consciousness' (Bottomley 307). When the Asian minority speaks, it needs to reclaim that space that 'has hitherto been obscured by the action of epistemic violence and culpable ignorance' (Varadharajan 138). Asha Varadharajan notes that the 'paradox of this space is that it is simultaneously empty and overdetermined' (138).

What I've tried to illustrate very briefly is how my methodologies in this study resemble, and differ from, those I've employed in earlier studies. In my work on late-eighteenth-century literature, I talked about representation and rescripting ideology. When Asian Canadians and Asian Americans engage in the process of 'returning the gaze' of dominant culture (Bannerji), they are also faced with the task of re-presenting, that is, to present again through filmic or textual narratives what has misrepresented. They have to 're-orient' and 'dis-orient' contemporary and prevalent myths of the Orient. At times, this entails a self-splitting of abject qualities – the backward and superstitious, the 'yellow peril,' and fetishized blossoms as depicted in literature, art, and film (see Jeffords, Kellner, Ling, Marchetti, and Wong). In their attempts to rewrite and re-present their subjectivity, they have recourse to myths, to personal and collective memories, to oral narratives, and to recorded as well as unrecorded history. For this reason, much ethnic writing was initially autobiographical. Betty Bergland notes that ethnic autobiographies are political because they are 'representative of the group' and because they also 'provide an image or symbol' (77). This representation of difference, however, is not the 'reflection of *pre-given* ethnic or cultural traits,' but 'on-going negotiation that seeks to authorize cultural hybridities' (Bhabha 2). David Eng reminds us that our political identities are not the same as our psychic identifications. He writes that 'to understand that identification is the mechanism through which dominant histories and memories often become internalized as our own – is to understand that we are all borrowers and thus not pure. It is to underscore that our social identities as well as our political intentions are not irreproachable, that political agency while a necessary goal must be continually interrogated for its slippages, thought of more as a variable process than a permanent position' (26).

My project is not meant to be a survey of Asian Canadian and Asian American literature. It presents readings of selected texts that actively engage with issues of otherness, visibility, and identification. Many of the narratives I examine are very much in the process of negotiation, working out how larger issues of representation, power, and history affect Asian North American subjectivity. Much work has been written in the last decade, especially by Asian American scholars. I hope my book contributes to the ongoing conversation started by Amy Ling, Elaine Kim, Shirley Geok-lin Lim, Sau-ling Cynthia Wong, King-Kok Cheung, Lien Chao, Epifanio San Juan, Jr, Lisa Lowe, David Leiwei Li, Robert Lee, Traise Yamamoto, Donald Goellnicht, Roy Miki, and others, from whose research I have benefited.

THE POLITICS OF THE VISIBLE IN
ASIAN NORTH AMERICAN NARRATIVES

Introduction

The dominant imprint I have carried with me since birth was of a Malaysian homeland. It has been an imperative for me to make sense of these birthmarks; they compose the hieroglyphs of my body's senses. We tell stories to bind us to a spot, and often the stories that make us cry knot the thickest ropes.

Shirley Geok-lin Lim, *Among the White Moon Faces*

Skin, as the key signifier of cultural and racial difference in the stereotype, is the most visible of fetishes, recognized as 'common knowledge' in a range of cultural, political and historical discourses, and plays a public part in the racial drama that is enacted every day in colonial societies.

Homi K. Bhabha, *The Location of Culture*

I was your house. And, when you leave, abandoning this dwelling place, I do not know what to do with these walls of mine. Have I ever had a body other than the one which you constructed according to your idea of it? Have I ever experienced a skin other than the one which you wanted me to dwell within.

Luce Irigaray, *Elemental Passions*

In one way or another, Asian North Americans deal daily with what Shirley Geok-lin Lim calls 'birthmarks.' There are visible hieroglyphs imprinted on our eyes, our black hair, our noses, our faces, and our bodies, the resonance of another tongue, the haunting taste of another culture, as well as the perception, real or imagined, of being from another place. As Asian Americans and Asian Canadians, these hieroglyphs, along with our yellow or brown colour, mark us indelibly as other, as Oriental, as exotic, subservient, mysterious, deviant, or threatening.[1] It is not simply skin, as Bhabha has noted in the case of blacks, that is fetishized, but a set of bodily markings, which include particular accents, a way of moving, culinary habits, and other cultural practices that are fetishized as Asian and which contribute to the shaping of our subjectivities.[2] What I call 'the politics of the visible' starts with the visual – a set of bodily attributes that has been represented in our culture as 'Asian,' filmic and pictorial representations of the Oriental – but moves beyond the visual to social, legal, political, and historical spheres. Some of these bodily attributes, such as our hair colour, the crease of our eyelids, the shape of our noses, can be changed,[3] just as certain Asian habits, such as acknowledging an elder person in the room by a small bow, showing courtesy to others at the dinner table by not taking the biggest piece of meat on the plate, and so on, can be unlearned. But these physical signs and cultural practices together create what we think of as 'Asian,' and in many ways influence what I identify as Asian North American sensibility.

Paradoxically, the politics of the visible is also about our invisibility. Until the last two decades or so, Asians have been almost invisible in mainstream North American public and cultural spheres. Our economic contributions and labour have not been made evident; our stories do not make prime time TV shows, and the distinctions between us are often effaced and overlooked. Historian Jun Xing notes, 'Despite their long (more than 150 years) and often dramatic history in the United States, the Asian American story remains virtually unknown to the average American' (18). In *Obasan*, Joy Kogawa laments, 'We are those pioneers who cleared the bush and the forest with our hands, the gardeners tending and attending the soil with our tenderness, the fishermen who are flung from the sea to flounder in the dust of the prairies' (112). We have lived in and been part of North America for centuries, but have remained in the shadows.

We have been invisible, yet we have been branded as 'visible' and minor. In Canada, the term 'visible minorities' was coined by the Canadian government under the Liberal leadership of Pierre Trudeau in the 1960s and 1970s to designate those persons, 'other than aboriginal peoples, who are non-Caucasian in race or non-white in colour.' Asians belong to this designated group, which differentiates racial minorities –

blacks from various parts of Africa, West Indians, Chinese, Japanese, Filipinos, Indians, Pakistanis, Sri Lankans, Koreans, Vietnamese, and so on – from ethnic minorities, such as Italians, Greeks, Ukrainians, Russians, Serbo-Croatians, and so on.[4] This term, aligning Asian Canadians with blacks, is most often used in governmental and legal discourses, in studies about employment, immigration, and labour. For example, visible minorities matter in the Employment Equity Act, in the Canadian census, in literature about multiculturalism. It has become a widely accepted term, but it was not, initially, a politically motivated nomenclature, unlike terms such as 'woman of colour,' Asian American, or African American.[5]

In the United States, racial politics plays out slightly differently.[6] In the twentieth century, and up until recently, American media and culture tended to refer to white and black America, leaving Native Americans, people from the Middle East, Southeast Asia, South Asia, and Mexico out of the generalization about races.[7] In his essay 'Is Yellow Black or White?' Gary Okihiro notes the 'construct of American society that defines race relations as bipolar – between black and white– and that locates Asians (and American Indians and Latinos) somewhere along the divide between black and white' (63). Okihiro observes:

> The marginalization of Asians, in fact, within a black and white racial formation, 'disciplines' both Africans and Asians and constitutes the essential site of Asian American oppression. By seeing only black and white, the presence and absence of all color, whites render Asians, American Indians, and Latinos invisible, ignoring the gradations and complexities of the full spectrum between the racial poles. At the same time, Asians share with Africans the status and repression of nonwhites – as the Other – and therein lies the debilitating aspect of Asian-African antipathy and the liberating nature of African-Asian unity. (75)

This disciplining has worked well, as studies outlining the similarities between African American and Asian American histories and culture, as Okihiro suggests, have been slow to emerge (see Cheung, '"Don't Tell,"' and Cheng).

As Asians in North America, we seem to be caught between the Scylla and Charybdis of categories and naming. By the official label, 'visible minority,' one is marked as racially different, rendered obvious, vulnerable, non-major. Though the term 'visible minority' was created to promote equity and diversity in hiring practices, it has the unintended, or perhaps the surreptitiously intended, effect of rendering all those cultures that are not European in origin marginal, as conspicuously minor against something that is articulated as dominant.[8] Himani Bannerji points out that, 'unlike the radical alternative political-cultural activists, the Canadian state was careful not to directly use the notion of color in the way it designated the newcomers. But color was translated into the language of visibility. The new Canadian social and political subject was appellated "visible minority," stressing both the features of being non-white and therefore visible in a way whites are not, and of being politically minor players' ('Paradox' 545). In America, as Okihiro points out, by not being included in the sweeping categories of black and white, Asian Americans, like Latinos, are not named, therefore invisible and, at times, rendered inconsequential in governmental policies and public discourse. Though 'visible minority' is not an official term in the United States, categories of black, white, Asian, and Hispanic are still very much predicated on the visible, or what David Palumbo-Liu has described as the 'physical sign' of otherness (*Asian/American* 86).[9]

To view this type of classification in another way, we could say that the Canadian government's system of classification is based on the modern episteme, while that of the United States is based on the older, classical episteme. In *The Order of Things*, Michel Foucault points out that in the classical age, roughly 1650–1800, systems of classification, such as Linnaeus's studies, were based on appearance. Plants were classified according to the structure, composition, and arrangement of their parts.[10] To talk about people in the United States as black and white follows this system of classification based on the pigmentation of one's skin. But Foucault stresses that what is visible is already a representation – it is given a meaning though language, through description. Of botanical gardens and natural history collections, Foucault notes that their importance 'does not lie essentially in what they make it possible to see, but in what they hide and in what, by this process of obliteration, they allow to emerge' (*Order* 137). Similarly, Palumbo-Liu argues that it is because of the physical sign that 'racial others are so "condemned" to "abstraction." Their physical difference renders them inaccessible *except* as a mental construct; racial phenotypology casts Asians into the realm of ideology' (*Asian/American* 86). This is consistent with Euro-American historical practices since the late seventeenth century. Similarities between European Americans and Africans were deliberately obfuscated, while their difference in skin colour, the visible sign of variation, was highlighted in order to justify slavery and the slave trade.[11] Even after abolition, this system of classification lingered in people's minds, and was one of the forces behind segregation in the United States and apartheid in countries such as South Africa. While Michael Omi and Howard Winant see this biological type of classification of races as the initial stage in the history of discourses on race difference (14–15),[12] other scholars, like Ruth Frankenberg, point out that such a paradigm shift has not occurred universally, as this kind of thinking can still be found 'in today's literature on race and racism in the United States and in the rhetoric of activists both for and against racism' (15).

In contrast, by classifying non-Caucasians – Nigerians, Ethiopians, Chinese, Filipinos, Indians, etc. – who do not look physically similar into one large group called 'visible minorities,' the Canadian government operates on slightly different assumptions. People are not categorized simply according to the visible, despite the term, but according to function. Foucault notes that from the end of the eighteenth century onwards, to classify 'will no longer mean to refer the visible back to itself, while allotting one of its elements the task of representing the others; it will mean, in a movement that makes analysis pivot on its axis, to relate the visible to the invisible, to its deeper cause, as it were, then to rise upwards once more from that hidden architecture towards the more obvious signs displayed on the surfaces of bodies' (*Order* 229). Foucault points out that 'henceforth, character resumes its former role as a visible sign directing us towards a buried depth; but what it indicates is not a secret text, a muffled word, or a resemblance too precious to be revealed; it is the coherent totality of an organic structure that weaves back into the unique fabric of its sovereignty both the visible and the invisible' (*Order* 229). In representing people of diverse origins and appearances as 'visible minorities,' the Canadian government organizes its citizens, its immigrants, according to the roles it believes they might play in society. Though this kind of classification ostensibly seems to be more progressive, as it is no longer predicated on race, it is more insidious and based on a hierarchy of cultures still dependent on visibility – who looks and does not look white or European.[13] Thus, mainstream Canadian society is an organic structure premised upon the privileging of the Caucasian. Implicitly, what is also assumed is that there is a coherence or organic similarity that links together non-Caucasians, who are people of very diverse backgrounds.

By comparing the two related but different modes of ordering Asian

Americans and Asian Canadians, I am trying to show the roles played by the visible and the physical in the construction of categories and differences. In both countries, what generates the classification and ordering of things is still predominantly appearance or the scopic drive. Though thinking about race has shifted and changed over history, to a large extent, visibility is still the basis for discourses about difference. Ruth Frankenberg notes of the consequence of this for white people: 'while discursively generating and marking a range of cultural and racial Others as different from an apparently stable Western or white self, the Western self is itself produced as *an effect of* the Western discursive production of its Others' (17).

The markings on our body have provoked from the dominant culture an array of responses that are predictable and overdetermined. Our Asian appearance continues to play a large role in determining how others read our identities, and it shapes, in ways both tangible and intangible, relations between Asian North Americans and non-Asians, as Frankenberg points out, and even relations between Asian Americans and Asian Canadians. The concern of mainstream North American culture with surface appearance is a lingering problem, and one that faces Asians and minority groups today. Consider the following e-mail, an inquiry sent in the spring of 2001 to the Asian American Studies list serve. It illustrates my point about America's obsession with the visible and the resulting problems with identity:

Hi all,

This question is not just a linguistic anthropological one, but maybe you will still have useful input. I am trying to help a student find literature that will help her illuminate her own highly complex identity. Her father is from Thailand, her mother from the Philippines. She grew up in the U.S. Her parents chose to teach her as little as possible about Thai or Filipino culture/language. So she speaks only English, and throughout her childhood regarded herself as simply 'American' – just like the other kids in the largely white upper middle class suburb where she grew up. However, she experienced the contradiction that other people often saw her as 'Asian' due to her appearance.

From this student's point of view, not speaking the first languages of her parents is a central aspect of her purely 'American' identity. But the way others react to her appearance has led to an almost DuBoisean double consciousness. My question is, is there a literature on this kind of issue?[14]

The student's 'American' identity seems invisible to the people around her; they can only react to the Asian hieroglyphs on her body. Their reading of her body becomes embedded in her subjectivity, contributing to the sense of double consciousness. As David Palumbo-Liu notes, 'concepts like "shame," "fear," and "pride" (i.e., those concepts that are the fabric of social, intersubjective being) have no meaning for us without the Other to confirm them ... We live fear, shame, pride, etc., only in seeing ourselves objectified by the Other; we can no longer freely assert a phenomenological Self, but are ontologically situated in being, transferred from "being-for-itself" to "being-in-itself"' ('Minority Self' 77). To use Irigaray's musings about woman that I used in the epigraph, this student could ask: 'Have I ever experienced a skin other than the one in which you wanted me to dwell within?'

In this case, as in the situation of many racial minorities, the student's feelings are akin to those expressed by the protagonist in Ralph Ellison's *Invisible Man*.[15] The invisible man feels that people around him cannot see beneath the surface, which renders him invisible; as he explains, it is 'a matter of the construction of their *inner* eyes, those eyes with which they look through their physical eyes upon reality' (3). People only see what they have been ideologically and culturally accustomed to perceiving and understanding, or, as Stuart Hall has observed, 'how things are represented and the "machineries" and regimes of representation in a culture do play a *constitutive*, and not merely a reflexive, after-the-event, role' (254). In our contemporary culture, a girl with Asian features cannot be 'American' but must be something else, must necessarily be other. David Palumbo-Liu links this pathology of the schizophrenic to the 'sense of being watched' (*Asian/American* 300). He points out that 'the ontological grounding for racial duality is produced by the fact that the racial subject is at once marginal *and* central, like *and* not like. The very fact that he or she can imagine being looked at *just so* means that his or her alienation is predicated upon a sense of difference installed *prior* to the act of self-consciousness – he or she has already internalized the dominant's point of view' (*Asian/American* 300).[16] The labelling or recognition of her identity thus has to be seen as a kind of misrecognition. Smaro Kamboureli writes: 'this identification entails a double recognition: recognition of the way ethnic subjectivity has been historically inscribed, and recognition of the fact that those historical designations involve misrecognition' (105).[17]

In Freudian psychoanalysis, the scopophilic drive, along with the oral drive, the anal-sadistic drive, the drives for cruelty, mastery, and knowledge, and the phallic drive are all constituents of the libido (Brennan 138). The obsession with the visible or the scopophilic is linked to voyeurism and exhibitionism. In 'Three Essays on the Theory of Sexuality,' Freud notes that 'visual impressions remain the most frequent pathway along which libidinal excitation is aroused,' but this pleasure in looking can become a perversion if it is restricted to the genitals, connected with disgust, or if instead of being *'preparatory* to the normal sexual aim, it supplants it' (251). Elizabeth Grosz points out that scopophilia has 'direct links to the desire for mastery (i.e. the conversion of the position of passivity in activity) and the desire to know (epistemophilia)' ('Voyeurism' 147). As I see it, the tendency in North America to mark and name people of colour is a manifestation of these drives that take pleasure in watching, in being able to master and to know the other. Teresa Brennan argues that 'the significance of scopophilia is that it is a means for formalizing the distinction between the subject and other people (as well as the fact that sight stimulates sexual desire)' (155). The 'distinct visualization of the other is a means for mastery in itself' (Brennan 155). In Orientalist texts,[18] in Hollywood films about the Orient, and in pornography featuring 'Oriental girls,' we have perverted forms of scopophilia. Scopophilia, along with the West tendency to orientalize the East, as well as factors such as poverty and overpopulation in Asia, accounts for much of the contemporary phenomenon of sex tourism in countries like Thailand, mail-order brides from the Philippines, and the like.[19] In my study of works by Asian North Americans, I argue that the ambivalent claims and powers of visibility create tensions and disturbing positions for authors who attempt to represent difference without falling prey to Western scopophilic fantasies. To resist the visible and the pleasures of scopophilia, to resist performing typically Oriental or ethnic roles without rejecting the everyday little acts that constitute one's self, become some of the biggest challenges of self-representation.

Articulating a similar problem in viewing and representation, in *The Four Fundamental Concepts of Psycho-Analysis*, Jacques Lacan has noted that 'what is profoundly unsatisfying and always missing is that – *"You never look at me from the place which I see you"* and conversely, *"what I look at is never what I wish to see"'* (103). For Lacan, 'in this matter of the visible, everything is a trap' (93) because vision always manifests as a 'labyrinth' where various fields intersect (*Four Fundamental Concepts* 93). In the constitution of the self, Lacan stresses that the subject not only looks at an object and simultaneously reproduces this object as an image, but the subject is also 'constituted as object by the Other' (Rose 190). Lacan uses two intersecting triangles to depict this relationship:

> ... in the scopic field, the gaze is outside, I am looked at, that is to say, I am a picture.
>
> This is the function that is found at the heart of the institution of the subject in the visible. What determines me, at the most profound level, in the visible, is the gaze that is outside. It is through the gaze that I enter light and it is from the gaze that I receive its effects. Hence it comes about that the gaze is the instrument through which light is embodied and through which – if you will allow me to use a word, as I often do, in a fragmented form – I am *photo-graphed*. (*Four Fundamental Concepts* 106)

Kaja Silverman explains, 'It is Lacan's way of stressing that we depend upon the other not only for our meaning and our desires, but also for our very confirmation of self. To "be" is in effect to "be seen" ... the subject is never "photographed" as "himself" or "herself," but always in the shape of what is now designated the "screen"' (*Threshold* 133). As Asian North Americans in the contemporary Western world, we are determined by the gaze or 'photograph' of dominant culture, but as I will argue in the following study, in turn, we can also intervene in the politics of this gaze, in the politics of the visible. One hears comments like 'Oh, what do you expect, they're Asian' or 'She's Chinese, I see.' What exactly is being explained is not articulated, but the assumptions act as a screen that very often supplants and mediates the constitution of Asian North Americans as subjects. Thus, what is gleaned by the visible marks on the Asian body places the spectator in a position of knowledge, mastery, and power. All the authors in this project attempt to disrupt visible signs dealing with the expectations of being Asian Americans or Asian Canadians, whether these are physical or cultural, thereby reinscribing the marks etched on their corporeal selves. They reciprocate the gaze and destabilize the set of meanings commonly associated with their Asian bodily features. By highlighting the means by which they are represented or 'photo-graphed,' they begin to shift the unequal balance of power that accompanies such structures and representations.

The chapters that follow examine the ways in which a selected number of Asian North American authors explore this large issue of the visible. In my use of the term, the 'politics of the visible' deals with the effects of being legally, socially, and culturally marked as 'visible,' and, paradoxically, with the experience of being invisible in dominant culture and history. In this study of nine Asian Canadian and Asian American narratives, I examine how these authors and filmmakers reinscribe their visibility and negotiate the dominant culture's mark on the Asian North American subject. Writers like Denise Chong, Shirley Geok-lin Lim, and Wayson Choy rescript the hieroglyphs of their bodies by reworking people's perception of difference as revealed in the sights, smells, dress, and other textures of their hyphenated lives. They reveal aspects of themselves that are not readily seen by the gaze of the other. Others, like Mina Shum, Bienvenido Santos, and Hiromi Goto, challenge the means by which the Asian North American subject is represented and constructed in the media and in everyday discourse. For other novelists, the act of dealing with the secrets of one's family and articulating one's desires becomes conflated with the larger concerns of one's community, and the politics of the nation.

In their re-presentations, the authors often have to juggle the identities and selves that emerge through the available, though sometimes competing, discourses of their ethno-cultural traditions, Asian and Euro-American notions of femininity and masculinity, good citizenship, the media, and popular culture. My study shows how selected novelists, auto/biographers, and filmmakers empower themselves and represent their various identities within the ideological, imaginative, and discursive space given to them by the dominant order. My view is that despite the seeming freedom and 'fluidity' of contemporary postmodern culture, minority authors are still, in many ways, circumscribed by interpretations, by the images and symbolic practices of the dominant order. Charlie Chan and Madame Butterfly are not necessarily dead.[20] Instead, they have been relegated to the dark realms of the unspeakable and the unconscious. At the same time, in reinscribing the meaning of the visible markings on their bodies, the authors succeed in making visible to the public or to historical records the experiences and stories of those who have heretofore been invisible to majority culture.[21] I have chosen texts that grapple in central ways with the logic of what seems; with the way in which the ethnic identity of the protagonists has to be reinvented or reconfigured against the expectations generated by the gaze of the other. They negotiate how differences are perceived through the odours and appearance of food, through clothing and its concomitant symbols of gender and class, through sex and sexuality, and through language and accent. What a number of these authors do is to recreate selves that have been effaced by the screen of the visible. For some, writing, producing a film, or telling a story becomes a struggle to avoid disappearing into oblivion; for others, it is a way to deal with the various selves that have been called into existence through spectacles of otherness, or through what Kristeva has called the powers of horror (1982).

Historical Reasons for Invisibility

As historians have noted, Asians have been present in North America for over 150 years (Takaki 3; Peter Li 3). Yet up until the last two decades or so, their presence in historical, cultural, political, religious, and literary spheres has been negligible. It is worth comparing the situations of Asians in the United States and Canada here to show the fascinating similarities in the contradictory and discriminatory practices of the two countries, what Lisa Lowe calls 'immigrant acts' (*Immigrant Acts* 6). Histories of Asian Americans and Asian Canadians are usually discussed separately, and their juxtaposition here reveals many noteworthy comparisons. The point of this review is to give a historically based explanation for the condition of invisibility today.

Before 1965 in the United States and 1967 in Canada, when immigration policy changed, Asian immigration to North America had been tightly controlled. Asian immigrants who came in the second half of the nineteenth century and at the beginning of the twentieth century had principally been miners, plantation workers, and contract labourers (see Sucheng Chan, *Asian Americans* ch. 1; Peter Li 20). In the 1850s, Chinese were lured to California and British Columbia because of their gold rushes. Between 1865 and its completion some four years later, many Chinese labourers were recruited to build the first transcontinental railroad in the United States, a project that 'employed more than 10,000 Chinese workers at its peak, many of whom were former miners' (Sucheng Chan, *Asian Americans* 30). Other work performed by the Chinese, and later the Japanese, along the Pacific coast in the second half of the nineteenth century included harvest labour, farming of labour-intensive vegetables, strawberries, and other small fruit, and factory work. The Chinese also operated laundries and restaurants, which enabled them to find an economic niche in towns and cities of the Midwest and along the Atlantic seaboard (Sucheng Chan, *Asian Americans* 32–3). In Canada, after the mining period of the 1860s and 1870s, between 1881 to 1884, it is estimated that about 6,500 Chinese were employed directly by contractors to build the western section of the Canadian Pacific Railway (Peter Li 21). After the completion of the CPR, many of these workers were discharged and took up casual employment in British Columbia's logging, mining, farming, and canning industries (Peter Li 22). From 1885 to 1909, most of the Japanese who came were unattached male peasants who took up fishing in Steveston or farming in the Fraser and Okanagan Valleys (Adachi 18). They also supplied cheap labour, sometimes underbidding Chinese labourers (Adachi 31). As Ronald Takaki, Sucheng Chan, Peter Li, and others have all noted, during this period a combination of exclusionary laws, discriminatory taxes, boycotts, hostility, and labour exploitation confined Asians to low-status menial work and reduced them to second-class citizens.

The United States and Canada mirrored each other in the way their governments and communities both made use of and yet discriminated against Asians in this period of the late nineteenth and early twentieth centuries. Sucheng Chan has identified seven categories of hostility against Asian immigrants: 'prejudice, economic discrimination, political disenfranchisement, physical violence, immigration exclusion, social segregation, and incarceration' (*Asian Americans* 45). For example, in 1875, the U.S. Congress passed the Page Law to forbid the entry of 'Chinese, Japanese, and Mongolian contract laborers, women for the purpose of prostitution, and felons' (*Asian Americans* 54). Chinese exclusion was extended in 1892, 1902, and 1904. On their part, the Japanese government consented to a Gentlemen's Agreement in 1907 whereby it would stop issuing passports to labourers. Attempts to stop the influx of Asian Indians culminated in the 1917 Immigration Act, while the strict Immigration Act of 1924 later barred entry of 'aliens ineligible to citizenship' to the United States, effectively preventing Chinese, Japanese, and other Asians who were ineligible for naturalization from immigration (*Asian Americans* 54). Filipinos were the exception because they were 'wards' of the United States after it colonized the Philippines in 1898. Filipinos, called 'nationals,' could enter America when other Asians could not (Lowe, *Immigrant Acts* 181). However, their entry, too, was curtailed by the Tydings-McDuffie Act of 1934, which promised independence to the Philippines but limited Filipino immigrants to the United States to fifty persons per year (Sucheng Chan, *Asian Americans* 54–6).

In Canada, according to Peter Li, 'Anti-Orientalism was exceptionally strong in British Columbia, where the Chinese tended to concentrate before 1900' (31). Before the enactment of the Chinese Immigration Act of 1885, there were numerous provincial attempts to disenfranchise the Chinese through special taxes or levies. As early as 1875, British Columbia had passed legislation to bar them from voting in provincial and municipal elections (Peter Li 32). By 1885, after the completion of the CPR, the first federal anti-Chinese bill was passed in the form of a head tax of fifty dollars imposed on all persons of Chinese origin entering the country. This head tax was raised to one hundred dollars in 1900 and to five hundred dollars in 1903. In 1923 the Canadian Parliament passed the Chinese Immigration Act, 'the most comprehensive legislation to prevent Chinese from entering the country and to control those already here' (Peter Li 34). Under the act, the only Chinese who could enter Canada were members of the diplomatic corps and children born in Canada to Chinese parents. It also stipulated that every Chinese person in Canada be required to register with the government. Initially, the Japanese, who were reputed to be 'highly civilized' and 'clean and frugal,' were viewed more favourably than the 'undesirable' and 'unclean' Chinese (Adachi 42). But by 1900, there were petitions to the Governor General of Canada to prohibit all 'Orientals' from entering Canada (Adachi 43).

Aside from official acts that made it difficult to enter North America, Asians who were in the United States and Canada at this time were subjected to violence and aggression. Often bereft of legal protection, the lives of early Chinese miners, for example, were not valued. Many were injured and killed, and records were not kept. A number were murdered because of racial fear and hatred (Sucheng Chan, *Asian Americans* 48). Chan documents outbreaks of anti-Chinese violence in a number of towns in the 1870s and 1880s, some of that were linked to economic crises and industrial upheavals that were occurring at the time (*Asian Americans* 53). Takaki records that Chinese, Japanese, and Korean newcomers to San Francisco were often pelted with bricks or rocks in the first decade of the 1900s (73). Later, a small outbreak of bubonic plague in 1900 became the reason for the cordoning off of San Francisco's Chinatown (Takaki 57). Every house in Chinatown was 'washed from garret to basement with lime, while gutters and sewers were disinfected with sulfur dioxide and mercury bichloride' (Takaki 57). From the late nineteenth century until well into the 1930s, Chinese children in the San Francisco area were barred from 'white' schools, and had to attend 'Oriental School' or schools set up for black children (Sucheng Chan, *Asian Americans* 58). Similarly, in Canada there were frequent outbursts of racial hostility against the Chinese and the Japanese. Serious riots occurred in Vancouver in 1887 and again in 1907 in which crowds vandalized the Chinese quarters and intimidated the Chinese to prevent them from competing for jobs with white workers (Peter Li 35). The 1907 riot was one of the largest anti-Asiatic demonstrations in the history of British Columbia. There were skirmishes reported between the white mob and not only the Chinese, but also the Japanese when the crowd swept into 'Little Tokyo.' People from the Asiatic Exclusion League were waving banners with slogans such as 'Stand up for a white Canada' (Adachi 72–3). After the riot, the Chinese went on an unofficial strike, while the Japanese worked a half-day (Adachi 76). Peace was restored, partly with the help of Mackenzie King's Royal Commission into property losses, but the riot resulted in the first concrete voluntary restriction of Japanese immigration (Adachi 81). Other anti-Asian sentiments can be seen in efforts to segregate the small number of Chinese children who were attending public school in Victoria in 1901, 1908, and 1922.

Because of the restrictive immigration laws, Asian immigration to North America between the 1920s and the Second World War, the period known as the exclusionary era, was almost halted. Those Asians who were already in Canada and the United States faced discriminatory labour practices – they were only allowed to work in menial jobs, and were paid less than their white counterparts for the work they did perform (Peter Li 48–56). For a great number of men, their social and familial lives were put on hold as their families were not allowed to join them. In California as in British Columbia, workers were not encouraged to bring their wives.[22] Labour recruiters wanted unattached male workers who were able to survive rough conditions. Under these harsh conditions, Asian workers felt that they could sustain their families in their homelands cheaper than they could in the United States (Sucheng Chan, *Asian Americans* 104), while the fifty-dollar head tax imposed on the Chinese in Canada prevented many from bringing women to the country. The early Chinese community in Canada predominantly consisted of married 'bachelors' who sent remittances to support their families in China (Peter Li 63; Sucheng Chan, *Asian Americans* 104). Many of the pioneer Chinese female immigrants were poor girls who had been sold into prostitution. These historical and political factors created a skewed and imbalanced community of Chinese men in North America, which has been represented in novels such as *China Men* by Maxine Hong Kingston and *Disappearing Moon Café* by Sky Lee. For example, in the United States in 1890, and in Canada up to as late as 1911, the sex ratio stood at 27:1 (Sucheng Chan, *Asian Americans* 106; Peter Li 67). It is not surprising that such a community could not integrate well with the rest of American or Canadian society. As Peter Li argues, it is not that Chinese immigrants were 'unwilling to identify with the host society because of a sojourner orientation,' but rather because the discriminatory practices, societal prejudices, and attenuated familial situations 'produced feelings of alienation, which in turn would have encouraged allegiance and attachment to the homeland' (64).

Before the outbreak of the Second World War, the Japanese fared somewhat better than the Chinese in this respect. While the first Japanese immigrant women were also prostitutes, they were later outnumbered by wives who were allowed to enter the United States and Canada. Married men could send for their wives, while bachelors could either return to Japan to get married, or else asked their relatives to find them brides. The last category of women, known as 'picture brides,' went through wedding ceremonies with absent grooms, had their names entered into their spouses' family registers, applied for passports, and sailed for America to join husbands they had never met (Sucheng Chan, *Asian Americans* 107). Though the influx of these picture brides was controlled, it nevertheless allowed for the Japanese in the United States and Canada to form families (Adachi 91). Sucheng Chan notes that the number of Korean, Filipino, and Asian Indian women who immigrated at this time was smaller. The sex ratio of Filipinos in 1920 was about 19:1. Filipino men were able to marry American women in states that did not have anti-miscegenation laws. A number of them settled in Chicago by 1930 and worked for the Pullman Company as stewards in railroad club cars. Because there were hardly any Asian Indian women in the United States before the Second World War, several Asian Indian men married Mexican women in southern California, producing children who were called 'Mexican-Hindus' (Sucheng Chan, *Asian Americans* 109).

Children of these immigrants in the United States had difficulty finding jobs commensurate with their education and training. They were encouraged to become farmers or merchants, rather than to enter into white-collar jobs. Many of the Chinese in Canada kept their families in China, where the cost of living was lower. When the children grew to working age, they often followed in their fathers' footsteps and sought work in Canada. Thus, the separated family helped the Canadian state reproduce another generation of cheap labour (Peter Li 76).

Because Japanese women were allowed to enter Canada as picture brides until 1928, there was a much more stabilized family life for the Japanese, which led to a network of institutions, shops, schools, churches, restaurants, mutual aid, and prefectural societies (Adachi 107). The Japanese, diligent and industrious, established themselves in the fishing industry, in lumber milling, and in pulp and paper production. By the 1920s, resentment against the Japanese was growing. In 1922, British Columbia asked the federal government to be allowed to pass a resolution prohibiting 'Asiatics' from acquiring proprietary interests in agricultural, timber, and mining lands or in fishing and other industries (Adachi 140). The Fisheries Commission recommended that licences issued to 'other than white British subjects and Indians' be cut by 40 per cent, and by another 15 per cent in 1925. The BC government also passed the Male Minimum Wage Act of forty cents an hour, which effectively restricted Asian employment because the Japanese were receiving not more than twenty-five cents an hour at the time. The act was eased in 1934 after complaints from employers who needed cheap labour.

These examples of exclusionary acts and legislation against Asians are by no means exhaustive. I have reviewed them in order to remind us of the different types of discriminatory practices that faced Asians in the late nineteenth and early twentieth centuries. As my brief survey shows, there were a number of parallel situations in Canada and the United States that contributed to the marking, or rendering visibly other, of the Asian subject in North America. Lowe titles her 1996 book *Immigrant Acts* to commemorate and name the 'immigration exclusion acts that restricted and regulated the possibilities of Asian American settlement and cultural expression' in this period up to 1965 (7). Peter Li calls these discriminatory acts against the Chinese 'institutional racism' because it was 'systematic and legal, and its practice was rationalized by an ideology stressing the superiority of white over non-white' (37). Li explains that 'Institutional racism involves social institutions that give a sustained meaning to superficial features of "race" and use "race" as the justification for disqualifying subordinate members of society from equal participation. In such cases racism is articulated as both a racist theory and a discriminatory practice, and its continuing manifestation in social institutions lends a false legitimacy to the use of "race" as a socially acceptable criterion for differentiating between individuals and groups' (37). The discriminatory practices against Asians worked and were intended to work in the same way as segregation did for blacks after the American Civil War. Alan Nadel contends that 'the South rather accommodated the guilt of failure by merely segregating the sign of that failure – the ostensibly free slave – making it an otherness, removing it into silence and invisibility in much the way that, in the preceding century, Europe segregated the mad' (11). Asians in North America were similarly segregated through these immigrant acts and rendered silent and invisible by not being allowed full participation in society.

Through these acts and bills that name the 'Asiatic' and the 'Oriental,' immigrants from different parts of Asia – Chinese, Japanese, Asian Indians, Filipinos, and Koreans – were constituted into a body, and into a threatening other. Frequently used as scapegoats in times of recession and economic difficulty, Asians in North America were forced to see their foreignness through these efforts to control and disempower them. Even as they resisted and challenged specific attempts at curtailing their work and rights, they saw themselves through white people's eyes, through British and European North Americans' modes of classification. It is through the controlling gaze of the white people already settled in North America that Asians entered into legal and social existence as subjects. Repeatedly hearing themselves labelled as alien and other, they became scarred by the obsessions and paranoia of European America and Canada. Like the newly liberated slaves in the American South, Asians were free, yet their rights to work, to own fishing licences, land, or small businesses, or to re-enter the country could be revoked at any time. The uncertainty affected women as well as men. Sucheng Chan notes, for instance, that an untold number of Chinese women in the early part of the twentieth century 'lived under a virtual reign of terror' fearing arrest and deportation. Immigration laws passed in the United States in 1903, 1907, and 1917 enabled immigration officials to judge and deport Chinese prostitutes ('Exclusion' 132). From 1923 in Canada and 1924 in the United States, naturalization of Asians was a slow and difficult process. Their physical features made them targets of racial slurs, violence, and hostility. These same features not only forced them to work at menial and low-paying jobs, but made many of them resign themselves to the fact that all they were allowed to do in the white man's land was to provide cheap labour.

Exclusionary acts that barred the entry of Asians, and legislation that prevented their votes, required them to register with the government, and created special rules for their businesses, all functioned to keep the Asian in North America in his or her place. These acts, along with the disparaging ideology of 'Mongolians' (which later included Malayans) as an inferior race, created the 'docile' worker – virtually a sexless and impotent machine.[23] In order to continue to maintain this white caste structure, a system of surveillance was created to keep Asians in North America in a secondary place. The constant attempts to regulate the activities of Asians – their work, their bodies, their sexuality, their social lives – suggest the volatility of the situation and the potential threat of the Asian man or woman stepping out of place. Asians in North America had to be 'disciplined' to order and morality not through force or confinement, though that was to happen to the Japanese during the Second World War, but through fear and the threat of further alienation and loss of privileges. Discipline became internalized in the same way that the discipline of the asylum effectively controlled the mad, as Foucault points out.

> fear no longer reigned on the other side of the prison gates, it now raged under the seals of conscience ... The asylum no longer punished the madman's guilt, it is true; but it did more, it organized that guilt; it organized it for the madman as a consciousness of himself, and as a non-reciprocal relation to the keeper; it organized it for the man of reason as an awareness of the Other, a therapeutic intervention in the madman's exist-ence. In other words, by this guilt the madman became an object of punishment always vulnerable to himself and to the Other; and, from the acknowledgment of his status as object, from the awareness of his guilt, the madman was to return to his awareness of himself as a free and responsible subject, and consequently to reason. (*Madness* 247)

Just as the madman in Foucault's asylum saw himself in the mirror as a madman, many Asians came to internalize the sense of inferiority and otherness, accepting work for substantially lower wages, doing jobs that white people shunned, believing that they were second-class citizens.

In addition, the difficulty most of the Asian immigrant workers had with the English language made them more silent and rendered many invisible as individuals. Ken Adachi notes, for instance, that though the Japanese who came to Canada were literate, their English was 'woeful, and did not improve to any significant degree for a long time' (29). Even after having spent a number of years in Canada, they could communicate only by gestures or in pidgin English. This was partly due to the little contact they had with English-speaking Canadians, and due to the structure of the community in which the early immigrants lived. They grouped together under a Japanese 'boss,' who acted as their intermediary with their employers. Not until they began to see their future in Canada as more than a temporary sojourn, did they feel the need to learn the English language (Adachi 29–30). Many Asians assumed the cloak of invisibility due to necessity. One type of work that entails silence, obsequiousness, and invisibility is domestic service. By the end of the nineteenth and the beginning of the twentieth centuries, large numbers of Chinese immigrant men had been driven out of the mining and farming industries and were hired into middle-class households as domestic servants. While the Chinese were indispensable as domestic labour, they 'represented a threat of racial pollution within the household,' and were thus represented in popular culture as both 'seductively childlike and threateningly sexual' (Robert Lee 10). As late as 1920, close to 50 per cent of the Chinese in the United States still worked as domestic servants (Espiritu 34). In the first decade of the twentieth century, Japanese immigrants worked during the day while living in Japanese-operated boarding houses. They cleaned houses, washed windows, prepared meals, washed and ironed clothes, tended yards and gardens (Sucheng Chan, *Asian Americans* 39). Filipino boys and men were also hired as household servants, janitors, bellhops, and doormen in hotels, and waiters and cooks in restaurants. Even today, 'hundreds of thousands of Filipinos swarm the world's airports, going back and forth to the Middle East, Europe, and Asia as contract workers, domestics, "hospitality workers" (mostly in Japan), and every conceivable kind of employment' (San Juan, Jr, *Philippine Temptation* 101).[24]

In order to be able to stay and eventually settle down in the host country, Asians in North America eventually learned to perform invisibility. But the trajectory of going from the visibly marked to the invisible was not straightforward. What Anne Anlin Cheng says of the process of racialization is true of the means by which one is marked as other, and becomes invisible: 'underneath the pop-psychological insight of an "inferiority complex" lies a nexus of intertwining affects and libidinal dynamics – a web of self-affirmation, self-denigration, projection, desire, identification, and hostility' (17). To be quiet, accommodating, and industrious made one desirable as a worker and acceptable to white society. To flaunt difference or to show too much success often risked endangering or curtailing the right to work or to fish. To display too much intelligence and ambition would be to incur the negative criticism of being 'aggressive' and competitive, as the Japanese in Canada did. What Asians in North American discovered was that to become invisible was the safest route if one wanted to stay in California and British Columbia. Like the madmen described in Foucault's asylum, many Asians resented their treatment, but hid their desires, their sexuality, their frustrations, and became silent, inscrutable, and invisible to outsiders. Foucault's comments about madness could also apply to this experience of being 'Oriental' and, thus, different: 'It is judged only by its acts; it is not accused of intentions, nor are its secrets to be fathomed. Madness is responsible only for that part of itself which is visible. All the rest is reduced to silence. Madness no longer exists except as *seen* ... The science of mental disease, as it would develop in the asylum, would always be only of the order of observation and classification. It would not be a dialogue' (*Madness* 250). In the case of madmen as in the case of early Asians in North America, to be invisible and anonymous was to be free. As surface was all that mattered, it made sense to appear docile and appeased. One couldn't literally efface one's facial features, but one could avoid highlighting other differences. As Wayson Choy notes, all the Chinatown old-timers used to say to each other, 'In Gold Mountain, simple is best' (*Jade Peony* 14). The narrator adds, 'there were, besides, false immigration stories to hide, secrets to be kept' (*Jade Peony* 14). It was to one's advantage to act the way Asians were expected to act, not to complicate matters by exhibiting one's aspirations, frustrations, and unfulfilled dreams, or to explain the web of relations that linked one person to another. Some stories were best left untold.

This adoption of the stance of docility and silence contributed to the ease with which the governments in the United States and Canada were able to carry out the evacuation and relocation of Japanese Americans and Canadians during the Second World War. Ken Adachi emphasizes these traits in Japanese Canadians: 'Most Japanese did not resist evacuation but co-operated with a docility that was almost wholly in line with their background and their particular development as a minority group ... The Japanese were inclined to follow lines of least resistance since their cultural norms emphasized duty and obligation as well as the values of conformity and obedience ... Disruptive behaviour was censured, discipline and obedience were mandatory so that self-control, resignation and gratitude were highly desirable' (225). What Adachi has described as the 'development as a minority group' is, I argue, the complex phenomenon of being marked as visible in North America and the ensuing desire for invisibility and acceptance. Adachi notes that the Nisei 'wished to prove that they were "Canadian" by co-operating fully with the authorities. Indeed, the demand that Japanese should show their "loyalty" to Canada by accepting evacuation and by co-operating with the authorities, and the conclusion that non-acceptance demonstrated "disloyalty," was perhaps the crudest device utilized not only by the proponents of evacuation but by Mackenzie King and his Cabinet' (226). As in the case of Foucault's asylum, punishment consisted not of force or violence but of an awareness of one's guilt, and the necessity of cooperation from a free and responsible individual. In *Obasan*, Joy Kogawa's protagonist, Naomi, reflects on this quality of obedience instilled in the Japanese, which became detrimental during the time of internment: 'It is always so. We must always honour the wishes of others before our own. We will make the way smooth by restraining emotion. Though we might wish Grandma and Grandpa to stay, we must watch them go. To try to meet one's own needs in spite of the wishes of others is to be "wagamama" – selfish and inconsiderate' (128). The fact that most Japanese Canadians did not actively resist the evacuation and internment made it easy for the RCMP to carry out its orders, which led to the dispersal of the vibrant Japanese Canadian community that was once in Vancouver throughout the villages of the Lower Fraser Valley and along the coasts of Vancouver Island (see Adachi 153). Kogawa laments the loss and the quiet disappearance of the people: 'We are the Issei and the Nisei and the Sansei, the Japanese Canadians. We disappear into the future undemanding as dew' (112).

Contemporary Politics of Visibility

Since the U.S. Immigration Act of 1965 and subsequent amendments, which abolished national-origin quotas, and since Canada changed its immigration requirements in 1962, Asians have entered North America in increasingly greater numbers. The newer group of Asian immigrants include people from India, Pakistan, Sri Lanka, Bangladesh, Thailand, Vietnam, Laos, and Cambodia, as well as those from the Philippines, Korea, Taiwan, and mainland China. According to the 1996 census, visible minorities make up about 11 per cent of Canada's 28 million people.[25] Asians make up about 7.5 per cent of the population, with large concentrations in cities like Toronto and Vancouver (Statistics Canada). In 2000 the U.S. Census Bureau estimated the Asian and Pacific Islander population of the United States to be around 11,279,000 out of a total population of 276,059,000, or roughly 4.1 per cent (U.S. Census). In spite of the increasing numbers of Asian Americans, and events such as the Los Angeles riot of 1992, which not only put black and white racial tensions in the media, but also placed Korean Americans in the limelight, Timothy Fong argues that 'precious little is known about Asian Americans in the United States' (1). For Fong, Asian Americans are visible only as 'stereotypes,' and invisible 'due to widespread ignorance of their distinct histories and contemporary experiences' (2).[26]

Thus far, I have been stressing the similarities between Asian Americans and Asian Canadians. However, it is important to note that the invisibility of Asian Canadians as a group is today more pronounced than that of Asian Americans. What Donald Goellnicht observes of Asian Canadian literature is true of Asian Canadians as a political and social entity – both have had a 'long labour' and a 'protracted birth' in comparison to their Asian American counterparts. Goellnicht gives several reasons for this delay, including the relative sizes of the minority population, the presence of the catalytic anti–Vietnam War movement in the United States, Canada's official policy of multiculturalism, and Quebec's agitation for independence ('Long Labour' 5–8). While the study of Asian Americans has been 'recovering, reclaiming, and reconstructing knowledge on Asian Americans over the past thirty years' (Kenyon Chan 17), Canadians of Asian ancestry are still attempting to find a cultural space, and a politicized voice, or 'Asiancy,' as Roy Miki asserts (101). Following Lisa Lowe, who argues that it is out of structural contradictions that resistance can occur, Guy Beauregard writes that the critical task is 'to recognize the complex ways Asian Canadian writers and cultural critics are working through these contradictions and rewriting these histories of attempted yet not absolute exclusion' ('Emergence' par. 10).

The Politics of the Visible in Asian North American Narratives is one such attempt to examine the complexities of location and identity, the rewriting of history by Asian North Americans. I pick up and extend the trope of visibility and invisibility as used by Traise Yamamoto in her study of Japanese American women. Yamamoto notes a number of ways Asian Americans are invisible. She says that Asian Americans are 'invisibilized' as 'model minorities' or 'honorary whites' (64), often conflated with Asian nationals, and that Asian American women are cast in an undifferentiated 'pool of Asian women' (65).[27] Similarly, in her study of whiteness, Ruth Frankenberg notes that 'racist discourse ... frequently accords a hypervisibility to African Americans and a relative *invisibility* to Asian Americans and Native Americans; Latinos are also relatively less visible than African Americans in discursive terms' (12). It is primarily through discourse that all these others are named. Both Asian North American women and men are affected and cast in an 'undifferentiated pool' of the Oriental, marked as other, yet invisibilized. By being labelled through the official discourse of government and labour as 'alien' or a 'visible minority,' one is psychically and socially marked as other, as visibly different, and less than the norm, which is white. In the United States, although the term 'visible minority' is not used, the classification of racial others works in the same way. Today, all European Americans are classified as whites with no distinction between different origins, such as English, Irish, Scottish, German, French, Italian, Dutch, Polish, Russians, Ukrainian, Croatian, Maltese.[28] Blacks and Hispanics are differentiated from whites and from Asians and Pacific Islanders, whereas Hispanics do not exist as a separate category in Canada. My point is that our subjectivities as Asian Americans and Asian Canadians in North America are in a state of dependency or nonbeing, comparable to the status of women in an androcentric society. As we can be defined only by what we are not, by our lack of whiteness, particularly in Canada but also, implicitly, in the United States, we remain, as feminist philosopher Luce Irigaray says of woman, in a state of 'unrealized potentiality,' as beings who exist 'for/ by another' (*Speculum* 165). For Irigaray, the issue is not simply a state of social inferiority but a psycho-subjective state of alterity. Just as having a phallus becomes the symbol of power for males, I argue that possessing white skin is fetishized and valorized in the same way in our culture. Those who do not possess the phallus or white skin are dispossessed and rootless in our symbolic order. Irigaray points out that in our culture, 'logic and rationality are symbolically male, and the female is either outside, the hole, or the unsymbolizable residue' (Whitford 69). The consequences are damaging for women and for Asians as they find themselves 'homeless' in this symbolic order (Whitford 69).

To state the problem another way is to use the terms of the marked and the unmarked. In her work on contemporary photographs, theatre, film, and performance art, Peggy Phelan describes the political binaries of Western metaphysics using male and female terms. Her observations here could apply equally to the relationship between whites and visible minorities: 'One term of the binary is marked with value, the other is unmarked. The male is marked with value; the female is unmarked, lacking measured value and meaning. Within this psycho-philosophical frame, cultural reproduction takes she who is unmarked and re-marks her, rhetorically and imagistically, while he who is marked with value is left unremarked, in discursive paradigms and visual fields. He is the norm and therefore unremarkable; as the Other, it is she whom he marks' (5).[29] As Asian Americans and Asian Canadians, we are the ones unmarked (with value), and yet rhetorically and imagistically remarked other. In addition, many of us are doubly marked. A number of authors I consider are women, already regarded as an other in Phelan's equation and in Western metaphysics, and marked as visibly minor. Some of the other writers, though male, are also doubly marked because they do not belong to the normative group of dominant white heterosexual culture. Yet the relationship between self and other, between the dominant and the other, is a continuous exchange, an interdependent arrangement. Phelan says: 'Identity emerges in the failure of the body to express being fully and the failure of the signifier to convey meaning exactly. Identity is perceptible only through a relation to an other – which is to say, it is a form of both resisting and claiming the other, declaring the boundary where the self diverges from and merges with the other. In that declaration of identity and identification, there is always loss, the loss of not-being the other and yet remaining dependent on that other for self-seeing, self-being' (13). It is this resistance and claim of the other, this divergence and convergence of self and other, that creates the most interesting and dynamic tensions in many of the works studied here.

It is my contention that the socio-historical and cultural situation of Asian North Americans has had serious psychic repercussions on our subjectivity. This line of thinking bears some similarities to the arguments advanced by David Leiwei Li in *Imagining the Nation* and Anne Anlin Cheng in *The Melancholy of Race*. Li sees two distinct periods of 'American Orientalism,' the first during the legal prohibition of Asian American citizenship from 1854 to 1943/65 when Asians experienced 'alienation,' and the second from 1943/65 to the present when Asian Americans were 'abjected' (5). According to David Li, in the first period, 'the "Oriental" was legally constructed as the most visible, most menacing kind of difference, as the Other to the (European) American self, and as the object of national prohibitions' (5). In the second period, Li asserts that 'the Asian American has been turned into an "abject," into that which is neither radical enough for institutional enjoinment of the kind in period I nor competent enough to enjoy the subject status of citizens in a registered and recognized participation of American democracy' (6). Part of Li's argument about abjection revolves around the discourse of the 'Asian American model minority,' which is a phenomenon peculiar to the United States. In Canada, race relations have not led to such a classification of Asians. I also do not share Li's notion of a sharp break between the two periods. As I see it, the conditions during the exclusionary period, though different from conditions in contemporary society, had the same effect of marking Asians as visible, and paradoxically rendering all their other qualities except their physical Asian features invisible.

Anne Cheng's more complex paradigm sees the process of racialization as a form of Freudian melancholy both for the dominant white culture that has introjected the other and for racialized peoples who have undergone the 'complex process of *coming* to racialization/socialization' (17).[30] Cheng insightfully sees parallels between the racialization of Asian Americans and blacks, and she examines the 'nature of racial fantasy and of racial melancholia' in order to alter 'how we conceive of ethics and politics' through the help of psychoanalysis (27). Her study looks at a group of Asian American and African American texts that I do not examine in this work. However, a number of Cheng's observations are worth highlighting here. For example, she notes that 'the pedagogy of discrimination is painfully installed in multiple stages. White preference is not a phenomenon that simply gets handed down from society to black women and then to black girls: instead it travels a tortuous, melancholic path of alienation, resistance, aggression, and then, finally, the domestication of that aggression as "love"' (17–18). What I call the politics of the visible is also a process that is layered and complicated, involving naming, interpellation, resistance, acquiescence, and the recreation or reimagination of subjectivity. What I focus on more specifically, however, is the primacy of the visible in the construction of the Asian Canadian as well as the Asian American subject. As I see it, what these texts are resisting is the facile categorization afforded by surfaces. They play with and contest visible features and ready assumptions, which have to be rewritten or reinscribed.

As noted earlier, I use the term 'invisibility' to denote a state of not being seen by the dominant culture, akin to what Ellison portrayed in *Invisible Man*. It takes many years of hard work and anguish – recuperation of history, resistance, mimicry, and sheer will – to undo the images of Orientals depicted in the media, in cultural practices, and in everyday discourse. It is the work of refocusing or reconstituting the gaze of dominant culture. The degree to which one experiences the oppressions of history varies, yet the many attempts to exclude and delimit the rights and privileges of Asians in North America invariably affect one's subjectivity. They form a facet of the set of markings that are inscribed on us.

In Part I of this study, 'Visuality, Representation, and the Gaze,' I focus on texts that explicitly examine and challenge the dominant culture's portrayal, and expectations, of Asian North Americans. The three narratives I have chosen play with visuality and emphasize the importance of the gaze. They attempt to represent their protagonists in terms that de-exoticize and humanize what has been othered and Orientalized. But invisibility for Asian Canadians and Asian Americans in North America is also a self-imposed and self-willed state of being, as in the case of domestic workers, people who arrive with forged identification papers, or immigrants who fear deportation, as the novels show.[31]

In Part II, 'Transformations through the Sensual,' the three works I study feature protagonists who negotiate their invisible status by acts of transformation. A number of characters attempt to transform outward 'visible' signs – one's body, the food one makes, one's accent – into things of power and of beauty. The pressures to conform and to assimilate begin a series of changes for the protagonists of these narratives.[32] Thus, transformation, which initially was a strategy for maintenance and integration with society, becomes a site of creative empowerment.

In Part III, 'Invisible Minorities in Asian America,' I deal with the minoritized groups within Asian America. In the past, in an effort to strengthen the bonds between Asian Americans, some differences between Asian groups have had to be elided. A pan-ethnic alliance has sometimes entailed the silencing of certain groups within the category of Asian American. In some cases, minimizing differences has been a means of survival. For example, during the Second World War, some Japanese Canadians and Americans tried to blend in with the Chinese to avoid being targeted.[33] After the war, some attempted to assimilate as much as possible to show their loyalty to their country, as illustrated in Hiromi Goto's Chorus of Mushrooms. For their part, Filipinos, whose home country was colonized by both the Japanese and the Americans, find themselves in the strange situation of now being equals with Japanese Americans through ethnic hyphenation. Their particular contribution in the field of Asian American literature needs to be better explored and historicized. In addition, one can be multiply invisible and minoritized because of one's sexual orientation and economic circumstances. As Bino Realuyo's The Umbrella Country shows, the combination of poverty and homosexuality exacerbates one's marginalization and vulnerability. The novels in Part III all struggle with multiple layers of invisibility as a result of the subject's position within the dominant culture and within Asian American culture.

A Note on Scope and Methodology

In studying Canadian and American narratives, I self-consciously move beyond national boundaries, a demarcation to which literary critics who write on Asian American texts have tended to subscribe.[34] My view is that there are too many commonalities in the situation of Asian Canadians and Asian Americans to ignore and that a cross-border comparative reading is fruitful and long overdue, especially in our transnational and diasporic world. The concerns highlighted by Chinese Canadian authors, for instance, are comparable with those of Chinese American and even Chinese Australian authors, though I do not study the latter group.[35] At the same time, this study does not purport to be comprehensive. I have not gone out of my way to choose representative texts from different ethnicities to work on, and there are obvious gaps. For example, I have not studied South Asian North American texts, or those written by Korean or Vietnamese Americans.[36] I have instead chosen narratives that stress and illustrate my points about the politics of the visible and its link to identity, with examples mainly from Chinese, Filipino, and in one case, Japanese North Americans. I have avoided canonical Asian North American texts, such as *The Woman Warrior* and *Obasan*, because there are already many excellent readings of these. My sense is that there is a richness in Asian Canadian texts that has not yet been explored. Similarly, Filipino American works are often under-represented in studies on Asian American literature. My study focuses on a number of these works, yet I hope to give some sense of the scope and breadth of the topic by not limiting myself to just one ethnic group.[37]

My book provides readings of texts that, for the most part, have not received much critical attention to date. As far as I know, these chapters encompass the first sustained critical writing for more than half of the works I have chosen to study. My project is also one of only a few to examine Asian Canadian and Asian American works together.[38] Part of my aim in writing about these texts is to create further interest in these works and their authors. Many critics who write about Asian American literature take Carlos Bulosan or Jessica Hagedorn as examples of Filipino American literature.[39] But there are obviously many other versions of Filipino American life that are worth analysing. Additionally, I have not divided the book into fiction and non-fiction. Rather, I prefer to look at all the works as narratives and representations of Asian American experience, recognizing that the lines between fiction, autobiography, and biography are not always easily discernable in Asian American writing.[40]

Lastly, my theoretical approach, which some may find rather eclectic, is a creative hybrid, like the approach of many of us who work as Westernized Asian academics. I have used Asian American and Asian Canadian socio-cultural history, feminist theories of the subject, psychoanalytic and psycholinguistic insights, postcolonial and poststructuralist theories. Rather than maintaining a single theoretical approach, I have borrowed from these various schools and used them where they illuminate and illustrate my points about the Asian North American subject and issues of visibility and invisibility. I hope that a study of the way in which the imaginary functions in historical and social contexts can produce changes and shift power relations in our culture. To borrow from Kristeva's essay 'Women's Time,' it is the 'mixture of two attitudes – *insertion* into history and the radical *refusal* of the subjective limitations imposed by this history's time on an experiment carried out in the name of the irreducible difference' in which I see Asian American and Asian Canadian writers currently engaged (*Kristeva Reader* 195).

PART I

VISUALITY, REPRESENTATION, AND THE GAZE

1

Writing Historiographic Autoethnography: Denise Chong's *The Concubine's Children*

In attempting to set down the story of her family – her mother's tales and memories, her grandmother's colourful life – Denise Chong has had to contend with a number of difficulties relating to issues of gender and ethnic visibility. Firstly, as Sidonie Smith has noted of autobiographies, normative definitions of the genre of life writing lie in the relationship of the subject 'to the arena of public life and discourse. Yet patriarchal notions of woman's inherent nature and consequent social role have denied or severely proscribed her access to the public space' (7). Few women have achieved the status of individual greatness, according to our androcentric culture's definition of the term. At the same time, 'to take a voice' and to call attention to one's distinctiveness has traditionally been viewed as 'unfeminine' (Smith 10). Traditionally, a woman who puts herself on display risks the loss of her reputation. Secondly, like other biographers and autobiographers, Denise Chong has to interpret and situate remembered experience, documented history, oral tales, and other elements, and to construct a narrative that seems to tell 'the story' rather than simply 'a story.' The selves that she creates in her story are, in Smith's words, 'cast in language and are always motivated by cultural expectations, habits, and systems of interpretation pressing on her at the scene of writing' (47). For female subjects in particular, these representations are always complicated by the prevailing culture's ideologies of femininity and gender, whether these stem from Euro-Canadian or Confucian Chinese traditions. Thirdly, Chong is faced with the demanding task of handling a delicate and potentially transgressive subject. Her grandmother, May-ying, is not only a concubine, but could also be labelled a 'sex worker,' or prostitute. Shannon Bell has noted that 'prostitute discourse itself is a contested terrain' and that 'modernity through a process of othering has produced the "prostitute" as the other of the other: the other within the categorical other, "woman"' (97, 2). Lastly, Chong has to battle the image of the Oriental woman, whom Lisa Lowe has pointed out is 'not a singular object but is variously and heterogeneously projected as at once sexual enchantress, productive machine, and racial inferior' (*Critical Terrains* 76). Writing, then, means challenging and reworking expectations of genre, of gender, and of female agency and subjectivity, and rewriting the dominant culture's misconceptions of ethnic differences.

The Concubine's Children (1994), based on oral history, family photographs, the author's encounters with, and memories of, her ancestral family, letters, and archival research, crosses many generic boundaries. The Penguin Canada 1994 back cover copy advertises the book as a 'portrait of a people' (*Globe and Mail*), a 'history' (*Vancouver Sun*), and a 'family saga' comparable to *The Joy Luck Club* (*London Free Press*). Yet it is, strictly speaking, neither a work of fiction nor a work of history. The autobiographical impetus for the work came from a trip to China the author made with her mother in 1987. Visiting the village where her grandfather was born, Chong discovered a need to learn about her family history, which she felt was rich with unearthed stories. In a public lecture, she explained that she felt then that her past was like the tea spilling out from an overturned teacup, and that she wished she could gather up the various little stories that moment in order to preserve them. Her own training as an economist in Canada had not adequately prepared her to write a memoir, and Chong modestly and humorously relates how she first learned to write by reading books on how to write crime fiction.[1]

For Chong, the family memoir is rather like a mystery, where one is searching for the truth, and finding different versions of it from the various suspects and people involved. In seeking out and recounting the facts and the events of the past, Chong is at once writer of fiction, biographer and autobiographer, and historian.[2] For *The Concubine's Children* is about herself, but it begins three generations earlier, at the turn of the twentieth century, and in mainland China. While the work is based on actual incidents, the writer nevertheless had to rely on others' accounts of what happened. Included in the work are photographs, which are traditionally used as evidence for the existence of people or things, but which, like narratives, can be manipulated and constructed.

Photographs, like narratives, are selective; they can be cropped, and they can serve to highlight only those elements that the author wants us to see. In many ways, the work is akin to postmodern forms that interrogate the limits of literature and history. Linda Hutcheon notes that 'historiographic metafiction suggests that truth and falsity may ... not be the right terms in which to discuss fiction' as 'there are only *truths* in the plural, and never one Truth; and there is rarely falseness *per se*, just others' truths' (*Poetics* 109). One could apply these observations to Chong's hybrid text.

This concern for truths and versions of truths becomes important when writers of ethnic origins tell their stories. Frequently, as in the case of Chinese immigrants to North America, their versions of history do not always coincide with the official records. In *The Concubine's Children*, May-ying, the concubine, is married off and moves to Canada in 1924, a year after the Canadian government passed its Exclusionary Act prohibiting any Chinese from immigrating. This act was similar to those passed in the United States in 1882, 1924, and 1934. Lisa Lowe notes that 'the period from 1850 to World War II was marked by legal exclusions, political disenfranchisement, labor exploitation, and internment for Asian-origin groups in the United States' (*Immigrant Acts* 9). Throughout the twentieth century, 'the figure of the Asian immigrant has served as a "screen," a phantasmatic site, on which the nation projects a series of condensed, complicated anxieties regarding external and internal threats to the mutable coherence of the national body: the invading multitude, the lascivious seductress, the servile yet treacherous domestic, the automaton whose inhuman efficiency will supersede American ingenuity' (*Immigrant Acts* 18). In Canada, the laws functioned in similar ways. Chinese males were allowed to enter the country as cheap labourers, but they were not encouraged to bring along their families or their wives until the repeal of the Exclusionary Act in 1947 (Peter Li 65). Consequently, women like May-ying became waitresses, hostesses, and later sex workers for economic and social reasons. Initially, May-ying had to work in order to pay off her passage to Canada. But more importantly, the shortage of Chinese women in Canada at the time made 'waitressing' and hostessing too tempting and lucrative for women to resist. The high proportion of Chinese bachelor men made it difficult to sustain traditional family life. Instead, large numbers of lonely bachelors relied on pretty waitresses in tea houses for entertainment.

Chong represents an ethnic and gendered other – one who is an other within the categories that construct white, Western women as the norm for women, and specifically an other within the interrelated systems of race and gender. She recuperates this figure – a woman who was a gambler, a 'tea house' waitress (29), and a concubine – in her book. One way she rewrites her reading public's cultural expectations of this other is by calling into question the veracity of history.[3] What is set down in history books is only one side of the story. She politicizes Chinese Canadian identity through her narrative, which is a work of historiographic autoethnography. I use the term 'historiographic auto-ethnography' to emphasize a consciousness of the act of writing history and to highlight the complexity of ethnic self-representation. Linda Hutcheon argues that historiographic metafiction's 'theoretical self-awareness of history and fiction as human constructs ... is made the grounds for its rethinking and reworking of the forms and contents of the past' (*Poetics* 5). I borrow this notion of historiography, along with Rey Chow's notion of autoethnography. In her study of Chinese film-makers, Rey Chow points out that for those who have been 'formerly ethnographized ... what are "subjective" origins now include a memory of past *objecthood* – the experience of being looked at – which lives on in the subjective act of ethnographizing like an other, an optical unconsciousness' (*Primitive Passions* 180). The term historiographic autoethnography, then, questions the way in which history has been narrated; what, and from whose viewpoint, it has been told; and, at the same time, it articulates an awareness of the unequal terms of Euro-American–dominated ethnography that reverberate in one's act of self-representation.

In representing what happened to her grandparents and parents in British Columbia in the years before her birth, Chong participates in the act of 'autoethnography' (see Pratt 7), or what Rey Chow calls 'ethnography of the self and the subject' (*Primitive Passions* 180). Chow points out that autoethnography necessarily involves the gaze of the dominant culture: 'what may be called "to-be-looked-at-ness" – the visuality that once defined the "object" status of the ethnographized culture ... now becomes a predominant aspect of that culture's self-representation' (*Primitive Passions* 180). Chong is placed in the position of observing and recording the cultural practices of the exotic and marginalized other of Western civilization, and of translating for herself and for her audience a past that is fraught with omissions and questions. Chong's even-handed account of May-ying's work demystifies and de-exoticizes the figure of the sexualized Oriental woman. She resists modern discourses and constructions of the prostitute body that, as Shannon Bell notes, 'dichotomize[] the female into the "good" and the "bad" woman in all her manifestations' (2). Contrary to popular conceptions of the Oriental woman, May-ying does not know any ancient sexual techniques, nor is she particularly servile. She is not dangerous, she does not lack morals, she does not possess uncontrollable desires or inordinately strong passions;[4] she becomes a waitress only because of existing socio-historical conditions.

Chong writes: 'As she became more desperate, May-ying finally went the way of many waitresses – when her shift was over, she no longer refused all the advances of her customers. Men had always been attracted to her ... Her motive in these casual liaisons was mainly to help ease her financial problems, yet it was not prostitution in the strict sense of a simple, quick exchange of sexual acts for money. The men would generously pay a gambling debt here or there or give her money to "buy herself something"' (83). By recontextualizing the conditions of May-ying's life, by breaking down the boundaries of what Patricia Hill Collins calls 'the public/private dichotomy separating the family/household from the paid labor market' (58), Chong forces her readers to see her grandmother from a more nuanced and historicized perspective. We do not see her as a prostitute, but we see the waitressing work as an extension of what Collins calls 'motherwork.' Collins argues that 'racial ethnic women's mothering and work experiences occur at the boundaries demarking' dualities such as 'oppression and liberation,' 'family and work, the individual and the collective' (59).[5]

Chong's novel has been praised as 'an unsentimental memoir that documents a personal history within the context of events taking place in both China and Canada' (Schatenstein I:3), but in some ways, *The Concubine's Children* is closer to a 'postmodern' text, in Hutcheon's definition of the term, than it is a straightforward memoir or family history. Hutcheon uses the term postmodern for historiographic novels that 'are both intensely self-reflexive and yet paradoxically also lay claim to historical events and personages' (*Poetics* 5). Chong's work calls attention several times to the nebulous quality of history, and to the fact that we have access to the past beyond recall only through different kinds of texts – oral histories, official documents, photographs, letters – that are all mediated representations of reality. In the foreword to the book, Chong writes, 'there are as many different versions of events as there are members of a family. The truth becomes a landscape of many layers in an ever-changing light; the details depend on whose memories illuminate it' (xiii). Similarly, in an address dealing with the difference between fact and fiction, she notes that 'non-fiction writers start with the premise that they are "not going to make things up." Yet, there is a certain randomness to fact-gathering that is not present in fiction writing' ('Fiction' 11). These statements reveal her awareness of the way truths are selectively produced and represented. The self-conscious inclusion of different materials demonstrates the hybrid nature of Chong's text. Various kinds of records – visual, oral, governmental – are needed in order to satisfactorily represent a woman's life. These materials, which produce contradictory versions of the truth in *The Concubine's Children*, formalize and thematize the historiographic and fictive nature of all representations of the past, whether public or private.

Although Chong's text differs politically and ideologically from that of Joy Kogawa, like *Obasan*, the book uses a structural technique that Manina Jones calls the 'documentary-collage.' Jones points out that this strategy, found in a number of contemporary Canadian works, 'is a "collage" technique that self-consciously transcribes documents into the literary text, registering them as "outside" writings that readers recognize both as taken from a spatial or temporal "elsewhere" and as participating in a historical referential discourse of "non-fiction." The works both invoke and undermine the oppositions between categories such as textual/referential, intratextual/extratextual, literary/non-literary, or fiction/non-fiction, and thus stage a kind of documentary dialogue' (13–14). This technique results in the challenging of conventional truths 'by fragmenting received texts, and then by translating them from one context to another' (16). In addition, Jones notes that it foregrounds the 'reader's position as ... interpreter of documentary evidence,' and makes us aware of 'the extent to which *we* are constructed *by stories*' (17–18). In *The Concubine's Children*, documents are linked to larger issues of identity, veracity, politics, gender, and race.

Through photographs and documents, Chong writes back and 'returns the gaze' of the other.[6] Though these materials usually denote authenticity, in Chong's text, photographs and official records have to be read with care and with a degree of scepticism. Often, these are but 'representations' of the truth, manufactured for a specific purpose and put together for a desired effect. Another technique Chong uses is the refiguring of what one would traditionally consider an 'abject' of society, in Julia Kristeva's sense of the term, through discourse. Kristeva notes that the abject is that which is 'radically excluded' in the formation of identity, and linked to the improper, the unclean (*Powers* 2).

Abject figures include the threatening others often depicted in Oriental stereotypes, as well as the immoral and the sinister. Throughout her biography, Chong carefully avoids referring to May-Ying in terms of the criminal or the lurid. She calls her a 'waitress,' a *'kay-toi-neu,'* which, though 'considered to be almost one and the same as a prostitute' (27), has a different connotation. Instead of focusing on her grandmother's work as a prostitute, she stresses themes of maternal duty, necessity, and sacrifice. These motifs work to counter the stereotype of the wanton and servile Oriental woman. Such images have been made popular in American culture through the figure of Madame Butterfly in opera and characters in contemporary musicals such as *Miss Saigon*, through the figure of the treacherous seductress in James Bond movies and films about Vietnam, the bar girl in the *World of Suzie Wong*, and others (see Josephine Lee, Marchetti, Uchida). As Robert Lee notes, 'what produces these stereotypes is not just individual acts of representation, but a historical discourse of race that is embedded in the history of American social crises' (12).

The most striking documents included in the memoirs are the photographs, mostly of the author's family, located in the centre of the book and on the cover. Chong constructs her memoirs around the 'pile of old black-and white photographs' found in the 'cedar chest upstairs' in her parents' bedroom (xi).[7] They were 'the only artifacts' of her grandparents' generation; 'anything else of value had gone the way of the pawnshop' (xi). At a basic level, photographs attest to the authenticity of the subject. However, like other documents, photographs can also be problematic in their ordering and reconstructing of the past. Because most family photographs are taken at formal occasions or celebrations, they tend to record moments of ineluctible joy rather than misery. Roland Barthes notes, 'what the photograph asserts is the overwhelming truth that "the thing has been there": this was a reality which once existed, though it is "a reality one can no longer touch"' (87). John Tagg points out, however, that Barthes's statement 'has to be read against the death of his own mother, his reawakened sense of unsupportable loss, and his search for "a just image" and not "just an image" of her' (1). The photograph, 'a material product of a material apparatus set to work in specific contexts,' is 'empty and cannot deliver what Barthes desires: the confirmation of an existence; the mark of a past presence; the repossession of his mother's body' (Tagg 3).

I suggest that this authentic and reassuring encounter with her grandmother (and mother) is also what Denise Chong desires. A sense of loss has similarly produced in her a longing for 'a pre-linguistic certainty and unity.' Her book seeks 'to make present what is absent or, more exactly, to make it retrospectively real' (Tagg 4). More than once in *The Concubine's Children* she remarks with nostalgia the passing of time and the changes it brings. She says, for instance, 'my mother's friends were the last generation of children to be raised in Vancouver's Chinatown ... It was not easy to find physical evidence of earlier generations'(xii). Similarly, the trips to China have a quality of urgency for her: 'I found the south of China to be changing even more rapidly. On the first trip to see our relatives, we reached my grandfather's village only after traveling three hours along back roads; on the second, an hour's ride by jet-foil took us to a terminal ten minutes from the village. Even as I researched and wrote the book, I felt as if the window of opportunity to get a glimpse of the past was closing' (xiii). These passages in the foreword give an *ubi sunt* motif to the book, lamenting the vanished past. The sense of the evanescence of existence is countered, firstly, by the physical presence of the photographs, and then, by the text itself, which acknowledges the life of May-ying, and thus fills the space left vacant by the grandmother's body.

Aside from a personal nostalgia for a past age and generation, there is an added impetus for Chong, that of collective remembering. The need to know about and recount the past is more pressing for many writers of ethnic or minority backgrounds because their histories in North America are often unrecorded. In *Beloved*, for example, Toni Morrison writes of the need to 'rememory' the sixty million and more Africans who perished during the American slave trade (215). Similarly, in *Obasan*, Aunt Emily tells Naomi, 'You have to remember, ... You are your history' (49–50). While the injustices recorded in Chong's memoir are not as horrific in scale or degree as those in Morrison's novel, they are, nevertheless, aspects of Canadian history and culture of which many Canadians today are largely unaware. Though the focus of the work is personal rather than ideological, it recuperates a neglected and painful aspect of the past as Morrison's and Kogawa's novels do. Lien Chao argues that 'although Chinese Canadians deserve the title of pioneers and nation-builders, systematic racism in Canadian history has denied them the recognition' (17). The photographs attest to the hopes and aspirations of a generation of Chinese immigrants who struggled to make a living in the fabled Gold Mountain that was Canada. Their desperation and need to circumvent the Chinese Immigration Act is evident from the first of the inset photos, that of 'May-ying affixed to

The concubine's eldest daughters, Ping and Nan.

the false papers she used to enter Canada in 1924.' These are the stories, Chong says, that 'serve to illuminate Canada's social history' ('Being Canadian' A29).

Usually, photographs serve to arrest the moment and stop the flux of time. They are, however, not real in themselves, and they only become meaningful read within specific historical and social circumstances. Pierre Bourdieu notes that popular social photography captures 'moments which have been torn from the temporal flow by virtue of their solemnity ... capturing people who are fixed, immobile, in the immutability of the plane' (76). However, 'photography captures an aspect of reality which is only ever the result of an arbitrary selection, and, consequently, of a transcription' (Bourdieu 73). The photographs included in *The Concubine's Children* are mostly portraits, showing people dressed formally and posed before professional photographers. Chong notes that the photographs she looked at in the cedar chest were mostly taken 'when Chan Sam and May-ying wanted to record a moment for posterity' (xi). Several of these are included in the book, along with some of her mother, Winnie (or Hing), in a nurse's uniform, and on her wedding day. While I have been arguing that photographs authenticate

May-ying's family portrait with Hing and newly procured Gok-leng.

and render tangible what has been there, the reader of the text will notice a disjunction between the photographs and the narrative. Most of the photographs represent a conventional, well-dressed, seemingly happy and comfortable middle-class family. They depict mothers, fathers, babies, weddings, and children. Absent are the 'squalid rooming house[s]' where Chan Sam and May-ying lived (48), the gambling dens where Winnie 'would sit in a booth by herself, waiting for her mother to finish' (91), and the 'daily ritual' of spankings Winnie had to endure as a child (106). In other words, the photographs are anaesthetized, cleaned-up versions of the biographical narrative. Looking at them, one only gets the presentable facade of the family history.

Referring mainly to present-day France, Pierre Bourdieu notes that 'photographic practice only exists and subsists for most of the time by virtue of its *family function* or rather by the function conferred upon it by the family group, namely that of solemnizing and immortalizing the high points of family life, in short, of reinforcing the integration of the family group by reasserting the sense that it has both of itself and of its unity' (19). He points out that 'the family photograph ... expresses the celebratory sense which the family group gives to itself ... the need to take photographs ... are felt all the more intensely the more integrated the group and the more the group is captured at a moment of its highest integration' (19). This statement might seem rather ironic applied to a family divided between two continents. Chan Sam's two wives and his children are an unusual family group, and not at all united. But what the photographs reveal is May-ying and Chan Sam's desire to be seen as a successful, respectable, and integrated family. The photographs show the way the traditional sense of 'family' interpellated their desires and their identities. In other words, in spite of her strong-willed and rebellious nature, May-ying conformed, at least in her pictorial narrative, to the image of the feminine valued by the Chinese – the delicate young maiden, the dutiful wife and mother. To complicate things further, some photographs were later cut and pasted in the album by Chong's mother, Winnie. Lien Chao notes that Chong 'makes no attempt to disguise the disparity that lies between ... the cut and pasted photographs (ix), and the reality that is shut out initially by the camera or later cut off by her mother's editorial scissors' (106).

Photographs provide a sense of family and lineage that may otherwise not exist for diasporic peoples. Benedict Anderson suggests that 'ethnic identities were maintained in the modern age of international migrations through the family photograph album.' According to Anderson, the 'photograph album replaces the graveyard as the site of ethnic identifications. Grandmother and grandfather are no longer buried in one's own local graveyard, they are buried in the family photo album. Thus, the photography album enables one to formulate and maintain an ethnic identity distinct from one's national identity' (qtd by Shawn Smith 86, n. 50). It was, after all, photographs, not tombstones, that aroused Denise Chong's childhood curiosity about her past, about her ancestors, and that ultimately led her to explore and write about her Chinese Canadian identity as an adult.

The most eye-catching photographs in the book are the images of May-ying, shown dressed in her *cheong sam* and wearing her dangling earrings. It is not surprising that the publishers chose to put her picture on the cover.[8] Her story as a concubine and later a prostitute, as well as her exceptional beauty, adds an exotic and fascinating element to Chong's family history. Like many children of immigrant families, Chong, who is a Canadian-born Chinese, is both inside and outside of her culture(s).[9] As a Chinese in the diaspora, her depiction of Chinese concubinage and marriage customs, filial and familial traditions, is as autobiographical as it is ethnographic. She demonstrates, in Chow's words, 'a culture's belated fascination with its own datedness, its own alterity' (*Primitive Passions* 145).[10] Before her decision to write her memoir, she thought of the China side of her family as something of a mystery. She recalls, 'To me, China was what was left behind when the boat carrying my grandmother, pregnant with my mother, docked in Vancouver ... China was where you'd find yourself if you dug a hole deep enough to come out the other side of the Earth' (220). She speaks of the strenuous effort she made as a researcher and storyteller to be accurate, to resist the temptation to 'leave things out, to censor, to ignore, to embellish, to glorify, to sentimentalize,' in short, to 'rise above the facts, and ascend to some greater truths' ('Fiction' 11) about her family and culture. Yet in some of her descriptions, there is a hint of the romantic. The sense of the alterity and otherness of her ancestors comes across at times in her telling, revealing the way she has internalized her own otherness. For example, in her first description of May-ying at seventeen, Chong writes, 'No man or woman who first came upon May-ying could help but stare fixedly at this tiny figure of a girl, who stood no higher than the average person's chin. Her delicate features, the bright round eyes and the much admired heart-shaped mouth, were set in pale skin that had retained its translucence ... But for her unbound feet, she had the body and features much imitated in Chinese porcelain dolls' (7). Here, life imitates an art form, porcelain dolls, which is stereotyped, stylized, and marketable, especially to foreigners.

The photograph, reinforced by the comparison of May-ying to Chinese porcelain dolls, has the paradoxical effect of making her at once familiar and other. Inadvertently, Chong participates in the Western colonial gaze as she voyeuristically dwells on May-ying's features, and later on her Oriental clothes and jewellery and her posture. As she renders tangible her grandmother, she also exoticizes and mystifies her as the female other. Gilles De Van argues that while 'exoticism is generally defined as the attraction for a civilization – manners, climate, social behavior, clothing – foreign to our own, far from us in time or space,' it can be defined as 'a process of knowledge that transforms into a metaphor of desire' (78). He notes that 'it is an impetus toward the other which becomes a mirror of the self, the search for a foreign land which changes into a reflection of one's own country, the quest for the different that sends us back to the same' (78). Hence, Chong's detailed and careful recreation of May-ying, who 'traced a part down the back of her head, bound the hair on each side with a filament of black wire and twisted it into a chignon above each ear,' is also, in part, a desire to

A photograph of Hing (Winnie, Chong's mother) dressed as a boy,
cut and edited by her.

uncover the beautiful and exotic in herself (5). While looking at her
grandfather's portrait, Chong wonders, 'Do I look like him? ... I was not
so bold as to think I resembled any image of my grandmother,' who,
everyone has told her, 'is so beautiful' (4). Her text is as much autobiographical as it is ethnographic in that it records her own dislocated self
within Western history, imagination, and culture.

Chong juxtaposes archival photographs of Vancouver's and
Nanaimo's Chinatowns with photographs that overtly call attention to
the unreliability of pictorial documentation. Included in the album is
one of Winnie (Hing) as a child, dressed as a boy. It is only upon reading
the caption and the narrative that we realize the gender and identity of
the child. The confusion concerns the sex of the child, but it also points
to the malleability of gender and our long-standing belief that clothes
make the man (or woman). What the photograph does not show is the
consequent heartbreak and pain – both for the mother who longed to
fulfil her destiny as a bearer of sons, and for the child who was forever
to see the picture as 'proof of her mother's disappointment that she was

not born a boy' (91). According to Chong, the image, 'the first ever taken of the concubine's third daughter, foreshadowed a childhood filled with fear and confusion' (91). This deliberate confusion of her sex is exacerbated by the other changes in relation to her identity. When Hing first attends school, she is asked for an English name. Not only does she have to make up a Christian name, and change from Hing to Winnie, but her last name becomes anglicized as Chin. Winnie's acceptance of these changes reveals her desire to avoid the conflict that would have been inevitable had she refused to adopt the anglicized names. Though at home she is Hing, at school she is Winnie, a fact that suggests a desire to dissociate herself from the dingy rooming houses and mah-jong dens of her mother's life. Later, when her parents separate, her sense of who her father is and who her mother should be with is similarly muddled. More than one strange man or family friend comes to share her mother's bed, and upon passing her father in the streets of Vancouver at one point, she is told by her mother, 'Don't call him *Baba!* ... He's not your father' (119). For the child Hing, there are no stable identities and indisputable facts. Her gender, her name, the identity of her father, are all subject to change, to interpretation, and to dispute.

Indeed, *The Concubine's Children* highlights the way official documents – birth certificates, immigration papers, government letters, death notices – are all unreliable sources. When May-ying prepares to come to Canada as Chan Sam's concubine, she takes on a new official identity with the help of a photographer: 'the photograph had to conform with the age on the false birth certificate,' so May-ying becomes twenty-four instead of seventeen on paper (9). This official identity remains with May-ying until her death, whereupon her family discovers that she died 'under the false name and age on the birth certificate she used to enter Canada' (264). In the *Vancouver Sun* the grandmother's death is reported as the 'city's third traffic fatality of the new year. The name was wrong, and so was her age; only the address of her rooming house was correct' (229). Not only are identities exchanged, bought, and sold, so are families. After trying to bear a son three times and failing, May-ying decides to adopt a boy as her own. The narrator notes that 'In Chinatown, putting children up for adoption was an accepted family practice, and these children were simply referred to as children "brought up by someone else" or children "using another family's surname"' (116). After her lover, Chow Guen, helps her pay Granny Yip three hundred dollars, May-ying is presented with a baby boy and a birth certificate: 'the name of his mother matched the name on the false birth certificate that had got May-ying into Canada; Chan Sam was named as his father' (117). Leonard comes into official existence with parents who do not match his false birth certificate in more ways than one. They are not his biological parents, but even the identity of his adoptive parents is questionable. Chow Guen, not Chan Sam, is the adoptive 'father' at this point, but he is not officially acknowledged. May-ying, his mother, is not the woman she is supposed to be according to her papers. These examples show the desperate measures that early Chinese settlers were forced to take in order to satisfy the requirements of the Canadian government and, at the same time, to fulfil the traditions of their culture. What becomes evident within the context of historiography is that the text underlines the way in which official records, those usually regarded by historians and biographers as verifiable 'sources,' can become less truthful than unofficial ones.

In another instance, identity papers become a source of income for Chan Sam. Towards the end of his life, one of the 'last of the family's assets' Chan Sam holds title to are the birth certificates of his daughters, Ping and Nan (191). He is able to sell these certificates, each 'worth several hundred dollars' (192), as false immigration papers to two women who are eager to come to Canada. Cumulatively, these stories of subterfuge, as well as those from Chong's family, serve to critique and politicize both the discriminatory acts of the Canadian government and the patriarchal customs of China. On the one hand, it is the Chinese Confucian ideology with its emphasis on the need for the continuation of family from father to son that causes May-ying to first dress Hing as a boy, and then adopt Leonard with the false papers. On the other hand, it was restrictive immigration laws that made it difficult for Chinese people to come to Canada that caused many to buy their way into the country with false documents.

Exclusionary acts, such as the five-hundred-dollar head tax and the Chinese Immigration Act of 1923, are mentioned by the narrator, but they do not enter the text as actual documents. Chong avoids overt denunciation of past prejudices against Asians in Canada, but weaves them seamlessly into her historiographic narrative. Her technique is to proceed from the particular – in her case, the familial, using the example of her ancestors – and to then move to the general – the historical canvas. For instance, she recounts details about Chan Sam's father's 'voyage from China to San Francisco ... financed by his clan society in his home country,' and his return to China in 1888 (12–13). At the same time, she includes information about the rise of the early Chinatowns on the West Coast in the late nineteenth century, due to the gold rush. The difficulties of these early settlers are reported: 'In the 1870s and 1880s, there were limits on the number of incoming Chinese per boat, bans against hiring men with pigtail-length hair and against the use of poles to carry baskets. There were special taxes levied on the Chinese for school and policing, employment, laundry, shoes, and even cigars' (12). Much later, when she relates how her mother sought to compensate for her unhappiness at home by throwing herself into her studies, she notes: 'She was studying Latin at school and in her spare time, for she had indeed set her sights on becoming a doctor. She did not know then that the University of British Columbia in Vancouver, then among the top schools in the country, had yet to admit a Chinese student, male or female, into its faculty of medicine' (153). The discriminatory practices are presented non-judgmentally, but not apolitically. The integration of history and personal narrative demonstrates that history is, as Fredric Jameson has pointed out, 'the experience of Necessity.' In Jameson's words, 'History is what hurts, it is what refuses desire and sets inexorable limits to individual as well as collective praxis ... But this History can be apprehended only through its effects, and never directly as some reified force' (*Political Unconscious* 102).

Chong's details of what happens to her family members who remain in China emphasize themes of survival and necessity. Events such as the Japanese invasion of China and the political upheaval that was to ruin her grandfather's hopes of economic success in China read more like a well-researched historical narrative than the first-hand accounts of what happened in Canada. The narrative is chronological, but understandably sporadic. Certain occasions and events are presented in detail, while there are large gaps in other years. For example, Chong only briefly relates the historic fall of Nanking in 1937 and the fall of Canton in 1938. These events form the backdrop of the lean years faced by Huangbo and the children, when they were down to 'one meal a day' (137). More interesting is her depiction of Mao Zedong's 'land reform' (184), where Chan Sam loses the *mau tin* for 'which he had sacrificed years of his life overseas and which he had purchased to provide for the future security of his family' (186). Instead of providing comfort for Huangbo, ironically, the land and showy house make her a target for the Work Team. The Communists accuse Huangbo and other landowners of exploiting the people, of being 'an enemy of the people' (186). Again, the events demonstrate how the past is subject to varying readings and misreadings. The grand house built by Chan Sam using the wages of May-ying becomes 'evidence' that his family was 'counter-revolutionary' (186). While Chan Sam had lovingly designed each part of the house, it was now condemned by the Work Team for its 'unsightliness,' and its excesses destroyed (186). The deliberate misinterpretation of 'evidence' shows how documents can be used to further one's ideological purposes. The Work Team 'removed all papers, letters and photographs' (186), that is, all recorded traces of history, leaving only their version of the past. In their hands, history is something that can be manipulated, and the past harnessed for propaganda.

The letters that survive and are included in *The Concubine's Children* do not always reveal much information about the past. More often than not, these letters are highly stylized and formal exercises in Chinese composition. They demonstrate the Confucian ethos of respect, obedience to elders, and familial obligation. For example, as part of Hing's Chinese studies, she is expected to write regularly to her family in China. The narrator notes, 'Each letter was virtually the same; the salutation and sign-off she had to copy out were invariably longer than anything else she wrote' (99). Reading Hing's letters, one would conclude that she was a well-behaved, obedient girl without much character, as she writes: 'Honorable Mother, I kneel before you with my head bowed and my hands clasped. How are you. I am a good girl. I listen to my mother' (99). In some cases, letters have to be decoded. During Mao Zedong's Communist regime, the 'communication between Chan Sam and Yuen became, in part, a charade to deceive the prying eyes of Communist authorities and villagers anxious to point the finger' (198). Chan Sam's letters contain the requisite Communist rhetoric: 'I hope things go well for China, that production will increase, that construction will increase, and people will live well' (198). The inclusion of these letters makes overt to the reader the difficulty of the act of uncovering evidence, and the need to interpret what is found. The reader shares the work of the writer as researcher, as she, too, must produce the truth, or a version of the truth, from the documents.

One of Chan Sam's last letters to his son contains nothing but 'a litany of Chinese proverbs.' He writes, 'When I see how fast the changes are in the world, I realize in the end that everyone has to die ... Looking back over life, there is no one who has not made mistakes ... Man's fate is rough. If you have money and power, you need have no fear of having no friends' (212). What is ironic is that this and his other letters are revered and held to contain authority and truth by the son in China.

When the author finally meets her uncle Yuen and his family, they act as if they already knew everything from the grandfather's letters. 'It seemed the last word on the family history was comprised of my grandfather's words from Canada, along with what happened to the Chinese family at home' (253). From their strong sense of respect for the father, they believe in reading his documents as literal truth: 'There was a presumption that my grandfather would have told the Chinese side of the family everything of importance about the Canadian side' (253). Yet Chong's book, with its competing discourses and textual evidence, reveals the ways in which that story is only a version of the truth, that 'they were living with an incomplete version of the Canadian family's history' (253).

Ultimately, the book shows that every source of information is subject to error or misreading and has to be carefully interpreted. Photographs, identity papers, letters, and other documents do not always divulge the truth for the writer who wishes to recreate the past. They make sense only when they are placed in a narrative, when they are textualized. Similarly, it is difficult to judge the actions of the concubine without placing her life into the context of history. What was probably one of the most useful sources of information for Chong is the first-hand account, the oral narrative. However, these narratives, too, have to be shifted and arranged. Chong notes of her mother's stories: 'There was nothing ordered about the vignettes from her past' (219). As the receiver of the tales, Chong acknowledges that she exerts some control over what is narrated. She remarks, 'I looked only for the happiness and the sadness. There was so little to laugh about that I would often ask her to repeat my few favorite stories. I liked best the one about how Mother actually got to name herself and chose the name Winnie. There was a lot to cry about ... the lasting impression I had from all Mother's stories came from the words they always ended with: "I had nobody"' (219–20). These comments support Evelyn Hinz's argument that 'although modern forms of auto/biography technically share a narrative element with prose fiction, the internal dynamics of life writing are much closer to dramatic art' (208). As the narratée of the tales, Chong shapes the recollections of the past by highlighting those stories she 'liked best.' Those stories are the ones that have the most dramatic power, and that provide the most interest for her and her readers. Though they may not be the whole story, they are the fragments that, stitched together by the author, form the biography, the narrative of a woman's life.

As well as serving her desire to recreate and come to an understanding of her mother's life, *The Concubine's Children* is also a vindication of her grandmother's troubled life on behalf of her mother. To the Chinese side of the family, her grandmother, May-ying, was simply a bad woman – a gambler, a drinker, and a cantankerous wife. Chong notes, 'To them, what elevated my grandfather to heroic proportions was the tragedy of his hard life in Canada. They cried for the anguish my grandmother caused him, and the separation he had to endure from his wife and family in China' (254). The book represents all that the mother couldn't say to her sister and half-brother in China: 'She did not tell Ping and Yuen ... that the house they cherished as a monument to her father had been built on her mother's back, on the wages and wits of waitressing and the life that came with it. She did not tell them that it stood for everything that had been so misunderstood about her mother, by them and by herself ... She decided it was better to let them believe that her mother brought their father only unhappiness, and that the other mother who raised them had been the superior wife' (254–5).

Chong redefines Western culture's notions of individuality and heroism by presenting us with a nuanced conception of ethnic identity. Though May-ying's occupation as prostitute renders her an abject of society, Chong's narrative emphasizes not her sexualized self but her valiant maternal self. This focus is achieved by the use of Hing's perspective in various parts of the book. Hing recollects that even in difficult times, 'May-ying made certain that her daughter was always clean and well-groomed' (126). She remembers being made to feel guilty because of her mother's constant lament that she has to raise her 'singlehandedly' (127) which was laborious. Scenes depicting May-ying's stoic grief at losing her daughter, Nan, balance those describing her drunken activities in the gambling dens and tea houses. By highlighting those acceptable gendered positions occupied by May-ying, by bridging domesticity and the public sphere, Chong revises and erases prior constructions of normative gender values and racialized notions of otherness and exoticism. She redefines the family for Canadians, by exploring non-traditional dynamics between members of the family.

Seen through the child Hing's eyes, the work of May-ying as a prostitute becomes horrible and painful, not at all glamourous. Hing remembers a time when her mother and one of her 'secret friends' (108) climb into bed beside her. For what 'seemed like an eternity,' Hing lies quietly, feigning sleep (109). In actuality, she is in agony from the recognition of what her mother has become, and also from having one arm 'pinned under' the bodies of her mother and her lover (108). As narrator, Chong shifts the focus of the scene from May-ying's sexuality to Hing, who suffers for her mother's sins: 'The pain of such knowledge revealed itself in her own ailments. She developed recurring stomach cramps, she'd get hiccups often, and she suffered from daily nose bleeds, sometimes severe enough to stain her dress front. Her hair started to thin. But the worse was the eczema on her legs' (109). With such narrative shifts Chong is able to deflect the voyeuristic gaze of Western eyes, to create not scopophilia or visual pleasure, but sympathy. Similarly, as the narrative progresses, Chong replaces May-ying's youthful beauty and porcelain doll figure with her aging and ill body. We witness May-ying becoming frail, suffering 'rapid weight loss' and 'bleeding ulcers' (208). In her old age, she is plagued with 'spitting-up blood disease,' or tuberculosis (215). These images counter whatever romantic notions the reader might have had about the Chinese concubine.

Another important way of de-exoticizing the Oriental other is by tearing away the veil and revealing the suffering beneath the 'painted' faces and perfumed bodies of the waitresses, their 'high heels and hats' and fancy *cheong sam* dresses (28). Chong notes that the young Chinese women who came to Canada expected 'an ordered Confucian society of house and household,' but instead were recruited into the tea house circuit where 'pregnancies were common, mostly unwanted ones. Some waitresses had a string of children by different men; most boarded out some if not all of their children' (29). What is revealed when the 'heavy powder on their faces' is removed are 'the bruises of their men's anger against them' (29). Again, what is emphasized is not the individual's quest for greatness, for freedom, or wealth, but a sense of familial duty and maternal obligation. The waitresses hand over their pay to their men and are left only with their 'tips, which was often all they had to support their children' (29). Hence, Chong positions these women as courageous subjects, without necessarily individualizing them, and without their having to enter into the traditional male sphere of public life and discourse.

By collecting information and writing *The Concubine's Children*, Chong is able to repossess her grandmother's body, textually if not physically. She provides a 'just image of her' to counter the wild stories in circulation in China. Through her historiographic textual act, she recuperates not only her mother's and her grandmother's life stories, but she also finds her own. Her book shows that the quest involved contending not only with the forces of history, but with her own sense of alterity, her divided subjectivity. Laying 'down the truth in all its dimensions,' as she calls it, meant grappling with various forms of documentary evidence, some of which prove to be contestable, as well as realizing when to let go of the past (Chong, 'Fiction' 11). Carolyn Heilbrun notes that while 'biographers of men have been challenged on the "objectivity" of their interpretation, biographers of women have had not only to choose one interpretation over another but, far more difficult, actually to reinvent the lives their subjects led, discovering from what evidence they could find the processes and decisions, the choices and unique pain, that lay beyond the life stories of these women' (31). Chong has 'reinvented' the life of her grandmother, and in the process has also suggested new ways of reading and recording women's lives and histories.

2

A Filipino Prufrock in an Alien Land: Bienvenido Santos's *The Man Who (Thought He) Looked Like Robert Taylor*

The bigger, brighter cities held him longer, New York, Washington D.C., Chicago. He thought it would be Washington to the very end until that day he came running to Chicago, where he had been earlier in his younger days. Fate must have spoken as it always did in his life. Chicago became home where the years came and went. Perhaps there would be time to return. Who could tell? All he knew now, the hour was late.

Bienvenido Santos, *The Man Who (Thought He) Looked Like Robert Taylor*

In Bienvenido Santos's *The Man Who (Thought He) Looked Like Robert Taylor*, Solomon King decides impulsively to retire from his job as a butcher and go 'discover America' (13) when he hears of the death of the Hollywood actor Robert Taylor. All his life, he has believed that he and Robert Taylor shared a mystical connection because of a series of coincidences and because he thinks he resembles the star. Though Solomon makes plans for travelling and fills his basement apartment with travel brochures, he remains, for most of the novel, in Chicago. In the past, he has told his co-workers that he is going away, only to spend his vacation time in his apartment imagining trips to 'Lake Tahoe and Yosemite Park, trout fishing in Lake Okoboji, midnight swimming in Higgins Lake in Roscommons, camping in Hiawatha country' (6). In actuality, he tries to save money, and stays in his apartment on Honore Street, 'part of an extensive area covering several blocks of a Polish colony,' where he feels most comfortable (8). Sol likes the 'Polish people, their sweetness, their fatness,' because 'like him, they were always talking of home, of the old country, and like him, they were making no move to return' (8).

This movement and non-movement is emblematic of the paralysed existence of Solomon King, an old man who senses that death is to come to him shortly. A Filipino American who repeatedly tells himself that *'Time was of the important'* (5),[1] Sol is like T.S. Eliot's J. Alfred Prufrock, who speaks of activity but is paralysed by his sense of inadequacy and fear. Like Prufrock, Sol spends a good deal of time worrying about his age, his health, and his looks. He is unable to enjoy life fully and enter into relationships. Symbolically, he chooses to be located in Chicago, in the middle of America, to which 'he found himself returning' again and again until he decided that 'Chicago was to remain his base' (15). While he 'loved the city,' especially the 'business district where there was movement and a spell and as far as he was concerned, without boundaries and directions' (15), he is also lost in it. 'Maps frightened him, particularly the map of Chicago, which looked, to him, liked a diseased epidermis with exposed veins and arteries in decay where the blood had long clotted in areas that were supposed to be parks and landmarks of a famous city' (15). Like Prufrock, Sol is attracted by the bustle and lack of boundaries of the city. Yet Sol is repelled by its vastness, by what he sees as the illness in the landmarks of the city. This ambivalent attitude towards Chicago is reflective of his attitude to America. Chicago is Sol's home, yet he is restless and does not feel at home in it. America becomes his home, but he is never completely at home in it.

In the last chapter, I looked at the ways Denise Chong recuperates her grandmother and mother, figures of gendered others, while at the same time resituating Chinese Canadians in Canadian social and cultural history. Here, I examine the alienation and dislocation of Filipinos who settled in America in the first half of the twentieth century. In both of these works, the lives of the protagonists in the latter half of the twentieth century have been affected by exclusionary laws, imperialist policies, and prejudices of an earlier generation. Understanding the historical and social conditions of Filipino Americans at the beginning of the century, then, is crucial to an appreciation of Santos's novel. *The Man Who (Thought He) Looked Like Robert Taylor* deals with the power of American film, advertising, and media on the protagonist, who is, in many ways, representative of Filipino 'old-timers.' Through Sol's story, Santos reveals how the culture of the United States has colonized and influenced Filipinos to such a degree that there is no subject outside of

the desires created by those illusions. For Sol, pictorial, literary, and
filmic renditions of people and places, largely created by American
institutions and corporations, become as immediate and as real as his
experiences in life. The very title of the book suggests the unstable
subjectivity of one who imagines he is a Hollywood actor. In the final
section, I discuss how ethnicity intersects with the theme of alienation
and how Santos grapples with issues of Filipino identity in a city that is
in the heart of America.[2]

In this novel, as in a number of his short stories, Bienvenido Santos
depicts the estrangement and isolation of Filipino old-timers in America,
those Filipinos who immigrated to America from the 1920s to the 1940s
(see Santos, 'Pilipino Old Timers'). For this group of Filipino Americans, identity is based on a series of psychic and emotional accommodations and deprivations. Full subjectivity and agency, in Paul Smith's
use of the term, is denied them (xxxv). These immigrants entered the
United States as male subjects, but the customary privileges of being
male in a patriarchal society are not conferred upon them. They are
caught in an undefinable space of being men in an androcentric society,
yet not being able to exercise rights enjoyed by other heterosexual men,
such as being able to marry, procreate, and raise and support a family,
because of America's anti-miscegenation laws at the time. Like other
Asian men, they are feminized in womanless households by having to
learn domestics skills,[3] sometimes having to work as domestics, and
condemned to a life of 'perpetual boyhood' in their own communities
(Kim 74). To complicate matters, their subjectivities have been heavily
interpellated by different aspects of American culture that stress individuality, freedom of movement, and masculine prowess.

This particular situation developed as a result of a number of factors.
Firstly, because of U.S.-directed education in the Philippines, English,
rather than one of the eighty-some indigenous dialects, became the
official language of the archipelago. Consequently, many Filipinos who
have had formal education not only speak, read, and write in English,
but often think in the language of their colonizer more 'fluently' than in
their own language. Secondly, American economic and cultural domination made U.S. products widely available and tempting. Groceries,
magazines, and, most of all, Hollywood movies created subjects who
not only desired the goods and values of Western society, but became
constituted by those very desires. Even before entering North America,
many Filipinos were already 'Americanized' because of U.S. occupation and control of the islands from 1898 to 1946.

Historically, Filipinos who entered America in the early part of the twentieth century were discriminated against by U.S. immigration and recruitment labour practices. Santos points out that these immigrants are special because they have had to endure what recent Filipino immigrants have not:

> Prior to World War II and as late as the 1950s, the Pilipino immigrant was unwanted wherever he went, in the big and the small cities of the United States. As Pilipinos came in increasing numbers, they caused mounting resentment, particularly on the Pacific Coast where riots against them flared, which gave rise to violence and accusations. Resolutions were passed, seeking to ban them from participating in constitutional pursuits. They were accused of spreading diseases and of living no better than animals. They were considered overly fond of white American women and openly suspected of being oversexed; their presence threatened the purity of the Caucasian race. Consequently, they tended to live among themselves or with other minority immigrant groups in labor camps. ('Pilipino Old Timers' 26)

In that period, the United States' capitalist economy needed cheap labour and recruited massive numbers of male workers from the Philippines to work, mostly on farms in California. These workers were treated as temporary labourers without social and familial rights. Immigration policies did not permit their families or Asian women to enter the country, and Filipinos were legally prohibited from marrying white women (see Espiritu 16–18, 22). The result was a community of young men in their prime who lived in lonely bachelor societies and who were then accused of having either excessive sexual appetites or of being sexless.

In *The Man Who (Thought He) Looked Like Robert Taylor*, Santos does not dwell on this aspect of immigrant life, but sets his novel in the later years of these early immigrants. His novel is what Jaime An Lim calls a 'requiem for an old timer' because its characters are already in their old age, retired or close to retirement, by the opening, which is set in the late 1960s and early 1970s. Lim notes that the novel contains a 'wistful evocation of *ubi sunt*' (265), a nostalgic longing for times past. Sol is constantly worried about the passing of time and whether there will be time for him to do what he wants. According to Jaime Lim, the novel 'tries to distill the essence of the life of Solomon King from his boyhood in Sulucan to his early years in Chicago, from the pre- to the postwar periods in San

Francisco and Washington, D.C.' (265). From a sprightly man with a
Filipino dream, he is now reduced to one who has pains in 'every part of
his body' (2). Like the map of Chicago, his body, though once without
boundaries, is now an interconnection of illness and disease.

The best-known Filipino American novel set during this time is
Carlos Bulosan's *America Is in the Heart.* Unlike the characters in Bulosan's
autobiographical work, which documents the difficult lives of migrant
Filipino farm workers, Santos's Solomon King has not worked in Alas-
kan canneries, or picked grapes or asparagus on various farms on the
West Coast. Solomon King's migratory life has been spent mostly in
cities. Historian Barbara Posadas has pointed out that, in general, the
Filipinos who moved into the major cities in the Midwest were a different breed than those who settled in California. For example, they were
slightly better educated than their West Coast counterparts. They tended
to labour as service workers rather than agricultural hands (see Posadas).
However, similar to Bulosan's protagonist, Santos's hero has had to
work at poor paying and unsavoury jobs all his life. In his younger
days, he had once tried to work as an assistant mortician because he
could find nothing else suitable for him. In one of the most detailed and
humorous vignettes of the book, Solomon's horror is described as the
mortician shows him how to pump blood from the cadavers and to rip
the 'internal organs' from the bodies (22). After a week at the job, he
quits. Earlier, he had also tried to work 'as an unskilled labourer on a
high-rise building under construction' when he had 'just arrived in
Chicago' and 'was running low on funds and desperately in need of a
job' (16). Sol arrives at his final and longest career as a butcher after
having 'been at many other jobs as he moved from city to city until
finally settling down in Chicago' (15). Like that of Bulosan's hero, his
career path is characterized by much horizontal movement without too
much advancement. Sol works himself up to the position of butcher
and overseer, but he had to start by cleaning the pens in the compound.

Cumulatively, these menial jobs demonstrate the extent of the abase-
ment, disempowerment, and abuse to which many immigrants had to
submit in order to survive. They often had to accept ignoble occupa-
tions in difficult and dangerous places. Sol moves from jobs where he is
queasy at the thought of heights and contact with dead bodies to one
where he has to slaughter hogs. By the time he starts to work at the
stockyards, his sensibilities have hardened. 'When he saw how the
hogs were butchered, he felt no qualms about the blood, the killing. It
was almost scientific unlike the way they butchered animals in the

Philippines' (15). The focus on blood and guts in both the jobs at the mortician and at the slaughterhouse is significant. These scenes point to the often unseen, but important, parts of our body that work unceasingly to keep the exterior alive. Migrant workers represent the blood and guts of America. Forced to work at menial and unappealing jobs, they are the unacknowledged and unnoticed core of white America. Associated here with them, one could say that the immigrant farm labourers, the domestic and unskilled workers, are metaphorically the innards of white America.

In Santos's work, Sol King is like Prufrock, whose romantic ideals fall short of reality. I bring in T.S. Eliot here because there are many echoes, explicit and implicit, of his work in Santos's. Sol is unhappy and ill at ease with the society in which he is placed. Unable to act, he is haunted by dreams of the past and by his own sense of failure. His various relationships with women have all ended in estrangement. Yet, Sol's alienation, unlike that of Prufrock, does not stem from a kind of modernist angst but from specific historical, ethnic, and cultural circumstances that have to do with Filipinos in the United States. The reasons for his alienation are due to immigration practices as well as social class. Because of the shortage of Filipino women in America in his younger days, Sol, like many Filipino males, is not able to develop traditional familial bonds. Posadas notes that Filipinos in Chicago before the Second World War often contracted interracial marriages with working-class women, many of them from immigrant families. Sol himself does not marry, but he does form short-term relationships with a number of these immigrant women who fit the pattern that Posadas describes. For instance, Sol has an affair with a working-class woman who is from a 'small town in Nebraska' (60). Morningstar, the name he gives her, 'worked nights and it took her an hour by bus to come home' (60). Because of their work schedules, their encounters are brief and take place early in the morning. She complains that his car arrives 'in front of the apartment every seven o'clock in the morning' and leaves 'again on the dot, a quarter before eight' (60). At times, she says, he even leaves the engine of the car going, doing 'everything rush rush, shove, shove, pant, finish, back to the car' (61). The scene is reminiscent of the lovers in T.S. Eliot's *The Waste Land* where at the 'violet hour' the 'human engine waits / Like a taxi throbbing waiting' (ll. 215–17). Like Eliot's office workers who make love unceremoniously and mechanically, Sol and Morningstar perform a sexual ritual that later becomes a 'dreadful habit' (59).

Instead of using mythic or Shakespearean comparisons to demonstrate the degeneration of modern man, Santos uses the discrepancy
between Hollywood movies and ethnic reality to reveal the absurdity
and irony of his protagonist's condition. Solomon compares himself to
Robert Taylor both onscreen and off. Repeatedly he asks Morningstar
and his other girls, 'whom do I look like?' (59), but the answer is never
what he wants to hear. He wants all his girlfriends to acknowledge his
'resemblance to Robert Taylor' (11). Taylor, whose career Sol has followed since 'he saw him in *Magnificent Obsession* in the Philippines in
the middle thirties' (4), is one of the few men 'left in America' whom Sol
considers to be like him, 'a beautiful manly man' (5). Sol's craze for
Robert Taylor reveals his own problematic obsession with masculinity
and identity. Like other minority males who lack power in the work-
place and the public sphere, Sol's male ego needs boosting. His attempts to model himself after the American actor also demonstrate the
difficult position of the ethnic subject in relation to the dominant culture. His plight can be seen as an example of what David Palumbo-Liu
has called the 'problematic of self-construction via the appropriation of
a set of symbols of the Other' ('Minority Self' 81).

Using Sartre, Lacan, and Fanon's notion of the other, Palumbo-Liu
explains the ways in which the 'minority Self is anchored by the gaze of
the dominant Other' ('Minority' 78). He argues that in self-representa-
tions of Asian Americans, we 'see the mediating power of the Other
prescribing implicitly and subtly the manners in which the Asian American can (imaginatively) fit into' the signifying order ('Minority' 79). In
The Man Who (Thought He) Looked Like Robert Taylor, we see the way the
dominant other is able to 'foist upon the minority Self a set of predeter-
mined and necessarily limited sites of representation' ('Minority Self'
76). Solomon believes that he can act like, and is like, the other by virtue
of his looks. He adopts the cavalier habits and dashing mannerisms of
his other, Robert Taylor, in order to validate his masculinity and his
identity. For instance, when his relationships with women go sour,
usually when they tire of him, he takes comfort by comparing himself
to the actor, who in the 1930s and 1940s was also 'kicked around by
women' (63). Sol thinks of Greta Garbo, who gave Taylor 'the cold
shoulder without explanation' (63), and Barbara Stanwyck, who 'treated
him as nothing more than a toy' (64). Coincidentally, Sol has also had a
lover named Barbara, so he ends his musings with 'Poor Bob! Poor Sol!'
(64). Again we see that, in his mind, there is little distinction between
himself and the actor.

During a fight with his girlfriend, Morningstar, 'a scene from *Johnny Eager* flashed before him like a quick change of slides ... He spread out his hands, and panting heavily, he stalked her as she retreated, his face as evil as it could get like Bob's' while Morningstar looked 'much more desirable than Lana Turner' (65). Yet Morningstar does not react as she is supposed to. She threatens to scream, and he thinks, 'this was not part of the script' (65). One way of interpreting the scene is simply to read Sol as a deluded man who fails to distinguish between life and art. He believes that he can control his relationships by simply re-enacting scenes and following the script. Sol also conflates Robert Taylor's life with his screen roles by recalling messy affairs Taylor had with women in films like *Wicked Woman* and *Gorgeous Hussy* (64). His conclusion is that both Taylor and he 'were soft. No matter how they blustered about, they were the ones who bled in the end ... Both of them were cardboard lovers' (64). In contrast to this softness, Sol thinks that the way to handle women is to be 'without mercy. Slap 'em around' (64), as Taylor did in *A Yank at Oxford*.

Jaime An Lim notes the irony of using Robert Taylor as a masculine ideal, for although Taylor was known onscreen for his virility, biographies of the actor reveal that he was 'a nice but weak-willed and submissive man whose first marriage to Barbara Stanwyck was basically engineered by MGM, a man whose sex life was clouded over with rampant allegations of homosexuality' (273). But I would like to read the delusion another way. I see it as the failure of the ethnic subject to freely adopt the subject position he wishes. Much as he wants to be like Robert Taylor, Sol's ethnicity and otherness restrict him. His girlfriends cannot see him for anything but an ethnic other. One of them, Ursula, says to him, 'You're a very special person. Are all of you Filipinos special persons?' (96). Her comments reveal how race and preconceived notions about racial difference can mark, condition, and circumscribe sexual desire. In another instance, when Sol tells her that Robert Taylor's wife is also named 'Ursula,' Ursula repeats her own name and says, 'I can't say it the way you do,' referring to his accent (96). In these moments we see the limits of ethnic self-construction. No matter how much Sol tries to be unlike a Filipino and to be like his Hollywood hero, the markers of his ethnicity, his accent and his looks, condition people's reactions to him. He cannot be like his ideals from the dominant culture simply by appropriating the symbols of Hollywood, and yet he cannot see his own desirability as a Filipino American without those icons. Thus, Robert Taylor's movies function as a screen that affects Sol's view of himself.

Palumbo-Liu points out that it is not only the other's regard, but also the ethnic subject's perception of the way he or she is regarded, that constitutes him or her ('Minority Self' 96). Sometimes, what happens is that the ethnic subject subscribes to the other's discourse inadvertently or unconsciously. Sol believes that he was a 'jealous lover. Abnormally so. Very possessive' (61). When he tries to explain this to Morningstar, he tells her, 'it was a matter of cultural difference' (61). Then he thinks, 'What the hell was that? He couldn't say. He had read and heard about it, that's all' (61). In his wish to excuse his behaviour, he resorts to the dominant order's facile way of understanding the other rather than probing the real reason for his behaviour.

Sol is an example of what Homi Bhabha has called the colonial mimic. Bhabha explains that colonial mimicry 'is the desire for a re-formed, recognizable Other, *as a subject of a difference that is almost the same, but not quite*' (86). Sol acts, thinks, and believes that he is like his colonizer. He is 'almost the same but not white' (Bhabha 89). When Sol tries to better himself by taking a freshman class in English, he encounters an incredulous admissions officer. Sol insists that he is a high-school graduate who lost his credentials during the war. He says. 'Some of my teachers were Americans ... I've read Edgar Allan Poe, William Cullen Bryant, Henry Wadsworth Longfellow, John Greenleaf Whittier. I know some of their poems by heart' (50). Significantly, Sol does not mention learning about any Filipino writers. His reading consists solely of American literature. Instead of being impressed by Sol, the professor is amused by his accent, 'I couldn't follow you ... I mean, I couldn't understand much of what you were saying, at first ... But ... I do get the drift of your speech' (50–1). Sol's efforts to be an authentic American results in what Bhabha calls the 'repetition of *partial presence*' (88). His knowledge of nineteenth-century American poets, coupled with his Filipino accent, renders him an anomaly. But his status as mimic also calls into question notions of colonial authority, classification, and cultural identity. He is a semblance who renders problematic the 'very notion of origins' and reveals 'discriminatory identity effects' in colonial practice (Bhabha 89, 90). The danger in Sol's mimicry is that the resemblance threatens to take over his whole identity.

Most of Sol's relationships in the United States have been with white women rather than Filipinas. Sheng-mei Ma, in *Immigrant Subjectivities*, points out that 'white female bodies have consistently served, in Asian American literature by male writers, to help define male subjectivity' (63). Following Fanon, Ma argues that 'by possessing the white female bodies, [the disadvantaged group] see themselves as temporarily merged with the center' (*Immigrant Subjectivities* 67). While this observation rings true for the most part, in *The Man Who (Thought He) Looked Like Robert Taylor*, Santos complicates interracial eroticism. As I have shown, Sol's involvement with women is influenced by filmic fantasies as well as the lack of Filipinas in the country. Because he lives in one of America's most racially diverse cities, Sol's 'white' women are not WASPs, but often immigrants themselves who are not from the 'centre,' as Ma argues. Sol has had Polish girls visit his apartment, and Ursula is from a 'now-lost Lithuanian coastal town' (100). But the relationship that is most lovingly delineated in the novel is Sol's two-week affair with Blanche Hardman. She, too, is not exactly from the 'centre' because though she is white, she is poor and helpless. What attracts Sol's interest in Blanche at the Greyhound bus depot in Chicago is the fact that Blanche, who is very young, has a baby with her and has 'green eyes' that conveyed a look like a 'wounded bird's' (134–5). Stranded in Chicago by a winter storm on her way to Dowagiac from Joliet, she arouses Sol's fatherly and charitable instincts. It is not from a desire to possess her or her body that he takes her and baby Jerry into his home, where they play at a makeshift family situation. However, like all the other women in Sol's life, this one, too, leaves him. Sol's basement apartment becomes rather like the Chicago Greyhound station, where the 'women come and go' without his forming any lasting bonds with them. Significantly, there is a link between his continual struggle to assert his male identity, to have a family, and his struggle to become the ideal American.

Aside from Hollywood images of masculinity, immigration, and demographic factors, Sol's problems with women stem from his negative childhood experiences. His inability to form relationships can be traced back to his past in the Philippines, and to his father, Daniel King. Sol's memories of his father consist of a 'scent' of 'cheap wine, cigarette butts, sweat dried on the skin in the sun,' and 'a gesture, a grimace: open palms lashing at him as Sol raised his hands, face averted against the blows' (34). He remembers his father's 'thin breath of curses as his blows found their mark or a whip crawled alive on Sol's flesh, tracing welts' (34). This father who beat him was an expert in native fencing, in the aggressive 'silent duel of no touch' (36). As Leonard Casper notes, 'Solomon's own life has been spent not-quite-touching anyone else, least of all himself' ('Paperboat' 168). He remembers with nostalgia a girl called Luz, but her image is tainted with rumours about 'American soldiers in her house, her own family selling PX goods in the black market' (10). It is as if there is no relationship for Sol unaffected by American colonialism – military, economic, or cultural.

Another way Santos reveals the power of the media and mediatic representations is through Sol's fake vacations. For Sol, there is almost no need to get out of his basement in Chicago. The world penetrates his apartment through his TV, his stereo, his collection of photos of Hollywood stars, travel brochures, magazines such as '*Time, Newsweek*, and his favorite tabloid, the *Enquirer*' (12). As his co-workers tell him of 'fishing in Spirit Lake, boating down the Mississippi, camping in the Black Hills or simply travelling around the country,' he feels that he 'had been to all these places – and more – that is, he had read all the literature about them' (6). Everything he 'knew about these places came straight from travel folders, advertisements and special travel numbers in magazines and newspaper supplements' (6). Santos is not just critiquing the insidious power of the media that affects people of all classes and ethnicities. Specifically, he demonstrates how 'Filipinos are quick to identify themselves as Americans' (San Juan, Jr, *Articulations* 117). E. San Juan, Jr, points out that 'the Filipino has been produced by Others (Spaniards, Japanese, the *Amerikanos*)' to the extent that 'the Filipino cannot possess any identity worth writing about' (*Articulations* 118, 123). Santos further highlights this problem through a number of short italicized segments that interrupt the main narrative. In one of them, a Filipino phones the consulate to ask for an authentic Philippine superstition. He is worried that there are 'no Philippine superstitions' because Filipinos are 'just copycats from the U.S.' (122). But all the consulate has are mediatic representations of the country – 'tourist guides, Philippine periodicals' (122). The quest for the authentic superstition is not found there.

In the same way, Santos shows that Filipino Americans have trouble determining their ethnic essence. Again, the question of Filipino identity is raised. Sol recalls the annual gathering of old-timers that is supposed to be a celebration of the 'independence of the Republic of the Philippines' (38). The date of this holiday has always generated some confusion, even among Filipinos, some of whom think that it falls on July fourth (37). At one gathering, the attitude to their homeland is rather blasé. Someone says, 'It's all the same, every goddamned time: organize, united we rise, divided we fall' (39). Aside from some women dressed 'in lacy mestiza garments' and one or two men in 'barong,' the affair does not look very different from any other (42, 43). The highlight of the evening is the opening dance by the 'honorable Consul General of the Philippine Consulate with the beautiful Miss Philippine Independence Day 1968' (42). Yet even this is marred by the fact that 'his honor was suffering from something like gout or had never learned to dance,' and Miss Philippine Independence Day's face 'shone with too much mascara that had begun to drip' (43). When some women attempt to entice Sol into conversation, he finds them speaking of their favourite programs on TV. These turn out to be American daytime shows like *Search for Tomorrow* and *Let's Make a Deal* (44). In his typical existential manner, Sol retreats to 'listen to his pains' (45).

As we have seen, like other Filipinos, Sol's subjectivity has been thoroughly produced by American capitalist ideology. But he does not possess the economic means to satisfy the desires created by the mediatic images. He cannot make himself go on a vacation, or form a stable relationship, because he is too cautious, too full of emotional and economic insecurities. Unlike Prufrock's quasi-existentialist condition, Sol's problems arise out of specific historical and economic ones. He develops a strong 'determination to save' because 'he had been a spendthrift in his youth. He had known men like him from the Philippines who ended up paupers in the United States because all they were after was a good time ... He had known what it meant to go hungry, without a cent in his pocket and forced to take dangerous and filthy jobs' (6). He becomes paralyzed into inactivity and impotence like Prufrock, but the reason is not just psychological, but also socio-cultural. Through vignettes of other Filipino old-timers, Santos shows how the problems encountered by Sol are replicated and ingrained in the Filipino psyche. Other characters do not share Sol's miserly and self-isolating existence, but they do experience the impossibility of the Filipino dream of America.

In the last half of the twentieth century, Filipinos immigrated to America in great numbers because of what sociologists have termed the 'push' and 'pull' factors. The 'push' factor is an economic situation in which 70 per cent of the population in the Philippines are extremely impoverished. The 'pull' factor is the perceived economic opportunities in the United States embedded by 'the American-patterned educational system and the dominance of American popular culture in the Philippines' (Strobel 32). E. San Juan, Jr, notes that 'for about a century now, Filipinos have remained subjugated bodies interpellated by a market-centered panopticon, dispersed as "warm body export" into the fetishized and commodifying space of international trade' (*Philippine Temptation* 92). Today, more than six million Filipinos, mostly in the

Middle East, Europe, and Asia, earn 'on the average $3.5 billion a year for the Philippine government' (San Juan, Jr, *Philippine Temptation* 92). Consequently, Filipinos at home have developed an idealistic and falsely exaggerated view of the wealth that can be garnered in the new land. They think that all immigrants roll in dollars, lead highly successful lives, and can send money to their relatives whenever there is a need.

In the novel, Santos shows some of the consequences of the high expectation of Filipinos back home on immigrants in the United States. The Filipino dream of success has added yet another level of anxiety to the immigrant, who is made to feel ashamed if he or she returns home without 'making it' in the new world. Two characters reveal their half-desperate attempts to live rather sham versions of the Filipino dream. One is Artemio Banda, whose wealthy parents sent him to the United States to study. But Artemio discovers that he is 'not really interested in going to school' and is more interested in 'the movies and the long-limbed girls with golden hair' in Los Angeles (88). By the time he meets Sol, he has been 'ten years in and out of schools on both sides of the Mississippi, staying in each long enough to buy the school's stationery and pennant to mail home to keep his doting grandparents believing that Artemio was, indeed, trying to get an education' (88). In the novel, Artemio figures as a comic character who puts Sol's sense of Filipino hospitality to the test. He appears coincidentally at mealtimes, empties Sol's fridge, and stays watching TV past midnight. After a while, Sol notices 'the look in [his] eyes' and wonders if 'he was no longer receiving money from home' (91). Artemio is caught in the impossible situation of his ineligible status in America. He has a 'student visa' that does not allow him to work, so he has to keep enrolling in schools. He has to sponge off people in order to survive. Yet to return home to the Philippines would be to admit failure.

Another character caught in the no-man's-land of the illegal alien is Monica, who appears in a digression from the main plot. This tale concerns another old-timer, Alipio Palma, who, unlike Sol, has been married and has recently been widowed.[4] Segments like this cause Leonard Casper to criticize Santos's novel as 'loosely connected,' 'desultory,' and 'unconvincing' in its form (169). Yet, as I have tried to argue, what Santos is doing is trying to show the results of American imperialism, immigration policy, and the extremely impoverished conditions of the Philippines on a group of people. He is interested not only in the portrayal of an individual, but in the socio-economic impact of these factors on old-timers collectively. As Jaime An Lim notes, there are many Filipinos who are 'rainbow-chasing, dream-making pilgrim[s] in America' (273). The dream affects females as well as males, and in Monica's case, she is willing to give up youth, sexuality, and freedom for the dream of a better existence in America.

Like many Filipinas who come to America or go to Europe and Australia as mail-order brides, Monica has no other product to exchange but her body. As a woman, her physical self becomes the precious commodity that has any trade value in the international market. In the short tale, all three women – Alipio's wife, Seniang; Monica's sister, Mrs Zafra; and Monica herself – have had to resort to marriage with virtual strangers many years their senior in order to have the right to stay in the country. Now in his sixties, Alipio explains how Seniang approached him and said, 'marry me and I'll take care of you' (79). At that time, 'she had to get married to an American citizen otherwise she would be deported' (79). Similarly, Mrs Zafra, upon leaving an order of nuns, has had to find her way to change her alien status. She recalls:

> The immigration office began to hound her, as it did other Filipinos in the same predicament. They were a pitiful lot. Some hid in the apartments of friends like criminals running away from the law ... Those who had transportation money returned home, which they hated to do. At home they would be forced to invent lies as to why they had come back so soon. They were defeated souls, insecure, and no longer fit for anything. They had to learn how to live with the stigma of failure in a foreign land all their lives. Some lost their minds and had to be committed to insane asylums. Others became neurotic, anti-social, depressed in mind and spirit. (77)

Monica, a teacher in the Philippines, has a similar plight. She has come to America as a 'temporary visitor' and has stayed on for almost a year by extending her visa. She and her sister visit Alipio to try to sell the idea of her eligibility to him: 'she's good, religious, any arrangement you wish, she'd accept it' (83). Alipio's 'gleaming dentures showed a half smile' as he understood the proposition. Though an old man, his lechery is suggested as he 'smacked his lips' looking at Monica's legs (84). For these women, commodifying their bodies by marriage, sometimes with men over twenty years their senior, is the only way to follow the Filipino dream of life in America.

Thus, Alipio, though limping and hard of hearing, is able to seize the moment and sing his love song in the way that the Prufrockian protagonist, Sol, is not. Sol remains trapped in his map of pains and disease, in his unfulfilled desires. He is restless and never completely settled, even in Chicago. As if by chance or fate, the city 'became home where the years came and went' (153). Sol lives in a cosmopolitan and metropolitan city, but he is locked in his own emotionally circumscribed world just as, physically, he chooses to be confined in his basement year after year. Though the bright lights of Chicago's business district attract him, there is actually very little of the marvels of the large city that he enjoys. Shirley Geok-lin Lim argues that the novel is 'chiefly a critique of desire as it operates in and is operated upon expatriate Filipinos in U.S. culture ... Desire in the novel is not unidirectional, exilic desire; it is also desire for the United States, assimilationary desire' ('Immigration and Diaspora' 306–7). Yet, at the same time, Santos raises questions about the consequences of assimilation and the high cost of desire. Chicago does not have London's 'yellow fog that rubs its back upon the windowpanes' (Eliot, 'Prufrock' l. 15), but it functions in the same way for a Filipino in the late 1960s and early 1970s. It is a city of vibrancy, culture, and animation, but one in which a racial and ethnic other has difficulty in participating fully.

Santos' protagonist is a failed, somewhat comic hero, a man who, like Prufrock, is not the prince, but 'at times, the Fool' (Eliot, 'Prufrock' l. 119). Yet the novel offers a serious critique of the insidious effects of U.S. cultural and economic imperialism. In the closing scene of the novel, Sol dreams of his parents and hears 'Poe's bells for the dead' (173). In his dream, his mother hands him a candy bar, which she tells him is a gift from his old sweetheart, Luz: 'She has been keeping it since liberation when a G.I. Joe gave it to her' (173). Luz wanted the candy bar 'to sweeten his way' (173). Yet, like other things that originate from America, this present is ambiguously coded. The presence of the GI in the Philippines taints the gift with overtones of militarism, violence, and imperialism. Though sugar sweet, the candy bar is emblematic of other legacies bequeathed to the country by America. Gifts like American literature and language, Hollywood films, stateside goods, and the American dream have created subjects who, like Sol, have become impotent by the inaccessibility and excess of their desires. Like Prufrock, they may 'have heard the mermaids singing' (l. 124) at some point, but they are unlikely to be the subjects of the exchange.

3

Rescripting Hollywood:
Performativity and Ethnic Identity in
Mina Shum's *Double Happiness*

Mina Shum's debut feature, *Double Happiness* (1994), is a film that challenges the scopic drive of mainstream Hollywood films by intervening in what Ann Kaplan calls 'dominant looking relations' (7). The film, the first feature produced by a Chinese Canadian woman, self-consciously plays with its North American audience's expectations of cinematic gaze, narrative voice, subjectivity, and racial stereotypes. In the opening scene, the central character, Jade Li, talks directly to the camera, comparing her 'very Chinese' family with that of the TV sitcom *The Brady Bunch*. But, she notes with irony, '*The Brady Bunch* never needed subtitles.'

Subtitles and the need for translation suggest a concern with cultural and artistic re-presentation. Similar to the last two authors I examined, who dealt with issues of alienation and dislocation, Shum grapples with misunderstandings due to one's ethnicity. However, she adds the dimension of staging and representation to the politics of the visible. Through the genre of comedy romance, Shum reveals the extent to which identity is constantly being performed – in Judith Butler's sense of the term, 'performativity' (*Bodies* 95). Racial and gendered identity are re-enacted and problematized together in *Double Happiness*. Shum uses humour to demonstrate the sometimes high and painful cost of assimilation of the other into normative Anglo-Canadian heterosexual society. She employs narrative techniques in her film that are stylistically self-conscious and critical of Hollywood practices. While the film is not overtly political, it uses parody and intertextuality to comment on issues about social life in modern-day North America. It engages with mainstream audience's expectations, reveals our culture's stereotypes and institutionalized racism, and highlights the importance of ethnic and minority representations.

To begin with, I contend that *Double Happiness* is doubled and layered in more ways than one. Ostensibly, the title refers to the Chinese wish for twice-blessed good fortune. As some critics have noted, double happiness is the 'Chinese symbol for marriage, which is literally two happinesses joined in union' (Harvey, Xing, 221, n. 36). Xing notes that the 'movie title is a pun about Jade, the leading character, in a futile search for two types of happiness: one that her family wants, and one that she wants' (221, n. 36). But the 'double' in the title could also refer to other layered aspects. Many of the characters in the movie lead 'double' lives, acting parts and changing identities, thereby critiquing both Euro-American and Chinese cultures and ideologies in the process. Doubly or triply marginalized, as Asian, female, and Canadian in a predominantly Americanized culture in North America, Shum reveals her awareness of the processes by which subjects are formed and constituted in our contemporary world in this witty *Bildung*.

Double Happiness highlights what Judith Butler calls the 'performativity' of racialized and gendered subjectivity (*Bodies* 95) by its metafilmic structure. Several scenes contest the notion of a stable ethnic subject by playing with accents, dress, and performance. A number of instances in the movie demonstrate that being Asian is a negative marker in Canadian society. Jade's Asian features engender certain expectations in the people she meets. In her initial encounter with Mark, she plays with these cultural stereotypes by meekly bowing, pretending not to speak English, and acting demure when he condescendingly assumes she can't speak English. Conversely, the Chinese director from Hong Kong sees Jade's Chinese features and expects her to be fluent in Cantonese and able to read her Chinese script, even though Jade was raised in Canada. Jade's inability to read Chinese causes the casting director to sneer at her. Both of these examples illustrate Ien Ang's point about being the problems of being a diasporic Chinese subject. Ang argues that in many parts of the world, being Chinese is an 'unchosen, minority status.' Chineseness imparts 'an externally imposed identity given meaning, literally, by a practice of discrimination. It is the dominant culture's classificatory practice, operating as a territorializing power highly effective in marginalizing the other, that shapes the meaning of Chineseness here as a curse, as something to "get used to"' (Ang 224).

The notion of performativity as a 'forced reiteration of norms' (Butler, *Bodies* 94) is illustrated more than once in the movie. As Butler has explained, performative citations are 'never merely the voluntary choices of a humanist subject; rather, they are the product of constitutive constraints that create identities, creative performances elicited under duress' (Kondo 7). Not only is the main character, Jade, studying to be an actress and depicted in various guises, her family and friends are shown to be 'performing' several roles – good Chinese man, Oriental goddess, and docile mother – to varying degrees. These performances show how identity is a daily and ritualized act that occurs both consciously and unconsciously. For example, one of Jade's friends, Lisa, willingly plays the role of the exotic Oriental for her boyfriend. She wears sexy, skimpy dresses and stays with him in what Jade calls his 'Oriental love den,' complete with its red, gaudy K Mart lanterns. While one could argue that Lisa 'chooses' to live with her 'rice king,' one can see the incident as Lisa's effort to assimilate and be accepted by the dominant culture. Being with a man who fancies Oriental girls and Orientalism is Lisa's way of escaping her family and becoming integrated into Canadian culture. Though she may be aware of the exoticism, it is less oppressive than being with her family and being a social outsider.

However, in the case of other characters, being model Chinese citizens and subscribing to the values of traditional Confucian culture can also generate difficulties. Through minor characters like Jade's mother and her Uncle Ah Hong, Shum illustrates the complications of trying to maintain an essentialist Chinese identity in the diaspora. Both discover what Ang notes, which is that 'being Chinese outside China cannot possibly mean the same thing as inside' (225). Jade's mother tries to be the obedient Chinese wife who unquestioningly follows her husband's decrees. This effort causes her anguish as it conflicts with her maternal desires in her dealings with her son, Winston. Because Winston has disobeyed his father by moving out of the family home, he has now become a ghost to them. Jade's father not only banishes him from the family, he instructs the family never to speak of him again. All photographs of Winston are removed. In effect, Winston's existence has been officially erased from the Li family. They make up lies about him when their friends and neighbours ask about him. While obeying the father's wishes on the matter, the mother nevertheless breaks the patriarchal injunction and attempts to contact her son by telephone. That she has to resort to subterfuge to talk to her own son shows the extent to which Chinese patriarchal customs conflict with her own desires and the extent to which she has to suppress these maternal yearnings in order to be a good wife. She performs the role of the strict authoritarian parent only because her husband expects it of her.

In a similar way, the arrival of Ah Hong, Jade's father's friend from Hong Kong, brings into the foreground the ways in which Chineseness as an identity is being reshaped and reproduced in the diaspora. The whole Li family believe that they have to consciously perform their Chineseness during his visit. Upon his arrival, Jade and her sister have to speak their best Chinese to impress him. They bow in greeting and wish him happiness and prosperity, acting the roles of good traditional Chinese daughters. What the film illustrates rather nicely, however, is that Chineseness itself is no longer a static essence. At the airport, Ah Hong surprises the girls by kissing their hands because he 'saw it in the movie on the plane.' He is also the one who introduces the karaoke machine to the family, which, though a machine that originated in Asia, is used to play American hits in the house. While the family believes that Ah Hong has preserved traditional Chinese values because he lives in Hong Kong, he later admits to Jade that he has not upheld traditional Confucian customs, either. He has illicitly fathered children with his maid, who is probably either a lower-class Chinese woman or a Filipina.[1] He has to maintain his ties to them surreptitiously. The relationship with the maid is considered disgraceful by Chinese standards, and Ah Hong keeps it a secret from his friends and relatives.

My point in bringing up the mother and Ah Hong's deceptive behaviours is to show how identities shift and accommodate themselves to the cultures with which they come into contact. Adapting Butler's theories, we have seen how racialized identity is a 'process of iterability, a regularized and constrained repetition of norms' (Butler, *Bodies* 95) and how subjectivity is not essential but constantly reprocessing itself. These instances show how difficult it is to embrace what Ang calls 'a truly diasporized hybrid identity, because the dominant Western culture is just as prone to the rigid assumptions and attitudes of cultural essentialism as is Chinese culture' (235). It is precisely these assumptions and essentialisms that Shum's film playfully mocks.

The most hilarious examples of how gender and ethnic identities are performed and subverted occur during Jade's dates with young men whom her parents consider suitable marriage partners. It is true that, generally, the custom of dating and courtship has evolved into a highly ritualistic game. One often puts on a performance or acts one's best on dates. But Shum's film reveals the particularly comic and pathetic elements in the courtship rituals of Chinese ethnic families. Diasporic Chinese parents, while no longer following the traditional custom of using matchmakers, nevertheless have great economic and emotional investments in their children's marriages and potential marriage partners. Both Jade's and Andrew's parents believe that marriage with a good Chinese boy or girl is the key to their son or daughter's future. Like many children of immigrant families, Jade and Andrew are caught between the values of their traditional parents and the more modern values of the dominant culture. But the film dramatizes the way in which external parental pressures impinge on one's sense of self; or, to put it in Foucauldian terms, the way in which power, sexuality, and desire are linked. It is not only fear of parental authority that forces Jade and Andrew to comply with their parents. It is also the collusion of normative heterosexual discourse about love and marriage, cultural expectations, and images from the media that make them go through the dating charade.

As Foucault has noted in *The History of Sexuality*, there is a complex overlapping of sexuality, knowledge, and power (81). Power does not simply emanate from above, in this case, Jade's parents, but comes from a network of relations. In the opening scene, even Jade's younger sister, Pearl, becomes involved in the deployment of normative heterosexuality and romance. She remarks somewhat contemptuously that Jade is twenty-two and still not married. Jade's parents are practising what Foucault calls the 'deployment of alliance: a system of marriage of fixation and development of kinship ties, of transmission of names and possessions' (*History* 106), which Foucault believes has been superseded by the deployment of sexuality. Yet both systems seem very much alive in the Chinese Canadian society Shum depicts. Shum comically chronicles the surveillance mechanisms designed to ensure Jade's marriage with a nice Chinese boy. Her dates are carefully arranged; her mother helps her dress; the whole family watches her leave; and the father tries to monitor her telephone conversations. The danger for Jade is that no matter how much she rebels at first, she starts to think like them, caught in the web of power and surveillance, deception and transgression. It is her inability to completely dissociate herself from the values instilled in her by her parents that creates much of the tension in the film, and makes it so difficult for her to move out and start her life on her own. For Andrew, while it may seem funny to constantly be devising schemes to thwart one's parents and aunts, to constantly defer the moment of truth, the earnestness with which the matchmaking takes place shows that compulsory identities have deep implications for the ethnic subject. His gay identity is something he cannot share with his Asian Canadian family and must continually suppress. To reveal the truth would put him in the same danger as Jade's brother, Winston, where defiance of authority and tradition meant banishment and erasure of identity.

In terms of narrative technique, Shum refuses to follow mainstream cinema's practice of locating 'the male voice as the point of apparent textual origin, while establishing the diegetic containment of the female voice' (Silverman, *Acoustic Mirror* 45). Kaja Silverman points out that 'classic cinema's male subject sees without being seen, and speaks from an inaccessible vantage point' (*Acoustic Mirror* 51). As an Asian woman, Shum is faced with two challenging issues in this project. One is what Sandy Flitterman-Lewis calls the problem of 'female authorship' in cinema (16). In her classic essay 'Visual Pleasure and Narrative Cinema,' Laura Mulvey argues that woman functions as 'image,' while man is the 'bearer of the look' in Hollywood films (19). She notes that 'traditionally, the woman displayed has functioned on two levels: as erotic object for the characters within the screen story, and as erotic object for the spectator within the auditorium, with a shifting tension between the looks on either side of the screen' (19). The notion of female authorship or enunciation in the feminine, as Flitterman-Lewis suggests, 'raises the question of female *desire*, indicating a terrain of representation from which various new positions can be engaged, scopic modalities which imply alternative conceptions of female subjectivity and desire' (16–17). Aside from this problem of female authorship, another related issue for Shum is what Aki Uchida calls the 'Orientalization of Asian women in America.' Uchida notes that the image of the Oriental woman as 'exotic, submissive, and subservient, or sinister, treacherous, and lecherous' still predominates and 'is present at all levels of discourse: from the level of mass media to the level of interpersonal interactions in everyday life' (167). And as Gina Marchetti notes, 'Hollywood's romance with Asia tends to be a flirtation with the exotic rather than an attempt at any genuine intercultural understanding' (1).

When Shum presents Jade, a young Asian woman, as the main subject of her feature film, the producer has to somehow engage her audience's interest, but engage it differently. Following Flitterman-Lewis, we ask, 'What happens when a female enunciating subject is posed, when the desiring look articulates a different economy of vision?' (19). Flitterman-Lewis suggests a number of possibilities for female enunciation, some of which Shum uses in *Double Happiness*. Among those I look at are 'a problematization of the enunciating subject itself and the indication of alternative positions ... a shift of emphasis in the quality and intensity of the controlling look – as well as in its object ... and, at the level of the diegesis, differing structures of point-of-view and identification as well as the creation of new possibilities for destabilizing the inevitability and homogeneity of the patriarchal narrative' (Flitterman-Lewis 17).

Shum uses various strategies to disrupt diegetic realism in her film. As critics have noted, what passes for realism in classical cinema involves 'certain practices of editing, camerawork, and sound that serve the reconstitution of a fictional world characterized by internal coherence, plausible causality, psychological realism and the appearance of seamless spatial and temporal continuity' (Stam, 'The Question of Realism' 225). Shum's refusal to adhere to these practices completely and to reconstitute an internally coherent world creates a film that makes us aware of the expectations we have come to associate with realistic films. Her characters are not containable in the traditional realist way. In the opening scenes of *Double Happiness*, Shum takes 'a lazy-Susan shot of Jade's family at dinner, with the camera at the centre of the table, swivelling through 360 degrees to track their conversation' (Johnson 44). We are made aware of the importance of camera angle and viewpoint through this technique. The question of who has the power to speak is playfully raised. It renders all the speakers at the table equally important. At the same time, the swivelling has the disconcerting effect of intimacy. The lazy-Susan angle is one way of shifting patriarchal enunciation and narrative control. Through the confusion and babble of voices, it also has the effect of de-exoticizing her heroine. She is shown in the midst of her middle-class immigrant family, having dinner, like a scene from *The Brady Bunch* and, paradoxically, unlike the Bradys.

Another technique Shum employs to disrupt the illusion of realism is the use of mock interviews or monologues. These monologues, delivered by Jade and her mother, father, and sister, interrupt the narrative flow of the story.[2] What is said in the monologues does not always have a direct relationship to the narrative moment, and tends to jolt the audience into an awareness of the conventions they often take for granted while watching most films. Jade's monologue is preceded by the call 'Take 6,' which highlights the artificiality of filmic process. In the monologue, which occurs after the initial meeting with Mark, Jade tells herself not to get involved with him: 'No, no way.' But she talks directly into the camera, making the audience her confidant. What is interesting about these monologues is that they do not have the same function throughout the film. While Jade's monologue is like a soliloquy that informs us of her thoughts regarding an incident that has just taken place, the ones spoken by her father and mother are recollections of the past. They work like narrated flashbacks. In his monologue, Jade's father looks back to his life in China as a kind of Eden, to a time when his father took him for walks in the garden. He remembers that his family had servants, that they had every kind of vegetable there was, and made many new dishes. Jade's father expresses a longing for the uncomplicated life, where the father is always right and sure, where Li family values never change. Yet this idyllic evocation of homeland is contradicted by the monologue of the mother. For her, China was not always so wonderful. The strongly patriarchal culture placed unequal values on women and men, on girls and boys. In her monologue she tells the story of a girl who couldn't speak, who was someone's second wife. When the woman delivered her firstborn, a female baby instead of a male child, the family was so disappointed, they placed the baby in a pig cage and drowned it in the river. Jade's mother interprets the story as a story of the loss of children, like her own Winston. She reveals her fear that her children will be taken away one by one. This memory of cruelty contrasts with the Edenic picture painted by the father in his monologue, and also gives us insight into the repressed feelings of the mother.

Similarly, Pearl's monologue is about her memories, this time, of the banished Winston. It is only at this point that she is allowed to remember her brother, of whom her father forbids the family to speak. Pearl harks back to a happier time in their childhood, when they used to play and make snowballs. Like the father's, it, too, is one of loss and regret. She misses her brother, and laments that Winston can't give her presents anymore. Through the monologue, we are presented with an alternative view of the absent Winston, a view that differs from the one authorized by the father. In this way, Shum breaks down the monologic nature of the narrative, employing a filmic 'heteroglossia,' to use a Bakhtinian term (*Dialogic Imagination* 324).[3] *Double Happiness* reveals the many voices and narratives it takes to tell the story of one family fully.

In visual terms, as Mulvey has argued, in many Hollywood films, the gaze is organized in such a way as to privilege dominant patriarchal order (16). The problem, as Flitterman-Lewis puts it, is how to 'define a "desiring look" when the position of looking is female' (16). In *Double Happiness*, I argue, Shum attempts to represent desire in the feminine. From the start of the film to the end, Jade is the 'figure of narrative movement' that assures the spectator's narrative identification (de Lauretis 144). She becomes both 'image' and the 'bearer of the look' rather than simply providing 'pleasure in looking' (Mulvey 19, 16). Through close-up shots, we participate in Jade's ardent desires for a man and for an Academy Award, to be nominated for a dramatic part, 'something hard and real,' as she says. Another way Shum makes Jade's desires come alive for us is through her two rather surreal rehearsal scenes. In the first scene, Jade is depicted reciting lines with a Southern accent in the style of Blanche Du Bois in Tennessee Williams's *A Streetcar Named Desire*, while in the second scene she is saying lines in the style of Joan of Arc in George Bernard Shaw's *Saint Joan*. Both passages are interesting because they provide intertextual commentaries on Jade's life and her aspirations.

While the first rehearsal scene is not a word-for-word rendition of Williams's play, it is obviously an audition piece in the style of *Streetcar*. Shum may have had to change the exact passage from Williams's play for copyright reasons, but the sentiments, setting, costuming, and style of delivery are identifiable with Blanche. The echoing of this fading Southern belle who romanticizes her life is significant here. Like Blanche, Jade is a socially transgressive figure who is struggling to reconcile her desires with what is socially acceptable. Both women wish to transcend their social status, to live a different life than that which is expected of them, and are constantly role playing. In Jade's case, this role playing is part of her identity as an actress, while for Blanche, the acting is unconscious and part of her identity. Jade plays several roles offscreen. For instance, she performs the respectable professional, looking like Connie Chung, when she goes out on dates, the good daughter who brings her father sweet buns, and the sexy vamp with Mark. When Jade rehearses for the role of Southern belle, her ordinary bedroom is transformed into an eerie stage set. Through lighting and make-up, Shum creates the illusion of another world. It is as if Jade's enunciation is enough to engender a space that is outside of her everyday landscape. The scene, which takes us momentarily away from the main plot, shows the intensity of Jade's desire. In Shum's utopian world, a woman's dream can create a kind of reality. It is a vision of a theatrical world where there is racially unbiased casting and equal opportunity to work for all ethnic subjects. What critics have said of Blanche could apply here to Jade. Gene Phillips says, 'Within the boarders of her little realm Blanche is able to create a soft, exotic atmosphere which veils the unpleasant realities of life which she does not care to confront .... To this end she covers the naked light bulb in her cubicle with a colored paper lantern which subdues the light' (69). In one of Blanche's well-known speeches, she says, 'I don't want realism. I want magic' (Williams 1638).

In addition, Jade is like Blanche, as critics have noted, a 'determined, strong-willed woman' who 'has her soft and sensitive side' (Phillips 65). She is a complex character, who has her illusions, but whom some people, including Tennessee Williams, consider 'rather noble' (qtd in Phillips 74). In North America, her Southern belle character would not normally be played by an Asian girl on the stage or in the movies. That Jade can perform Blanche well, but will probably never play her, is the point Shum wants to make. It is not uncommon in Broadway and in Hollywood to see white actors playing in 'yellowface,' in Asian parts. For example, in such diverse works as Charlie Chan movies, *Madame Butterfly*, *The King and I*, *Miss Saigon*, and others, white actors play lead roles, but the reverse is not true (see Josephine Lee 12, Marchetti 81, Ty, 'Welcome'). Asian actors rarely get featured in important roles as white characters. This inequity and the lack of opportunity for Asian actors has often been expressed by frustrated Asian Americans and Canadians who are tired of the usual roles of Fu Manchu villains, Suzie Wong, or Vietnamese whores. One actor is quoted as saying: 'I will never play Suzie Wong or a Vietnamese whore again. I want to play Blanche and Nora, Medea and Desdemona. I have a lot to contribute, but ... they won't cast me' (qtd in Josephine Lee 14–15). When Jade auditions for a part in a movie, she is faced with the usual typecasting. The casting director is not amused or impressed by Jade's versatility as an actress, her ability to imitate a Parisian accent. He only wants her to play the Asian woman who speaks with a heavy Chinese accent.

Similarly, in the second rehearsal scene, Shum uses fire, smoke, and other lighting effects to create a surreal world simulating the in-between of heaven and earth. Again, the strength of Jade's desire and the power of her acting transform the ordinary setting of her bedroom into an incandescent stage. Jade recites, 'I am alone on earth but not in heaven,' a paraphrase from Shaw's history play. In the play, the line comes at the moment when Joan has been warned by the Archbishop that she stands alone, trusting her own 'conceit ... ignorance ... headstrong presumption' (Shaw 74). In spite of the warning, Joan is defiant and says, 'I have always been alone ... Well, my loneliness shall be my strength too' (Shaw 75). Nicholas Grene notes of the passage that it is 'one of the greatest speeches in Shaw' (243). He says, Joan is 'horrified and bewildered by the threats that are made against her. And yet out of that horror and bewilderment, out of the realisation that she is alone, she draws ... strength' (243).

For Jade as for Shum in real life, to be an Asian Canadian actor and filmmaker is to constantly be challenged, to be on trial in as difficult and as heroic a situation as that endured by Joan the martyr. Yet out of that bewilderment, she emerges strong. Like many children of Asian immigrant parents, Shum had to struggle with familial and cultural opposition when she wanted to work in the performing arts. In an interview, Shum said that her 'parents were critical of her pursuit of the Arts, acting and directing in particular' (Harvey). Even today, she stands 'alone'; she is known as the 'Chinese-Canadian filmmaker from Canada' (Harvey). In Shum's film, like Joan, Jade does not pursue the womanly path expected of her. Joan defies convention by cross-dressing. Jade rebels against her parents who do not take her acting career seriously, and would rather she concentrate on her marriage prospects. Jade's father tells her that in order to keep Andrew interested, she must be more feminine: 'you mustn't act the way you do... you've got to be gentle, soft.' But like Joan, Jade does not comply with the advice of the authority figures. Though not burned at the stake, Jade is forced to choose between following her acting career and sacrificing the approval and company of those she loves. Like Joan, she decides to listens to the 'voices' from within rather than to give in to society's dictates.

Grene argues that throughout the play, 'Shaw is bent on demystifying the figure of Joan. She is to be seen as plain-speaking, buoyant, unabashed, unreverent' (236). At the same time as he was 'determined to remove the glamour of the legendary Joan, he highlighted 'what was truly extraordinary in her character – the energy, the resolution, the unswerving will' (Grene 236). These comments could apply equally well to Shum, who is determined to remove the exotic, Oriental, and mystery out of the Asian girl. Like Shaw, Shum wants to highlight what is extraordinary about her character, Jade, as an individual – her energy, vibrancy, and pluck. Shum may have also been attracted to the character of Joan because of her 'exploring spirit, single and free' (Morgan 256). In her final prayer, Joan asks, 'O God that madest this beautiful earth, when will it be ready to receive Thy saints? How long, O Lord, how long?' (104) Margery Morgan remarks that this 'final cry marks her as an impossibilist, a utopian' (256). Jade is a contemporary and somewhat comic version of this heroine.

A final intertext used by Shum is Grant Wood's painting *American Gothic* (1930). In one scene, Shum has Jade's father hold a pitchfork that recollects the stance of the man in Wood's painting of rural life. Wood depicts a Midwestern farmer and his spinster daughter in a way that suggests their rigidity and Puritanism. Shum playfully recreates the image in her film, parodying the painting on several levels. The parody can be read as a criticism of the father, who is as austere and forbidding as the father in *American Gothic*. In addition, though ostensibly referring to an architectural style, the title of Wood's piece can also evoke a kind of insidious barbarism in America. Shum's imitation of the pose highlights the fact that there exists this same archaic excess underneath the well-meaning customs of Chinese parents. They expect an outdated Puritanical behaviour from their children, and when their expectations are not fulfilled, they behave like Gothic monsters. Jade's father is a man who does not accept compromise and change. In one of the final scenes of the film, he takes away Jade's key to the house, symbolically her access to her family, because she has decided to move out and live on her own.

Finally, the parody highlights the problematics of racial identity, an issue that Shum has raised since the opening lines of the film. At one level, the Li family is 'American' – read North American or Canadian. Their trials and tribulations are like those of the Brady Bunch. But at another level, they are like Gothic spectres, haunted by the ghosts of what they ought to be as well as the ghosts of a nostalgic past. The father has accepted the fabulation of Chineseness, a situation where 'the ontological distinction between active self-determination and passive internalization of an imposed idea or norm no longer holds' (Pheng Cheah 146). He has taken a notion of Chineseness, even though this no longer resembles the ethos of the homeland, and attempts to embody this ideal through his daily habits and roles. His identity becomes fixed and immutable, but nothing more than a spectre, according to Derrida's sense of the term.[4] Like Sol, who has taken Robert Taylor's characters in Hollywood movies for the real thing and acts according to what he believes the characters would do, the father has idealized the notion of Chineseness and rigidly imposes Confucian beliefs on his family. Like the tyrannical uncles in eighteenth-century Gothic fiction, he wishes to lock up his daughter or banish her from his sight when she does not obey him without question.[5]

Produced mainly for the English-speaking world, such films as *Double Happiness* made by Asians in the diaspora are important because they contest not only the dominant Euro-American culture's representations but also its power to represent. In another context, Rey Chow has argued that 'film serves as a major instrument for making the visuality of exotic cultures part of our everyday mediatized experience around the globe' (*Primitive Passions* 27). What Shum has succeeded in making familiar to film audiences is the gendered and racialized, and at times exoticized, experiences of Asians living in Canada. Though Lisa Lowe has stressed the 'heterogeneity and hybridity' (24) of Asian American (and presumably, Canadian) identities, in Hollywood films, we are only a step away from Orientalist images of 'the pollutant, the coolie, the deviant, the yellow peril, the model minority' (Robert Lee 8). A film made by a woman from a minority culture 'changes the traditional divide between observer and observed, analysis and phenomena, master discourse and native informant' (Chow 28). On the issue of minority representation, Trinh T. Minh-ha has noted that these questions of representation are always complex. It is not always clear who is subject and who is object, or if is there such a thing as an authentic native informant.

Trinh Minh-ha argues that 'the moment the insider steps out from the inside, she is no longer a mere insider (and vice versa). She necessarily looks in from the outside while also looking out from the inside' (145). It is this ambivalence and doubleness that creates the interests and tensions in Shum's film. *Double Happiness* reveals the indeterminacy and some of the yet unresolved problems of Asian Canadian who choose to represent themselves. In Trinh Minh-ha's words, Shum undercuts 'the inside/outside opposition, her intervention is necessarily that of both a deceptive insider and a deceptive outsider. She is this Inappropriate Other/Same who moves about with always at least two/ four gestures: that of affirming "I am like you" while persisting in her difference; and that of reminding herself "I am different" while unsettling every definition of otherness arrived at' (145). Shum's *Double Happiness* ends with Jade in her own apartment, hanging up curtains with pictures of Marilyn Monroe on them. Using Marilyn Monroe here as an icon is in keeping with the ambivalent spirit of the film. Monroe was successful in becoming a star, something Jade wants, and yet her life was fraught with difficulties. In the final scene, in a rather suggestive gesture of drawing the curtains, Jade is at once inviting us to participate in her life at the same time as she is closing off the gaze of the outsider.

PART II

TRANSFORMATIONS THROUGH THE SENSUAL

4

To Make Sense of Differences: Communities, Texts, and Bodies in Shirley Geok-lin Lim's *Among the White Moon Faces*

'Chineseness' is a homogenizing label whose meanings are not fixed and pregiven, but constantly renegotiated and rearticulated, both inside and outside China.

Ien Ang, 'On Not Speaking Chinese'

Like the other works we have seen thus far, Shirley Geok-lin Lim's autobiographical *Among the White Moon Faces* reveals the complexities and politics of diasporic Asian identity. Lim's diverse ethnic and cultural background exemplifies what Lisa Lowe has termed 'heterogeneity, hybridity, and multiplicity' ('Heterogeneity, Hybridity, Multiplicity' 24). Lowe's article points out that Asian American culture as a whole is heterogeneous rather than homogeneously 'minor' against a dominant hegemony, but I borrow her terms to describe the multifaceted conjunctions of cultures that mark the subjectivity of Lim. Of all the authors I study in this book, Lim is the one who best exemplifies transnationalism. Lim is a Malayan-born Chinese, 'assimilated into Malay and Western cultures,' she writes in *Among the White Moon Faces*, who, in her youth, was comfortable with a 'mélange of Chinese, Malay, Indian, Portuguese, British, and American cultural practices' (4). Her mixed heritage and community identifications are shown to be a result of historical conquests, immigration and labour policies, and cultural and religious imperialisms.

Lim's memoir reveals how Asian identities in the diaspora are marked by a kind of 'erasure.' In Derrida's use of the term, what is placed under erasure 'is effaced while still remaining legible, is destroyed while making visible the very idea of the sign' (40). While Lim, like many other Asian people, appears 'Chinese,' the sign is an inadequate signifier of her identity. Many aspects of her identity are invisible to those who do not know the particularities of her socio-familial, political, and historical circumstances. There is often a large gap between the majority culture's understanding of what constitutes Chinese American subjectivity and the layers of real and imagined affiliations that make us who we are. Lim's memoir, which begins with her 'Malaysian homeland,' attempts to 'make sense of the ... birthmarks' as they 'compose the hieroglyphs of [her] body's senses' (231). Her body becomes an important site of familial, national, and international penetrations, confluences, and traces. She is at once subject and object, resisting agent and colonized other. Through her narrative and her photographs, Lim represents her multiple subjectivities of daughter, student, rebel, mistress, scholar, lover, immigrant, community worker, teacher, mother, and feminist. As she lives through these various identities, she forms alliances and communities that lead to self-empowerment and enable her to combat the markings of her body and her sense of otherness in her homeland and in America.

Lim is othered in various ways – as a Chinese in Malaysia who did not grow up in affluence and could not speak Hokkien, as the only female in the family, as an Asian studying English, and later as an Asian immigrant in America. Otherness marks her body in a number of visible and striking ways. Lim overcomes her sense of not belonging by forming alliances with those who are similarly marginalized and alienated. Using similar techniques to those of Denise Chong, Lim reconfigures alien spaces into the familiar through the use of photographs and by providing a history filled with sensuous details. In doing so, she is able to create a position of authority and becomes the narrative centre of her memoir. Places and spaces in *Among the White Moon Faces* become important. The traditional geographies and affiliations of nation become difficult for someone like Lim who has a global upbringing, and is, in many ways, a transnational subject. Her relocation forces her to transform herself from a colonized other into what Aihwa Ong calls a 'flexible' citizen (6).

Two of the strongest recurring motifs in *Among the White Moon Faces* are absence and otherness. In chapter one, Lim begins by noting her marginal status: 'I have become transformed, and yet have remained a renegade ... the unmovable self situated in the quicksand of memory ...

is a fugitive presence which has not yet fossilized' (9). On the last page, she ends her memoirs with, 'Everywhere I have lived in the United States ... I felt an absence of place, myself absent in America. Absence was the story my mother taught me, that being the story of her migrant people, the Malacca peranakans' (232). The problem for the author is, how to insert an othered and still nebulous self into a text? How to infuse the *bios* (from Greek, meaning life) into the gap that is one's life? To put it in the terms I have been using in this book, how does one transform absence or invisibility into a meaningful and vital representation? These are the challenges facing Lim as an autobiographer and they are questions that I explore.

Like other writers and critics of autobiography, Lim has to contend with problems of language and referentiality, issues raised by post-structuralist theorists. As Sidonie Smith notes, for structuralists and post-structuralists, 'the autobiographical text becomes a narrative artifice, privileging a presence, or identity, that does not exist outside language' (5). The danger of following this line of thinking is that the writing self is seen to be without agency, is seen to be a self that is constructed solely through language. As a woman and as a member of a racial minority, Lim resists this negation of selfhood by insisting on the materiality of the body, by giving detailed textual and photographic evidence of embodied subjectivity, and by highlighting sensual specificities. These details and particularities, as well as the feminist mothers and sisters who shaped and helped her, engender Lim as a subject in the end.

As a 'multiply colonized subject,' Lim does not see 'oppressions as coming from a hegemonic centre. Instead, she sees 'a colonial subject as the cultural site for the contradictions inherent in the intersections of multiple conserving circles of authority' ('Asians' 35). Yet there are 'liberatory movements precisely *where* Confucianism, Catholicism, feudalism, and colonialism intersected' (*Among* 36). She explains: 'My cultural world was not monological but multilogical. Given the multiplicity of cultures, the extraordinary subjective feature remained that none of them offered the girl-child a stable established supporting society ... I remained between and outside the statements of these systems: non-male, non-Malay, non-Catholic, non-British colonial' (38). This sense of not being in the centre is ironically what propels Lim to U.S. feminism, which holds the promise of community to women of colour: 'American feminism appears to offer a counter-community. Commanded by its rhetoric of the privileging of difference, it promises a community that paradoxically is constructed not on commonality but on difference' (39).

Given this situation where she is always different and outside of systems, it is not surprising that the most striking element of the memoir is its self-conscious sense of otherness. Lim is aware throughout her narrative of the way in which cultural, gender, and racial differences indelibly mark one's physical body. More so than the other writers in this study, Lim lyrically describes how the body receives signals otherness. She writes, 'Every cultural change is signified through and on the body. Involuntarily the body displays, like a multidimensional, multisensorial screen, the effects of complicated movements across the social keyboard. And conversely, bodies are players, passionate amateurs, mobile, and nubile, and culture is the scene in which their continuous, promiscuous, nervous performances unfold' (89). It is through the body and bodily experiences that she remembers her mother, that she first learns of exclusion and otherness, and that she later assimilates into American culture. Her focus on the sights, smells, and tastes of her childhood accentuates her otherness, at the same time as it renders the unfamiliar familiar. Experiences that may be alien to readers are rendered in sensory terms. In order to create a visual image, Lim's early descriptions of her mother use metaphors, catalogues of objects, mostly Asian, and romantic associations. As with Chong's descriptions of her grandmother, the depictions sometimes have the unintended effect of exoticization. Lim describes her mother's speech, her clothing, her perfume, rendering her mother, and by extension, herself, into a spectacle. Of her speech, she tells us that her mother spoke 'the Malay spoken by assimilated Chinese – the idiomatic turns of her ethnic identity, was a waterfall whose drops showered me with sensuous music ... in memory it is my mother's speech but not mine; it was of my childhood but I do not speak it now' (12). Because Lim no longer speaks this language, it becomes associated with loss, with nostalgia, even though her relationship with her mother was not always positive.

In another instance, the child's fascination with her mother is rendered through the ritual of grooming and make-up. The mother becomes goddess-like in her throne, surrounded by her strange containers:

One was filled with sweet-smelling talc and a pink powder puff like a rose that she dipped into white powder and lavishly daubed over her half-dressed body, under her armpits, around her neck and chest, and quickly dabbed between her legs like a furtive signal. Another was a blue-coloured jar filled with a sugary white cream. She took a two-finger scoop of the shiny cream and rubbed it over her face, a face that I can still see, pale, smooth, and unmarred ... Her face shone like an angel's streaked with silver, and when she wiped the silvery streaks off, the skin glowed faintly like a sweet fruit. Later, I would discover that the blue jar was Pond's Cold Cream, the tub of powder, Yardley Talc. She was immersed in Western beauty, a Jean Harlow on the banks of a slowly silting Malacca River, born into a world history she did not understand. (13)

This passage is at once familiar and exotic, profound and yet ironic in its simplicity. Lim's technique is to observe carefully and recount in detail the colours, textures, and objects of her past. Even insignificant gestures from daily life take on momentous implications. She uses the common act of putting on face cream to comment on her mother's ignorance of the socio-historical world around her.

The passage is also interesting in its revelation of the fluid boundaries between what we traditionally see as the East and the West. The solemnity of the description and the fact that it is taking place in Malacca leads one to expect that the mother is putting on some special, secret Asian concoction. Lim does talk later about *badak*, which is a refined rice powder used on the peranakan female face (13). But here, the substances are Pond's cold cream and Yardley powder, which have been indigenized as part of the peranakan ritual.[1] The examples underscore Lim's point about being assimilated into Malay and Western cultures in her youth. For the child, mystery does not always comes from Eastern practices, but also from products that are familiar to Euro-American consumers.

In another passage, the mother's dress is associated with a cultural otherness for her Western readers, as well as for her Westernized present self: 'My mother wore *nonya* clothing, the *sarong kebaya* ... Some days she dressed us both elaborately, herself in a golden brown sarong and gleaming puce *kebaya*, and I in a three-tiered, ruffled, and sashed organdy dress with a gold-threaded scarlet ribbon in my hair. We rode in a trishaw' (13). These recollections function to separate and to restore the author's past for herself and for her readers. Lim deliberately does not translate the Malayan words, forcing her readers to acknowledge her difference at the same time as they are getting to know her through her text. The foreign words compel us to acknowledge cultural difference, but in a way that reveals our ignorance. These recollections are especially poignant and powerful because the past is no longer readily accessible. Susan Stewart points out that 'as experience is increasingly mediated and abstracted, the lived relation of the body to the phenomenological world is replaced by a nostalgic myth of contact and presence. "Authentic" experience becomes both elusive and allusive as it is placed beyond the horizon of present lived experience, the beyond in which the antique, the pastoral, the exotic, and other fictive domains are articulated. In this process of distancing, the memory of the body is replaced by the memory of the object, a memory standing outside the self and thus presenting both a surplus and lack of significance' (133). Objects, clothes, and smells become important as metaphors not only for the mother's body and the mother, who disappeared when Lim was eight, but also for her Malayan motherland, which is also no longer within her grasp.

In a comparable way, Lim's memories of her father are linked to her feelings about her homeland and these memories affect her in a visceral manner. When she emigrates to the United States and hears that her father has been diagnosed with throat cancer, she notes, 'Food stuck in my throat whenever I thought of Father. The thought was like a fishbone, sharp and nagging' (162). Her reaction to his death is one of disbelief: 'It was unimaginable that Father, the source of whatever drove me, that total enveloping wretchedness of involuntary love, my eternal bond, my body's and heart's DNA, had been dead for almost a month' (162–3). Thoughts of both her father and her mother affect and mark her body. They are linked to her Malayan past and to the parts of her life over which she has no choice. At the outset, she tells us, 'Before I could learn to love America, I had to learn to love the land of unconditional choice. The searing light of necessity includes my mother and father, characters whom I never would have chosen had I choice over my history' (10). As a child, she 'adored' her father's body, slept with her parents, and used to take comfort in his 'warm and solid' body beside her (31–2). Yet he has marked her body physically in more than one way. He used to beat her with a cane on her legs, shoulders, and back so that the 'raised welts were ... deeply grooved and bloodied' (32). Some of these beatings were his attempts to make her conform to his expectations of how a girl ought to behave. She recounts them as she recounts her hunger, poverty, and isolation, as part of her Malaccan childhood that renders her different from the people around her.

The father's writing on her body affects Lim later at various stages in her life. At eleven, she finds herself impulsively hitting her seven-year-old brother until he 'buckled at the knees and almost fell over' (192).

After the incident, she thinks, 'there is this access to violence in my body, that I have inherited, like an alcoholic gene, and that I have to keep in sight of, vigilant, never to let loose' (192). Much later, she finds herself involuntarily hitting her own baby, Gershom. After each incident, she feels 'shame and defiance, mixed with panic' (202). She realizes how she is re-enacting her family history: 'I was repeating those very scenes of brutality that my father had wreaked on me' (202). It is only by aligning herself with feminists that she is able to stop the cycle of family violence: 'I could only unravel the repetitions of fear and rage by understanding myself as a woman: a girl-child seizing autonomy rather than suffering damage, but damaged still by that premature forced growth, a young woman fearing independence but fearing dependency more' (203). Lim is able to detach herself from the ever-powerful and loving, but at times, destructive, familial bonds by choosing a community of feminist scholars and activists.

In *Imagined Communities*, Benedict Anderson argues that 'nationality' and 'nationalism are cultural artefacts of a particular kind' (4). He points out that what we call a 'nation' is largely 'imagined' into existence (7) through various ways. Before the eighteenth century, people were linked by religious communities, often further tied by a sacred language, and dynastic realms (chapter 2). But from the eighteenth century onwards, Anderson believes that print culture and 'print capitalism' replaced these earlier ties. While Anderson's observations provide a good starting point for discussing the origins of national consciousness, in Lim's case, as in the case of many diasporic people, national affiliation becomes a complex series of negotiations between the familial, the local, the ethnic, and the global.

As Lim observes early on, racial or national affiliation is particularly problematic for her as a Chinese Malayan. Though she feels at one point 'the sense of Malacca as [her] home,' which she does not experience again elsewhere (20), even there she feels like an outsider. One way in which she experiences alienation is at the level of language. In her paternal grandfather's house, Hokkien is spoken, but it was not the language spoken to her by her mother. She says, 'This language of the South Chinese people will always be an ambivalent language for me, calling into question the notion of a mother tongue tied to a racial origin' (11). It divides her from those who look like her: 'Hokkien laid out a foreign territory, for I was of the South Seas Chinese but not one of them. Hokkien was the sounds of strong shadowy women, women who circled but did not welcome me' (11). If we go back to Anderson's argument that communities were at one point linked by a sense of dynasty, as a diasporic Chinese, Lim is considered *huaqiao* (overseas Chinese). The term comes from *huá* or *wâ*, meaning splendid, magnificent, the best. David Yen-ho Wu notes that 'among many educated Chinese today' the idea of Chinese is still linked to *Zhonghua minzu*, meaning from 'the five major stocks of the Hua people of the middle land' (151). Lim comes from this ancient dynasty, yet she is an abject member. In Kristeva's terms, the abject 'does not respect borders, positions, rules.' It is 'the in-between, the ambiguous, the composite' (*Powers of Horror* 4). She is ostracized by Chinese-speaking Malays, called 'Kelangkia-kwei or a Malay devil' because though she looks Chinese, she cannot speak Hokkien (11). Ironically, like many people from colonized countries, the language that she eventually becomes most fluent in is English.

Another factor that contributes to her sense of otherness in her Malayan homeland comes from Euro-American cultural imperialism. Lim's father found 'his pleasures in films and Western music' (20). He 'seldom saw a movie that was not in English and imported from Britain or the United States' (22). As a child, Lim remembers her home filled with 'newspapers, magazines, and omnibuses of *Reader's Digest* ... *National Geographic* ... *British Tatler* and *Tid-Bit*' (20). Since these magazines, pop songs, and images come into Lim's home, they permeate her identity and reinforce her sense of herself as other. Not only is she named Shirley 'after Shirley Temple,' at her confirmation, she chooses the name Jennifer from Jennifer Jones,' the Hollywood actress who 'had breasts, dark hair, a sultry look' (4). What is significant about these choices is that they reveal the ways in which one constructs and lives out one's imagined community affiliation and identity. Ella Shohat and Robert Stam note that 'the contemporary media shape identity; indeed, many argue that they exist close to the very core of identity production. In a transnational world typified by the global circulation of images and sounds, goods and populations, media spectatorship impacts complexly on national identity, political affiliation, and communal belonging' (145). Through his consumption of Western films, magazines, and records, the father has brought the colonizer's values and standards of beauty into their home.

In an essay about autobiography, Lim notes, 'The Asian woman writer, like women everywhere, continues to be constituted by a Male Other. When we look at ourselves in maturity, the gaze we have reconstituted from our culture is male' ('Semiotics' 444). One could add

Western to male here. This process of identification is akin to what Homi Bhabha describes in an essay called 'Interrogating Identity.' Though Bhabha was theorizing about the relation between blacks and whites in a colonial condition, the effects on the colonized subject are similar. Bhabha notes, 'First: to exist is to be called into being in relation to an otherness, its look or locus. ... Second: the very place of identification, caught in the tension of demand and desire, is a space of splitting. The fantasy of the native is precisely to occupy the master's place while keeping his place in the slave's *avenging* anger' (44). Lim's narrative reveals some of these tensions, as she negotiates between her Chinese Malayan family, images of woman from the media projected by American culture, and her British colonial education.

As we have seen in Denise Chong's work, photographs play a crucial role in the construction of the self that the author wants to project in an autobiographical work. Linda Rugg notes that 'the presence of photographs in autobiography cuts two ways: it offers a visualization of the decentred, culturally constructed self; and it asserts the presence of a living body through the power of photographic referentiality' (19). Most of the photographs included in Lim's memoir are typical poses one sees in family photograph albums. Except for the family portrait that depicts her mother in a *cheong-sam*, the photographs reflect the already internationalized childhood of the writer. Of the ten items included, three highlight education: her ballet dancing, her convent school, and herself as scholar in New York. The accomplished side of Lim is evidently what she wants to stress through her images. Similar to Chong's biography, the visual narrative does not tell of the anguish and the poverty Lim experienced in her early years. The photographs simply reflect a happy and confident young woman who pictorially seems to belong to the family and communities with whom she is photographed. The visual narrative ends with her son, Gershom, and like her textual narrative, it is relatively silent about her American home and marriage. She has excised the assimilated American out of her photographic sampling to preserve her family's privacy and to highlight the more interesting part of her life. Instead, she favours pictures set in Asia, either of her growing up there or returning there. The photographs, like her narrative, stress her otherness and how difference has made her who she is. Photographs, as Rugg points out, represent more for us than 'the objects and persons contained within their frames. They introduce a new arena for visualizing the structure of history, and they perform as metaphor for the processes of perception and memory' (25). Through the photographs as well as the detailed and sensual descriptions of her mother, her home, and her Malayan homeland, Lim represents, but also enables us to 'remember,' something that does not belong to our specific past.[2] Part of this past entails Lim's negotiations between her Chinese heritage, her American upbringing, and her British colonial legacy.

In her memoir, Lim stresses how Euro-American culture is projected onto Asian spaces. However, despite the globalization of Western culture, there are traces of resistance and alternative practices. For instance, in her prologue, Lim recounts her first exposure to Shakespeare. It occurs not in a public theatre, but in the guise of a joke. 'Romeo, Romeo, wherefore art thou, Romeo?' is followed by 'chortles and sly looks' in her experience (1). 'Romeo was both an English and a Malayan word' and becomes a kind of performance of 'Western romantic love' (1). As a child, Lim equates the term 'Romeo' with sex and with a 'male effect – erotic heat combined with suave flirtation, distributed promiscuously, promising a social spectacle and unhappiness for women' (1). This adaptation of one of the best-known works of a canonical English writer is a interesting hybridization and indigenization of European culture. Yet this transformative practice has its limitations. While Romeo denotes 'the zany male freedom permitted under Westernization ... there were no Malayan Juliets, and sexual males were always Westernized' (1). It is only later in her teens, through rock and roll music, that Lim is able to express sexuality through her body. As she says, 'My Westernization took place in my body. As a young woman I wanted movement: the freedom of the traveler, the solipsism of the engine, the frenzy of speed, that single intensity inseparable from danger. I was drawn to motorbikes the way I was drawn to fast music' (89). The physicality of rock and roll music meant freedom, and 'freedom ... signified pleasure, a forgetting of social responsibility in the irruption of the sensuous to the surface' (89). She observes that 'the percussive drums and orgasmic rocking and rolling, the suggestive lyrics and gestures of Bill Haley and His Comets, Chubby Checker, and similar American pop singers, effected a visceral Westernization of Asia that years of reading Shakespeare's plays had not achieved' (89). Pop music became her way of rebelling against the restrictions of Confucian ideology.

During her formative undergraduate years, Lim's reading, from her mainly British colonial education, consisted mainly of canonical British writers: 'mandatory Chaucer, Shakespeare, Augustan, Romantics, and other traditional survey courses' followed by exposure to 'Mark Twain,

Ralph Waldo Emerson, Walt Whitman, and Henry James' (119). Commonwealth literature was introduced in a very limited way. This grounding in English and American literature creates an Asian subject who has a split consciousness, a fragmented sense of belonging, and divided feelings about national identity. Bhabha argues that it produces an unconscious that 'speaks in the form of otherness ... It is not the colonialist Self or the colonized Other, but the disturbing distance in-between that constitutes the figure of colonial otherness – the white man's artifice inscribed on the black man's body' (45). On the one hand, Lim feels the 'physical sensation of expansion in the chest, even in the head, as [she] read a profoundly beautiful or mindful poem' by a British writer (120). On the other hand, she is told that she cannot hope to 'understand Wordsworth' without having been to the 'Lake District' (120). In her essay on autobiography, Lim notes wryly, 'My story as a writer is also that of a colonized education in which the essential processes of identity formation are ironically the very processes stripping the individual of Asian tradition and communal affiliation' ('Semiotics' 449). If language and texts shape one's imagined sense of belonging, then Lim's literary repertoire positions her problematically as insider and outsider of both Western and Malayan cultures.

In an essay titled 'The English-Language Writer in Singapore (1940s–1980s),' Lim discusses the special problem of language for many writers of her generation. After Singapore separated from the Federation of Malaysia, English became Singapore's working language, the language of dominance, because it was perceived as a bridge language between the Chinese, the Malays, and the Indians. Yet English 'carries with it British and Western traditions and ideals; it is a strong transmitter of cosmopolitan values' (115). Used as a first language, it breaks down 'ancient ethno-linguistic identities' and threatens what Clifford Geertz called the 'primordial sentiments' of the community (115). As Lim notes, 'the obvious danger in this loss of traditional social identity is that of anomie, the condition in which individuals lose their traditional points of references and do not know who they are, where they belong, what their position and role in life are' (115). In effect, Lim is faced with the difficult position of being rendered as an other in her own culture. She writes of English-language writers, 'English cannot be a "mother tongue"; it expresses Western debased values; it is useful only for international trade and technological purposes ...; and not having mastery of his mother tongue (whether Mandarin, Tamil or Malay) signifies inadequacy, deprivation and deculturalization. He or she thus faces a

severe handicap in legitimizing his or her place in the national culture'
(116).

Instead of seeing her as a figure caught 'between worlds' (Amy
Ling), Lim's life, as documented in *Among the White Moon Faces*, can be
read as an example of what Aihwa Ong calls the 'transnational.' Ong
emphasizes that '*trans* denotes both moving through space or across
lines, as well as changing the nature of something' (4). She relates the
transnational to the '*trans*versal, the *trans*actional, the *trans*lational, and
the *trans*gressive aspects of contemporary behaviour and imagination
that are incited, enabled, and regulated by the changing logics of states
and capitalism' (Ong 4). Multiple geographies and cultures inscribe on
and engage with Lim's subjectivity, but she, in turn, reconfigures and
changes a number of these sites. While in Malaysia, she feels 'stratified
by race, religion, and long-standing familial bonds'; when she emigrates to the United States, she finds that there are more and different
possibilities for reshaping one's identity and alliances.

In America, Lim's sense of displacement and otherness is exacerbated by her race and her status as an immigrant. Upon her arrival, she
feels like 'an empty-handed transient, dependent on the charity of
strangers, without resources, adrift, wholly without community, yet
burning with pride and shame' (140). Her first American friends remark on her small size and on her foreignness. Over the course of her
life, she experiences a number of minor, yet memorable, discriminatory
practices that remind her over and over again of her otherness. What is
remarkable in almost every case is how Lim garners strength from
these incidents and empowers herself rather than becoming dejected
by them. Ong argues that 'transnational mobility and manoeuvres
mean that there is a new mode of constructing identity, as well as new
modes of subjectification that cut across political borders' (18). While
Ong examines 'the flexible practices, strategies, and disciplines associated with transnational capitalism' (19), I borrow her paradigm to look
at some of the ways Lim juggles her intellectual and cultural capital as a
transnational subject.

One of the first problems she encounters in her new home is isolation. She remarks: 'What had preserved me in Malaysia, the struggle for
an individual self against the cannibalism of familial, ethnic, and communal law, was exactly what was pickling me in isolation in the United
States. In the United States I was only a private person. Without family
and community, I had no social presence; I was among the unliving'
(155). Lim counters this early on by becoming a dormitory counsellor at

the Castle in Brandeis, a segregated dormitory. Here she finds comfort in a community of women. She observes that though 'such communities are ephemeral ... where women marry, bear children, and enter their husband's house to work,' nevertheless, the 'recognition of the possibility of sisterhood ... has remained steady' (156). For Lim, sisterhood is 'not only the necessity for coalition and the work of solidarity but also the sensibility of support that grows when social gender is recognized as a shared experience' (157). Aligning herself with this and other groups of women cutting across racial differences is an example of how Lim, as a diasporic subject, reconstitutes the familial and national communities that she had lost.

Aside from women, Lim tries to find friendship and support from other areas. She remembers thinking rather distantly of herself during those early difficult years in the United States: 'she views herself through the eyes of citizens: guest, stranger, outsider, misfit, beggar' (160). As an instructor in English at the City University of New York, Queens, she finds the freshmen unresponsive and resentful. She notes, 'with my long straight Chinese hair and accent, I was not any young American's image of Socrates. It must have been discomforting for some of them to find a "foreign" graduate student explicating Thoreau' (165). At this point, she is regarded by those around her as something Bhabha would call a colonial mimic, 'almost the same but not quite' (89). Her presence disturbs and questions authority. The description of herself suggests that she saw herself through others' eyes, seeing strangeness in her own body, hearing an accent in her own speech.

Her sense of herself as inhabiting multiple subjectivities is expressed in a poem called 'Modern Secrets,' published in 1980 in *Crossing the Peninsula and Other Poems*. She writes: 'Last night I dreamt in Chinese. / Eating Yankee shredded wheat/ ... The sallow child / Ate rice from its ricebowl / And hides still in the cupboard / With the china and tea-leaves' (50). The speaker of the poem sees her Chinese past as something of a secret to be hidden in a closet. The dream reveals a moment in her life when her Malayan and Chinese past are still very much part of her identity, though she perceives it unconsciously as an experience that must be buried. Interestingly, in a poem called 'Visiting Malacca' from the same collection, the speaker returns to 'the old house,' and finds it familiar yet changed. 'I am losing / Ability to make myself at home' (93), she notes. These two poems articulate her position of being outside of both cultures at this juncture, still struggling with her recent hyphenated identity.

Similarly, in her memoir, she recounts how slow and difficult it was for her to find her place in the United States in those years. Though she does not find 'intellectual commonalities with [her] students' at Queens (166), she does succeed in establishing bonds with the students at Hostos Community College in the Bronx. Of this teaching experience, she says, 'We were liberals, committed to helping our brown and black students succeed' (171). But she quickly learns that she has to adapt her teaching skills and use non-traditional classroom methods for her largely black and Puerto Rican students. Intense sessions at the writing centre that she sets up, as well as working with the students on their journals and on a student yearbook, 'felt right' (172). After a while, the students grow 'closer' to her than had her 'father's children in Malacca' (172). This comparison of the students to her step-siblings reveals how Lim sought, albeit unconsciously, a substitute family or community in those years. It is interesting that the highlight of this experience for Lim was a dinner party she hosted. Though she wrote her memoirs some twenty years later, she is able to give elaborate details of the food: 'I made rice and curry; Lucinda, a shy and graceful African American, barely twenty, brought a southern dish her grandmother made – vanilla biscuits, banana slices, and a pudding mix. William brought beer, Evie brought plantain fritters, and Josefina, a Peruvian Indo, brought matte tea from the Highlands' (172). Sneja Gunew has noted that an exchange of ethnic food is the first step of immigrant food on the road to assimilation: 'We have embarked on the process that transforms the nauseous taboo food into ethnic cuisine, a desirable marker of gastronomic richness and diversity that also acts as proof that the nation is an open and tolerant one, a guarantee of its cosmopolitanism' (150). But in this scenario, it is not the dominant culture that eats the ethnic food and by extension the ethnic other, as Gunew argues. The party is made of many immigrant cultures. The exotic origins of their food are matched by the diverse ethnic origins of the people. This gathering, noticeably non-European American, is significant as it represents the first of many coalitions of peoples from the margins. These associations and communities provide Lim with the energy and support she needed at various times of her life in America.

When Lim lives in Brooklyn, she similarly becomes part of a community that is multiracial. In an effort to improve their street, Lim and her neighbors form a 'block association' (176). The group includes 'West Indians, Polish, Jews, Asian' people who had 'nothing in common beyond property interests drawn together to secure these interests'

(177). She notes of this coalition, 'the necessity for political action ... could create community where none existed before, thus contributing to the continuous fresh construction of civic identities' (177). The block association does improve the neighbourhood, at the same time as it creates something of a 'public square' of their street (179). But the street does not give Lim the privacy she needed. However, the experiment is important as it reveals her ability to construct different 'civic identities.' It shows her ability to realign and reimagine her alliances and communities. This skill enables Lim and other diasporic Chinese to survive and to enjoy what Ong calls 'flexible citizenship' in the transnational world (6).

Ultimately the catalyst that changes Lim's view of herself as outsider and alien is motherhood. She observes that 'Birth changes a place to a homeland: birth land, children, our childhoods, where our parents have buried our umbilical cords, where our children will bury us and will bear their children. There are homelands of the memory and homelands of the future, and for many of us, they are not the same' (191). For her, the birth of her son is a transformative experience. She writes: 'I became an American politically with the birth of my child. I may have been a blackbird, flying into Boston a dishevelled traveller uncertain whether I was choosing expatriation, exile, or immigration. But I had no such doubts about my unborn child. He would be an American child of Jewish and Asian descent' (194). In her discussion of assimilation into American society, she presents herself as a valiant maternal figure, willing to do anything in order for her son 'to have a pride of belonging, the sense of identity with a homeland' (197). She describes the endless children's birthday parties, shopping for Mattel educational toys, brand-name products, and trips to department stores that seem trivial, yet are the daily and cumulative little acts that contribute to one's sense of identity and belonging.

As Lim dutifully carries out these daily rituals, she can be said to be 'performing' the role of American motherhood in order to be fully assimilated. As noted earlier, Judith Butler has pointed out that gender identity is not inherent, but is constructed through 'a regularized and constrained repetition of norms' (*Bodies* 95). Butler stresses that 'performance' is 'a ritualized production, a ritual reiterated under and through constraint, under and through the force of prohibition and taboo, with the threat of ostracism and even death controlling and compelling the shape of the production' (*Bodies* 95). In the same way, racial identity can be seen to be performative. It is enacted under and through constraint, or with the threat of ostracism, as Lim notes. Though America is a country full of immigrants, she has felt the 'stiffness and tentativeness, the distinct charge of distance that marked one as alien and outsider, ... directed chiefly to those who did not look white European' (199). Her care in, and performance of, the mothering role seems to have had its desire results. Her son, in his teens, has become '100-percent American,' the 'quintessential American consumer' (210), she notes with satisfaction and irony.

Along with her son's American upbringing comes her sense of herself as an Asian American scholar and writer. In order for this to have developed, Lim notes that she 'needed more than books and a room of [her] own' (227). She writes, 'I needed a society of scholars, an abundance of talk, an antagonism of ideas, bracing hostile seriousness, and above all a community of women' (227). She ends her memoirs optimistically, having found a community of students interested in Asian American studies and blessed with a supportive feminist community. Though happy to be in America, whose Constitution endows 'every citizen with equal rights without regard to race, gender, religion, public association,' she is 'always conscious of speaking as an immigrant, from a short hopeful personal past, and of the voices of others whose lives still bear the consequences of a U.S. history of genocide, war, racism, and other violences' (230). It is this consciousness with its 'simultaneous images' (231) that is characteristic of many Asian Americans in the diaspora today. *Among the White Moon Faces* reveals the ways in which a diasporic Chinese subject has triumphed and survived the shifts and changes of the transnational world. As with Shum's protagonist, Jade, who had to struggle with her Chinese appearance at auditions, the transformation of the visible signs of Lim's body and her Asian self was not without difficulty. But by remaining flexible, by constantly rescripting her subjectivity, and by reconstituting her community, Lim has been able to look back and to 'make sense' of her 'birthmarks' (231).

5

'Some Memories Live Only on Your Tongue': Recalling Tastes, Reclaiming Desire in Amy Tan's *The Kitchen God's Wife*

> My tongue doesn't taste things the same way anymore ... Do you know why that is? Why do some memories live only on your tongue or in your nose? Why do others always stay in your heart?
>
> Amy Tan, *The Kitchen God's Wife*

Like her first novel, *The Joy Luck Club* (1989), Amy Tan's second novel, *The Kitchen God's Wife* (1991), depicts the lives of older and younger generations of Chinese and Chinese American women. These two novels juxtapose present-day American culture with the folkloric, mythic way of life in China before the 1950s.[1] In both novels, the stories are told by a set or sets of mothers and daughters, with the mother representing the Old World and its traditions, and the daughter associated with the New World and its values. In both cases, the most compelling narratives are presented by the mother figures, who have often survived emotional and psychic trauma due to bad marriages, war, immigration, and severed familial ties. These accounts, revealing the strength and wisdom of a somewhat mysterious and exotic East, are structured as flashbacks and are linked to the Western sections through memory and storytelling.[2] Similar to many of the narratives in this study, remembrance and the subsequent act of narration become vital not only to the structure of the novel, but also to the ethnic protagonists who are seeking to render tangible their 'hybridized' subjectivities in the new world.[3] Though Chinese Americans are not historically colonized or postcolonial people, their status as a minority in North America ren-

ders them other in ways similar to colonialized subjects. They occupy
that space of the hybrid, or in-betweenness, where, as Homi Bhabha
puts it, 'what is at issue is the performative nature of differential identities' (219). The most common activities in America, such as playing
mah-jong, shopping for treats, or making a meal, become symbolic,
'overdetermined' gestures in Amy Tan's world.[4] Performed by the
mothers who have emigrated from China, they signify resistance and
survival. In the novel they become markers or visible signs that signal
the ethnicized lives of the characters. For Tan, as for many writers of
minority cultures in North America, simple quotidian acts such as
cooking and eating become crucial ethnographic indicators. Virginia
Woolf has pointed out that 'often nothing tangible remains of a woman's
day. The food that has been cooked is eaten; the children that have been
nursed have gone out into the world. Where does the accent fall? ... Her
life has an anonymous character which is baffling and puzzling in the
extreme' ('Women and Fiction' 56). These little, nameless, unremem-
bered acts have no slight or trivial influence on the lives of the women
in Tan's novels. Indeed, for the protagonist of *The Kitchen God's Wife*,
food, cooking, and eating become ways of determining one's role in
life, and of reconfiguring one's subjectivity.

    In an essay on *The Joy Luck Club* titled 'Memory and the Ethnic Self,'
Ben Xu suggests that 'identity, as well as the implicated self-definition
and self-narrative, almost certainly will be activated from memory' (4).
However, what he and other critics do not point out sufficiently is the
role food plays in Tan's books to create this racialized identity.[5] As
Carole Counihan and Penny Van Esterik note, 'Food marks social differences, boundaries, bonds, and contradictions. Eating is an endlessly
evolving enactment of gender, family, and community relationships'
(1). Descriptions of food are activated not only by the visual, olfactory,
and gustatory senses, but also in part by remembrances, while particular tastes are often linked to specific memories of the past. In North
American culture, food, and particularly food prepared for certain
special occasions and holidays, is often used to differentiate, sustain,
and celebrate ethnicities and cultures, especially for displaced and
dislocated immigrants.[6]

    In previous chapters, I looked at the importance of visual images
such as photographs and Hollywood movies in the construction of
ethnic identity. In this chapter, I explore another way in which ethnicity
and difference are represented and embodied. Here, memory and
selfhood are constituted by the appearance, taste, and texture of vic-

tuals in a novel where cooking is suggested in the very title. As Weili says in *The Kitchen God's Wife*, 'some memories live only on your tongue or in your nose' (296). Other critics have noted the importance of food and motifs of eating in Asian American literature. Sau-ling Wong argues compellingly that 'many Asian American writers use the motif of eating to symbolize a survival-driven act of assimilation, with the word *assimilation* reinterpreted (however obliquely and implicitly) to oppose the meaning most common and expected in the minority context' (*Reading* 77).[7] Eating is linked to the ability to swallow bitterness, pain, and humiliation, and it becomes a way of revealing one's character or testing one's endurance. In addition, the ideological assumptions associated with the preparation of food, the metaphors of consumption and appetite, eating itself, all serve not only to reflect but to shape female desire. This association of food with women is scintillating, but becomes problematic, especially in the case of the mother, Weili, whose identity is based to a great extent on her culinary skills. It becomes evident to her daughter and to the readers that in China, though she is a celebrated cook, she is perpetually in a position where she is supposed to efface her own desires and hunger, become invisible in order to serve others, particularly her voracious first husband. The mother and the originary culture she represents are depicted ambivalently in the novel. For the daughter, Pearl, the mother is a model of strength and resistance at the same time as she is an example of the self-sacrificing, dutiful traditional Chinese woman. She grows up in awe of her mother and her abilities but, like the daughters in *The Joy Luck Club*, has matrophobic fears of becoming just like her. In the novel, little domestic acts and tropes serve to construct, to liberate, but also to delimit a sexualized subjectivity, particularly for Asian women in both the Old and New Worlds.

In *The Kitchen God's Wife*, food, rituals of cooking and feasting, and gustatory images not only permeate the narrative, but structure it. According to Sau-ling Wong's critique of how some Asian American writers make 'a living by exploiting the "exotic" aspects of one's ethnic foodways,' Tan is guilty of what Frank Chin has termed 'food pornography' (qtd in Wong, *Reading* 55). In a number of scenes depicting meals and eating, Tan employs the 'tourist guide' approach, supplying 'the white reader with amusing but not too taxing glimpses of the mysterious ways of the Chinese' (Wong, *Reading* 66). It is through the rich and evocative language of appetite and sensuality that Tan replicates and creates the sense of nostalgia for the 'primitive' Orient.[8] However in other instances, Tan uses food imagery with more nuance, to reveal her protagonists' temperament or to differentiate between characters. As the kitchen god's wife, Weili constructs a narrative of her life based on the sights, smells, tastes, and textures of food. Although Weili's story is told, for the most part, in chronological order, the dominant characteristics are associative and interjectory. The narrative does not strictly follow a linear pattern, but involves a complex layering of one vignette or, more appropriately here, one ingredient followed by another. This technique is important because Weili's narrative consists of the main body of the novel, and is her *apologia pro vita sua*, or defence of her life. She reveals vital information about her past that she has concealed thus far from her daughter. Weili's methods as a storyteller parallel her cooking practices. She says with pride, 'I know how to make each dish delicate tasting, yet the flavor is clearly distinguished from other dishes – not everything bland or everything hot as the same roaring fire' (249). In the same way, her flashbacks are a feast, delicately balanced, with some sweet recollections, some spicy tales, and some sour ones that bring tears to the reader's eyes. We learn, early on in the novel, that Western, teleological notions of objectivity and historical veracity are not as important to Weili as the final result or presentation. Referring to her long-time friend Helen, whose Chinese name is Hulan, she comments, 'She doesn't remember. She and I have changed the past many times, for many reasons. And sometimes she changes it for me and does not even know what she has done' (69). Helen and Weili often have contradictory stories and remembrances of the same event. They both choose, consciously or unconsciously, to construct, and to transform, their pasts and their identities in ways that make sense for them and their present lives in America.

The different ways in which they reconstruct their pasts are reflected in the different attitudes they demonstrate to food. The ways in which food is presented and consumed by Weili and Helen are suggestive of their characters, formed in part by their mothers' influences and their particular economic situations and experiences as young girls. Weili, who comes from a family with more pretensions and fortune than Helen, recalls lessons in the way food must be handled. Her adoptive mother, Old Aunt, acts like a general in the kitchen:

> She was ordering the cooks to chop more meat and vegetables. And then she checked all her supplies. She lifted the lids on jars of peanut oil, soy sauce, and vinegar, smelled each one. She counted the number of fish

swimming in a wooden bucket, the number of ducks and chickens peck-
ing in the courtyard. She poked the sticky rice cakes filled with date paste
to see if they had steamed long enough. She scolded a cook's helper for
letting too many clouds of fat float in the chicken broth, scolded another
one for cutting strips of squid the wrong way. (136–7)

From these exacting methods, Weili learns important lessons in life. She
explains to her daughter: 'When I was young, I already knew everything must look good, taste good, mean good things. That way it lasts
longer, satisfies your appetite, also satisfies your memory for a long,
long time' (137). For Weili, appetite and desire are created by the visual
as well as the gustatory. Quality, as well as quantity, of food is of the
utmost importance. Aesthetics is closely linked to good taste, and good
food can provide present as well as future pleasures.

   From her own mother, Weili also learns to develop a taste for fine
living. One of the few memories Weili has of her mother is of her
fondness for English biscuits, which are 'hidden on top of her tall
dresser ... These biscuits were her favorites, my favorites too – not too
sweet, not too soft' (106). Weili's mother has exquisite and expensive
tastes: 'My mother had many favorites from different countries. She
liked English biscuits, of course, and also their soft furniture, Italian
automobiles and French gloves and shoes, White Russian soup and sad
love songs, American ragtime music and Hamilton watches. Fruit could
be from any kind of country. And everything else had to be Chinese, or
"it made no sense."' (106). From Old Aunt and her mother, then, Weili
has received subtle and overt messages about pleasure, desire, and the
pursuit of one's longings. While these messages are different, as Old
Aunt emphasizes that a woman's role is to serve and feed others, while
the mother is a rebel figure, it is the maternal figures in her life who
teach her about them. These pleasures, mostly sensual and bodily ones,
become linked in her mind to her earliest memories and to mothers. For
this reason, as an adult, Weili continues to associate having good food,
'freshest bean sprouts, the tastiest duck eggs' (372), with bliss and
contentment. She notes that 'during wartime, if you were lucky to have
money, you didn't think about saving your luck. A chance to taste
something rare or new was like your saying "Eat, drink, be married."
You could still have something to look forward to, even if life ended
tomorrow' (372).

   In contrast, her friend Helen, who comes from a poorer family in a
country village, looks at food as a means of survival and struggle. She

remembers how her family 'almost starved to death when she was a young girl' (362), and this experience teaches her to cling to life tenaciously and stubbornly. Helen does not have the luxury to distinguish between good and bad food, between the smells of good quality or poor quality peanut oil or soy sauce. Her past is one of scantiness and lack. For instance, one of her vivid memories is of a year when her family's fields were ruined by flooding: 'we had nothing to eat, except dried kaoliang cakes. We didn't even have enough clean water to steam them soft. We ate them hard and dry, wetting them only with our saliva. My mother was the one who divided everything up, gave a little to the boys, then half that to the girls' (362). This hardship teaches Helen many hard lessons about life. She experiences the immediate, physical consequences of the Chinese custom of favouring male offsprings.[9] She comes to understand the necessity of putting one's own interests ahead of others', of the positive and negative consequences of selfishness and self-protection. Shortly after the flooding, Helen steals a whole cake and eats it by herself to assuage her hunger. For this act she was punished by being deprived of food for the next three days. She recalls, 'I cried so hard, my stomach hurt so much – for a little kaoliang cake hard enough to break my teeth' (363). This more pragmatic and minimalist attitude to food characterizes Helen, marks her, and explains much about her actions later on in life. In contrast to Weili, there is little of the visual and the sensual in her descriptions of food. Her brush with near-starvation creates in her an enormous appetite. At one point during the war years in China, Weili notes that upon seeing a young beggar girl in the city, Helen 'put more food into her own mouth. She added fat onto her body the same way a person saves gold or puts money into a bank account, something she could use if worse came to worst' (363). Unlike Weili, who learns to be fastidious, Helen eats indiscriminately in order to stave off fear, to forget the remembrances of dark things past. Sau-ling Cynthia Wong notes that one of the major alimentary motifs in Asian American literature is 'big eating to the point of quasi-cannibalism, typically associated with the immigrant generation' (*Reading* 55). This tendency for 'big eating' is a 'survival strategy ... warranted by circumstances but also susceptible to excesses' (*Reading* 55). Though Hulan's extravagant eating occurs in China rather than in America, her voracious appetite, like those of the Asian American immigrants, is due to her years of struggle and poverty.

Weili is also distinguished from Helen through the ways they read and assess food. Tan uses food as a text to be analysed in a number of instances to show the two women's contrasting outlooks on life. The way Weili and Helen read the meaning of food in the markets and on the table is suggestive of the multifarious levels of interpretations, a theme Tan highlights in both *The Joy Luck Club* and *The Kitchen God's Wife*. Weili believes that though Helen 'was born poor ... she has always had luck pour onto her plate, even spill from the mouth of a three-day old fish' (68). To illustrate this point, she gives the example of the flat pom pom fish with an eye that Weili describes as 'shrunken in and cloudy-looking' (67), but a fish that Helen pronounces as 'juicy, tender' (67). As the fish turns out to be sweet rather than rancid, the incident becomes indicative of how the two women's 'thinking is too different' (78), their different ways of viewing opportunities as well as handling life's difficulties. For Weili, it becomes symbolic of the impossibility of predicting what fate has in store for women. Reflecting on the choices she has made in her life, Weili thinks, 'Maybe I made a mistake, such a simple mistake, saying no to one, yes to another, like choosing a fish in a tank. How can you know which one is good, which is bad, until you have tasted it?' (78). Helen, however, only sees things in simple terms. When Weili asks Helen what happens when fish are 'three days old,' Helen replies, 'They swim out to sea' (78). While for Weili, three-day-old fish have ominous and quasi-mythical resonances, for Helen, fish 'three days old' are merely going through life's natural process of birth, growth, and maturity.

This scene with the pom pom fish, which appears early in the novel, is a good illustration of how Amy Tan evokes the mystique of the fatalistic Orient, yet demonstrates how it is problematic for women. Through these metaphors that resonate with double meanings, she links the quotidian aspects of modern-day life with ancient and ritualistic practices and beliefs. Descriptions of feasting and discussions of food work at several different levels in the novel. For example, Weili recounts one of her attempts to be a good wife to Wen Fu during their stay at Yangchow. With Helen's help, she prepares a lavish dinner for fourteen people using her dowry money to buy all the food. She selects 'good pork, fresh clover for dumplings, many catties of sweet wine, all very expensive during wartime' (247). Though it is an extravagant meal, Weili spends the money willingly. Her attitude to the comfort value of this food indicates her apocalyptic mentality, caused by the war. 'If their luck blew down, those men might not return for the next meal. And with that sad thought, my hand would hurry and reach for a thicker piece of pork, one with lots of good, rich fat' (247). Similar to

Helen's gobbling down of food, Weili sees food as a means of living life to the fullest. But unlike Helen, she chooses her dishes carefully, noting their symbolic importance: 'sun-dried oysters for wealth; a fast-cooked shrimp for laughter and happiness; *fatsai*, the black-hair fungus that soaks up good fortune, and plenty of jellyfish, because the crunchy skin always made a lively sound to my ears' (248). There are several ways of interpreting this lavish meal being prepared by Weili. It forms a central part of Weili's narrative, and the many details she gives of this event, which happened many years ago, indicate its primacy in her life and in the formation of her identity.

On the one hand, the meal can be seen as a kind of Bakhtinian feast where heroic feats are connected to food. In *Rabelais and His World*, Bakhtin points out that in the oldest system of images, 'food was related to work. It concluded work and struggle and was their crown of glory. Work triumphed in food' (281). Indeed, Weili describes her banquet in hyperbolic and excessive terms reminiscent of the terms of festivity and carnival: 'Back home, I told the cook girl to boil enough pots of water and to chop enough pork and vegetables to make a thousand dumplings, both steamed and boiled, with plenty of fresh ginger, good soy sauce, and sweet vinegar for dipping. Hulan helped me knead the flour and roll out the dough into small circles' (248). Like Old Aunt, who checks her supplies and ingredients methodically, Weili is here depicted as the efficient and expert figure of authority who organizes the elaborate meal. Her narration emphasizes her skills and the pride she takes in her work. According to her, she is the one who has the best sense of taste and smell, unlike Helen, who 'was good at only those kinds of laborious cooking tasks: kneading, rolling, stuffing, pinching' (248). All their friends praise her cooking that night, 'told Wen Fu how lucky he was. They said it was impossible that a man could have both a beautiful wife and a talented cook – yet their eyes and tongue told them more differently' (249). The evening constitutes one of the moments of glory in Weili's unhappy first marriage. Through the preparation of the banquet she becomes the highly coveted and desirable woman in the eyes of the men around the table.

This triumphant evening is as significant as the dinner parties in Virginia Woolf's novels. In *Mrs Dalloway*, for instance, the preparation of the dinner party takes on a philosophic and social significance. The party serves to unite disparate and isolated individuals momentarily. Similarly, one could compare Weili's feast to Mrs Ramsay's Boeuf en Daube, which is a 'perfect triumph' (Woolf, *To the Lighthouse* 97). Just as

Mrs Ramsay feels 'a coherence in things, a stability' as she helps her dinner guest to a 'specially tender piece, of eternity' (Woolf, *To the Lighthouse* 97), Weili's delicious dumplings, 'steamed, water-cooked, or fried' (249), allow her to create a moment where everyone can 'eat and play together' (249). The feast becomes suggestive of their many struggles during the war years, of life prevailing over death, of order over chaos. In both Woolf's and Tan's novels, food becomes a way of warding off despair and death caused by wars, and political and social upheavals. Weili says, 'I was always ready to cook a good meal, even though the men usually returned home without telling me ahead of time – and sometimes, with fewer pilots' (249). The banquet can be seen as a woman's act of creating meaning out of a meaningless world, of her attempt to communicate with and touch those around her.

In her essay 'In Search of Our Mothers' Gardens,' Alice Walker writes of the necessity of recognizing the genius and creativity of our mothers and grandmothers. Though Walker is speaking of black women in America who were deprived of opportunities for becoming artists, her observations are applicable to women of the past who have been denied public means of expression. Walker encourages her readers to look not only in high places, but to look 'high and low' (2379) in order to find the creative spirit of our mothers. She suggests that women's artistry manifests itself in domestic and informal arts like quilt-making, gardening, cooking, singing, and storytelling. In the light of Walker's observations, Weili's 'big celebration dinner' (246) and the subsequent feasts she describes where 'each man ate thirty dumplings, loosened his belt and sighed, then ate thirty more' (250) can be seen as manifestations of female creativity and art. These meals are to be described in exaggerated and almost fantastic terms, which suggests their relation to myths, parables, and legends rather than historical veracity.

However, a darker reading of the same scene is also possible. In using food and the preparation of meals as a way of finding self-fulfilment, Weili, and hence Tan, runs into the danger of valorizing the very roles Chinese patriarchal culture has prescribed for women. Weili herself acknowledges that 'in those days, I was still trying to please Wen Fu, to act like a good wife, also trying hard to find my own happiness' (249). Finding happiness through cooking elaborate meals becomes problematic from the perspective of the contemporary feminist reader, as self-sacrifice, subservience, and domestic work are ways in which a woman becomes a good wife, according to Chinese teaching.[10] As part of the *lie nü*, or tradition of virtuous women, Chinese women were expected to be chaste, submissive, devoted to their families, and skilled at domestic duties. Through numerous biographies of virtuous women, young girls were taught 'pleasing speech and manners, to be docile and obedient, to handle the hempen fibres, to deal with the cocoons, to weave silks and form filets, to learn [all] women's work; how to furnish garments, to watch the sacrifices, to supply the liquors and sauces, to fill the various stands and dishes with pickles and brine and to assist in setting forth the appurtenances for the ceremonies' (*Li Chi [Book of Rites]*, qtd in Chow, *Woman* 60).

As Tan celebrates Weili's cooking skills, she inadvertently participates in the promotion of female identity based on these age-old notions of what constitutes a good wife. In her novels, it is never clear whether the scenes in prewar China, where the first-generation women are taught domestic skills, are meant to be critical, or merely descriptive, of tradition. In *The Joy Luck Club*, for example, Lindo Jong learns at twelve years old how 'to be an obedient wife' (*Joy Luck* 50). She says: 'I learned to cook so well that I could smell if the meat stuffing was too salty before I even tasted it' (*Joy Luck* 50). At another point it seems as if Lindo's whole subjectivity is based on whether or not she is a good cook: 'What was happier than seeing everybody gobble down the shiny mushrooms and bamboo shoots I had helped to prepare that day? ... How much happier could I be after seeing Tyan-yu eat a whole bowl of noodles without once complaining about its taste or my looks? (*Joy Luck* 51). Even though Lindo eventually escapes from this household, the tone of the narrative at the moment when she recalls her mastery of kitchen duties is a mixture of pride, bitterness, and irony. The traditional skills she had to learn distinguish her from her American daughter and make her account fascinating to readers, yet they also attest to her oppressive life in China.

Similarly, in *The Kitchen God's Wife*, Weili learns from her mother-in-law how 'to make [her husband] a proper hot soup, which was ready to serve only when [she] had scalded [her] little finger testing it' (207). Weili is taught that to suffer 'pain for a husband was true love' (207). These scenes constitute a large part of first-generation Asian American women's ethnicized identities, and they are narrated with painstaking and loving detail. For most readers, they evoke not only indignation and pity, but also wonder. They function as exotic pieces, or what Rey Chow calls 'a new kind of ethnography,' an 'accessible form of imaginative writing about a "China" that is supposedly past but whose ideological power still lingers' (*Primitive Passions* 143–4). They are melodramatic and mythic, and serve to incite as much amazement as horror at the primitive practices of the Chinese. Hence, while they can be read as testimonies of our mothers' creativity, as Walker suggested of her mother's garden, the exoticization of a domestic task such as cooking in this context remains problematic. In *The Kitchen God's Wife*, Weili more often than not cooks in order to please her husband, or in order to show what a virtuous wife she is. Despite the liberatory possibilities found in these scenes of excess and heroism, I argue that these scenes have the simultaneous effect of reinscribing patriarchal ideologies and circumscribing female desire.

Food as an art form also links the artist to what Kristeva calls the abject, to the 'powers of horror.' In her essay on abjection, Julia Kristeva argues that food designates 'the other (the natural) that is opposed to the social condition of man and penetrates the self's clean and proper body' (*Powers* 75). It is linked to the formation of identity because food, along with 'waste and the signs of sexual difference,' is one of the ways by which the subject distinguishes herself from the other (Grosz, 'Body' 89). For Kristeva, 'it is only through the delimitation of the "clean and proper" body that the symbolic order, and the acquisition of a sexual and psychical identity within it, becomes possible' (Grosz, 'Body' 86). Food is one of those objects that generate abjection, particularly 'if it is a border between two distinct entities or territories' (Kristeva, *Powers* 75) and reminds the subject of 'its own corporeal limits, its own mortality' (Grosz, 'Body' 90). There are a number of images of eating and appetite in the *The Kitchen God's Wife* that evoke abjection or oral disgust. These scenes are important because they show another use of the food metaphor. Rather than a celebratory use of food and feasting, they bring out how food can be linked to scenes of horror and the unspeakable. They add another dimension to the whole question of Asian female subjectivity, as the kinds of food that are linked to the abject inevitably become associated with the racialized and gendered protagonist.

One example of abjection occurs in the short opening section of *The Kitchen God's Wife*, which is narrated by Pearl, Weili's American-born daughter. Pearl's Westernized voice introduces the reader to her somewhat quaint and primitive Chinese mother. Pearl recounts a scene from a wedding in San Francisco in which Weili feeds her granddaughter, Cleo. Cleo opens her mouth 'wide like a baby bird,' and Weili drops jellyfish into it while telling her that Pearl used to compare them to 'rubber bands' (32). Cleo reacts by shrieking and wailing, 'the half-eaten jellyfish dribbling out from her pouting lips' (32). Looking at her mother's dismay, Pearl thinks: 'And I feel so bad for her, that she's been betrayed by her memory and my childhood fondness for rubbery-tasting things. I think about a child's capacity to hurt her mother in ways she cannot ever imagine' (33). The depiction of the half-chewed, stringy, and rubbery jellyfish dribbling out of a child's mouth is an interesting illustration of the in-betweenness of food that Kristeva argues is linked to the abject. The dish is both food and non-food, positioned in and out of the young bird/girl's body. It is an exotic dish, suggestive of Chinese people's tendency to consume whatever flies, crawls, walks, or swims. Weili is hurt by Cleo's indignation and horror, which is a rejection not only of her offering of love, but also of things Chinese, and of her memories of Pearl. Here the refusal of the delicacy becomes a way of establishing an Americanized, perhaps 'civilized' as opposed to barbaric, identity. Food is used as a demarcation of ethnic alliances, as a way of signalling boundaries of the self and other. The consequence, however, is that the figure associated with Chinese culture is categorized as the other that must be abjected, rendered strange, or ridiculed.

Another scene in which food is associated with horror occurs much later in the novel during the war. News about the Japanese soldiers at Nanking comes in the form of exaggerated rumours: 'Raped old women, married women, and little girls, taking turns with them, over and over again. Sliced them open with a sword when they were all used up. Cut off their fingers to take their rings. Shot all the little sons, no more generations. Raped ten thousand, chopped down twenty or thirty thousand, a number that is no longer a number, no longer people' (295). Weili has 'very bad dreams' for many months after hearing of these atrocities (295). She feels terror and guilt because her own plight has not been as tragic. In her dream, she returns to Nanking, where the cook tells her, 'You didn't have to leave Nanking to see such things, to taste such good food' (296). Then the cook sets down 'a dish, piled with white eels, thick as fingers. And they were still alive, struggling to swim off [her] plate' (296). This dream echoes the scene of the 'best' meal they had eaten, where they feasted on 'platters piled high with eels cooked whole, as thick as our fingers' (285). In the dream, the fear of violence, rape, dismemberment, and chaos is enacted through food. The eels, a symbol of plenty, become linked to the chopped-off fingers of the victims of war. The struggling eels become nightmarish versions of the 'raped ten thousand' who are struggling between life and death. In Weili's mind, what was abundant has become tainted and destroyed.

Years later, in America, she refuses Helen's offer to go to a restaurant that specializes in 'this same kind of eels, cooked with chives in very hot oil' (296). The taste is forever associated with the deaths of people at Nanking, and she does not 'have an appetite anymore for that kind of eels' (296). Here, the association of horror is not overtly linked to the protagonist's identity as in the first example. However, that the unspeakable acts return in the form of surrealistic images, as one of Weili's favourite foods, is a striking comment on her perception of herself. The abominable and the adored become intertwined in her mind after the war. The eels are suggestive of a kind of Proustian sweet remembrance of things past that can no longer be experienced with pleasure by the mature Weili. She notes, 'My tongue doesn't taste things the same way anymore' (296). Food here acts as a way of signifying the loss of innocence and an entry into a world of increasingly more complex experience.

In a similar way, Tan uses food to depict Weili's domestic situation, which becomes more and more intolerable. Just as the abundance of food was indicative of Weili's relatively happy state in her early years, the paucity and monotony of food become tangible evidence of the deterioration of her marriage in the early 1940s. After enduring Wen Fu's infidelities, as well as emotional, sexual, and psychological abuse for a number of years, Weili notes that her situation was no different from that of the whores that Wen Fu used: 'It was the same life, the same kind of torture, pulling me apart, inch by inch, until I no longer recognized myself' (356). It is around this point that Wen Fu tortures her by killing her appetite. A dish of 'pork with a kind of sweet cabbage' (358) that she used to enjoy becomes a form of punishment. One summer, when the cabbage is bad, the dish turns bitter like 'the flavor of the bad water it drank' (358). To satisfy his sadistic tendencies, Wen Fu orders the cook to prepare the dish of bitter cabbage night after night for Weili until she praises it. But she resists, and 'after two weeks' time, [her] stomach proved stronger than his temper' (359). This scene is only one of many examples of Wen Fu's ill-treatment of Weili. It is important, however, because it explicitly links food, subjectivity, female desire, and power. Life, with all its good and bad elements, is something that must be 'tasted' or experienced in a literal manner more than once in the novel. Here, as Weili notes, it might seem 'like a foolish thing, to be so stubborn over a bad-tasting cabbage,' but not fighting would be like admitting that 'life was finished' (359). In *The Kitchen God's Wife* then, women have the power to cook up and serve dishes for good fortune and happiness, but it is also possible to force them to swallow bitterness. The preparation and eating of food can empower the female subject, but consumption and appetite can also be used to shape the female body into docility, or at least obedience.

Ultimately, Weili must learn what her mother tried to teach her when she was just six years old. Before her mother left her, she taught her that there is a proper time and place to satisfy one's desires; that it is sometimes necessary to pay a high price in order to have one's wishes; and that female desire is not to be ignored. These lessons are presented in part through tropes of eating and appetite. In a rather enigmatic flashback, Weili recalls the very last day she spent with her mother:

> That day we also went to all the places where the best things in the world could be found. To Zhejiang Road, where she said they made the best French-style leather shoes; she did not buy any. To Chenghuang Miao, where she said they sold a beauty tonic of crushed pearls. She let me put some on my cheeks, but she did not buy this either. To Bubbling Well Road, where she bought me the best American ice cream sundae; she did not eat any, told me it was 'too messy, too sweet.' To Foochow Road, where she said you could buy any kind of book, any kind of newspaper, Chinese and foreign too. (111)

On this memorable day, Weili sensed that her mother wanted to her to 'open [her] eyes and ears and remember everything' (110). She learns about restraint and indulgence, about good quality food and merchandise, and about the possibilities of getting the best life has to offer.

However, more importantly, she also learns that desires and tastes are shaped by the textures and contexts of one's life. Her mother takes her to 'Little East Gate, where all the best seafood vendors put up their stands' (111). She looked for a delicacy, a 'rare little fish, called *wah-wah-yu*, because it cried just like a baby' (111). But upon finding the fish, the mother only says: 'Long ago I loved to eat this fish ... so tender, so delicious. Even the scales are as soft and sweet as baby leaves. But now I think it is sad to eat such a creature. I have no appetite for it anymore' (111). Weili thought at the time that her mother was letting her know something crucial: 'So many desires to remember, so many places to find them. I thought my mother was teaching me a secret – that my happiness depended on finding an immediate answer to every wish' (111–12). However, what Weili later discovers is that the secret is not that of instant fulfilment, but of timing. The best-tasting things in life, the finest luxuries can only be enjoyed by one who is ready for them, and who believes that she is worthy of them. The mother who ran away from her oppressive marriage was teaching Weili not just about satisfying cravings, but also about self-worth. She was telling her daughter that she was worthy of the best things in life. The incident is also enlightening for Weili in that she realizes that she does not have to be content with whatever is given to her. The mother's refusal to be circumscribed by the limits set by others becomes an example later for Weili. Just as the mother chooses between her own desires and that of her family, Weili later also chooses to leave her abusive husband, even though she knows that she will hurt her aged father in the process. Weili's mother demonstrates that there are different paths open for women, and this becomes her legacy to her daughter, who is poised between two cultures. One has only to reach out and take one of the hundred dishes one is offered to savour, and be ready for the consequences. The kitchen god's wife finally learns that life holds many delicacies and pleasures, and that, contrary to Chinese indoctrination of female passivity, self-effacement, and invisibility, it is sometimes necessary to put one's own desires and tastes first.

6

'Each Story Brief and Sad and Marvellous': Multiple Voices in Wayson Choy's *The Jade Peony*

Grandmother told that story, and then another, each story brief and sad and marvellous. There were seven pieces of jade, carved in the shape of ancient symbols. The one she held most dear, we knew, was a coin-sized one, an exquisitely carved peony of translucent white and pinkish jade; its petals were outlined in a simple, carved relief against a perfect round of stone.

Wayson Choy, The Jade Peony

Wayson Choy's *The Jade Peony*, winner of a Trillium Book Award, is set in Vancouver's Chinatown in the late 1930s and 1940s. Like Chong, Shum, Goto, and others in this study, Choy grapples with issues of ethnic identity in North American society, and the ways in which collective memory, history, and storytelling interact, and sometimes clash, with the gaze and expectations of the dominant culture in the construction of this identity. Structurally similar to a number of Asian American and Asian Canadian works published before it, such as Amy Tan's *The Joy Luck Club* (1989) and Sky Lee's *Disappearing Moon Cafe* (1990), *The Jade Peony* employs a series of narrators to give their particular version of the struggles and joys of living and growing up as a cultural minority. However, unlike works such as Louis Chu's *Eat a Bowl of Tea* (1961) or Ang Lee's film *The Wedding Banquet*, the conflict between what Lisa Lowe calls 'nativism and assimilation' is not figured simply in the topos of 'generational conflict' (*Immigrant* 77). In *The Jade Peony*, Choy illustrates the complexities of racialized subjectivity not only by way of friction between grandparents, parents, and their children, but also through protagonists who are of the same generation. Through the structure of 'multiple monologue narratives' (Souris 99),[1] which, like the 'exquisitely carved peony,' reveals layer after layer of wonder and delight, Choy illustrates how factors such as gender, economic status, and position in a family affect the ethnic subject.

Like *The Joy Luck Club*, ethnic identity is imagined and realized in *The Jade Peony* through the use of multiple voices. Though individualized, three voices are blended to give versions of the same story – that of growing up as other under the strong matriarchal influences of Grandmother Poh-Poh.[2] The device of multiple narrators is sustained in Choy's work, unlike Shum's sporadic use of monologues, as the novel is divided into three almost equal parts. The effect is to create a fuller and more complex picture of the family in a way that a focus on one protagonist does not. Choy links the three sections through the theme of metamorphosis. There is a scene of transformation in each of the three sections of the novel. These moments of metamorphosis occur when the protagonists change or transform what they have, who they are, or what I have been calling visible signs, into things almost magical and fantastic. Each of the objects transformed is linked to markers that are identifiably Asian North American, so the fantasy of transformation becomes symbolic of larger ethnographic and ethnic issues and potentials. In addition, these scenes are crucial to novel because they are emblematic of some of the protagonists' key characteristics and tendencies – they suggest Asian Canadians' ability to shift and invent, to create wonder out of necessity. Though in many ways the novel is about the struggle to survive and the difficult decisions of belonging,[3] this *motif* of transformation acts as a contrapuntal movement that celebrates the power of creativity and resistance, and the possibility of ethnic reinscription.

The three-part structure of the work and the multiple narrators enable Choy to depict differences within ethnic Chinese in Vancouver.[4] Ethnicity, by definition, needs the identity of the other in order to exist. In his introduction to *Writing Ethnicity*, Winfried Siemerling points out that 'Because ethnicity ... arises with the construction of cross-cultural identification, every notion of ethnicity implies an act of "ethnogenesis," a communal identification whose emergence is marked ... as different from the previous, seemingly unmitigated cultural identity to which it refers – yet which it cannot but name, remember, and construct from its new perspective' (2). Siemerling argues that 'because such acts of ethnogenesis imply simultaneous identification by both contrast and cross-cultural implication, they are marked by hybridity and invention' (2). In the novel, Choy juxtaposes the three narratives, creating a polyphonic effect that emphasizes the heterogeneity and hybridity of ethnic identity. Thus, Choy explores not only cross-cultural identification, but also the construction of subjects simultaneously marked by ideologies of race, family, gender, sexuality, and class. Political questions of exclusion, inequality, and immigration are ever present and serve as reminders of the history of Chinese communities in Canada, though these issues are often subsumed by the narrative's more dominant concern with the *Bildung* of the protagonists. While Jook-Liang, Jung-Sum, and Sek-Lung are brought up in the same family, they react differently to their ethnic heritage and are assimilated into the surrounding Canadian and American cultures to varying degrees. Their hopes and desires, fears and anxieties reflect their acceptance of, and also resistance to, their perceived identities, to the sense of being perpetually 'foreign' in the country where they were born.

Texts that deal with multiracial subjects often have a tendency to be what Fredric Jameson has called 'allegorical,' where even when narrating private stories, the public sphere is metamorphosized, and where the personal and the political, the private and the historical, become inextricably linked ('Third' 69).[5] As Shohat and Stam note of representations of colonized people, 'within hegemonic discourse every subaltern performer/role is seen as synecdochically summing up a vast but putatively homogenous community' (*Unthinking Eurocentrism* 183). Choy's book, with its repeated references to 'false immigration stories,' 'secrets to be kept' (14), 'paper years' that are 'always different from Chinese years' (49), can be read allegorically and negatively as typical of the mysterious and sinister quality of the Chinese. Choy's use of the three voices serves, in some ways, to counter this tendency to view all Chinese Canadians in the same light. In addition, instead of viewing them as stereotypes, one can more fruitfully read the accounts as a record for posterity of the hardships and suffering of early Chinese immigrants. As in Denise Chong's work, these difficulties are contextualized, shown to have arisen because of governmental policies and the 'yellow peril' threats that underlie the protagonists' world in the first part of the twentieth century. Christopher Lee remarks that 'the family itself functioned, to use a psychoanalytic term, as a fantasy, masking conditions that remained politically unknowable' (21). The choices that the children make, in games they play, the movies they watch, and the people they idolize, do not simply represent choices that children make when they grow up in a bi- or tricultural milieu: they also reveal the complex web of relations between public policy, economic status, and ethnic strategies of survival. Choy avoids any simplistic reduction of Chinese versus white Canadians by giving us specificities of Chinese Canadian cultural practices that produce identity. Lisa Lowe notes that the 'processes that produce such identity are never complete and are always constituted in relation to historical and material differences.' Cultural identity 'is not something which already exists, transcending place, time, history and culture.' Rather, these identities 'undergo constant transformation' (*Immigrant Acts* 64).

In the novel, the character who most resists change is the grandmother, called Poh-Poh by the children. Liang says that she 'became the arbitrator of the old ways,' being 'one of the few elder women left in Vancouver' (14). But even she is willing to adapt old ways to new ones. Instead of retaining the complex naming of kinship and relationships in Canada, she tells the children, 'In Gold Mountain, simple is best' (14). Her beliefs and proverbial sayings render her an ambivalent figure of authority for the hybridized children born in North America. She is full of the wisdom of the Old World, yet she is also the one to perpetuate Chinese androcentric views in the family.

Like Amy Tan and many other writers from immigrant families, Choy represents the daily textures of ethnicity through exotic foods and medicine, storytelling, and superstitious or supernatural customs. Most of these skills and practices are associated with Poh-Poh, the Old One. In the use of food, feasts, and the preparation of food as ethnicized markers, Choy is much more restrained than a writer like Tan. He does not indulge in what has been called 'food pornography,' or the exploitation of 'one's ethnic foodways' (Wong, *Reading* 55).[6] For instance, in the first section, Liang describes the groceries Father buys for the special dinner in honour of Wong Suk: 'a bare long-necked chicken's head, freshly killed, hung out of the bag he had carried home. Poh-Poh also unwrapped a fresh fish, its eyes still shiny. Once it was cooked, Kiam and Jung would fight over who would get to suck on the hard-as-marble calcified fish eyes. I wanted the chicken feet' (18). While food is certainly used to differentiate between Chinese Canadians and Canadians of other origins, it does not symbolize the knowledge of the old mysterious East to the same degree as in a film like Ang Lee's *Eat Drink Man Woman*. In Lee's film, the father, who is a master chef, prepares elaborate banquets every Sunday for his daughters. The close-up shots of his culinary skills are filmed in such a way to suggest a divide between the art of an older generation and the Westernized life of the young daughters, one of whom works for a fast food outlet. In Choy's work, because the children are as eager to have the 'calcified fish eyes' as their parents, food here suggests a shared experience rather than a generational difference. The enthusiastic anticipation of dinner indicates a familiarity with this aspect of ethnic life. Food is not a spectator sport, nor is it described as a quaint practice for the non-Chinese tourist.

In descriptions of Poh-Poh's medicine, a similar sense of acceptance is shown by the young narrators. Liang sees Poh-Poh slip 'mysterious pink pellets, like tiny BB's, into the warm honey-sweetened chicken broth' (32) for Sekky, who slowly becomes stronger. Later Sekky remembers Poh-Poh when he finds her shelf of herbal remedies: 'the valuable dried sea horses, the rare hard black nugget of bear spleen, the squat bottle of ground deer antler ... On the shelf were these: the still mysterious seeds like peppercorns with tiny spikes, the packets of bitter thick-veined leaves and mandrake roots, the tube of BB-like pills, the tiny cosmetic pots of sweet-smelling ointments' (193–4). The different kinds of medicine, though strange and exotic, are not used here primarily to give readers a sense of the protagonists' otherness or ethnicity. Instead, they are used to create the sense of loss that young Sekky feels after Poh-Poh's death. Stumbling upon the shelf, he remarks that 'Familiar fragrances, sharp and bitter flavours, made my tongue and nose go moist with anticipation' (193). Afterwards, rather than reacting with wonder, horror, or awe, Sekky, who was closest to Poh-Poh, feels 'revitalized by the medicinal scents' (194). His position as the sickly baby of the family, whom Poh-Poh nursed to good health, enables him to appreciate things about the Old One that the other members of the family do not.

Choy uses storytelling in the novel to hint at the richness of the stories of the Old World. We know from the children that Poh-Poh tells magical narratives of 'wild storms and parting clouds, thunder, and after much labour, mountains that split apart, giving birth to demons who were out to kill you or to spirits who ached to test your courage' (21). But the fables themselves do not form part of the narrative proper as they do in a work like Maxine Hong Kingston's *The Woman Warrior*. Whereas the chant of Fa Mu Lan actually takes up a large section of Kingston's autobiographical narrative, Grandma Poh-Poh's myths of the Monkey King and ghost stories are alluded to, but not narrated. Myths are only one kind of literature among many with which the

Chinese Canadian children grow up. Chinese myths and fables are often inseparable from other narrative forms in the novel: biographical and historical feats, Chinese opera, Hollywood movies, and English children's books. The tales from China are not only translated, they are also transposed and become part of North American culture. When Liang sees Wong Suk, she immediately believes that he was 'the Monkey King of Poh-Poh's stories' (23). At the dinner table she thinks: 'here ... right beside me in his patched-up shirt, with his soft eyes, like liquid – sat the marvellous Cheetah of the matinee movies; Cheetah, Tarzan's friend. Poh-Poh had educated me about his. After Jung took Grandmother and me to the Lux to see my first Tarzan movie, Poh-Poh announced that Cheetah was another one of the Monkey King's disguises' (27). Similarly, when Liang has fantasies, they are a combination of Eastern and Western tales: 'I mimicked the Chinese Opera heroines: the warrior-woman, the deserted wife, the helpless princess. And lately, in my movie costumes, I tapped steps as deftly as Shirley [Temple] herself' (38).

Among the stories that we do hear are the real-life, heroic tales told by various members of the family. Liang hears of how Poh-Poh became house servant to the First Concubine in Old China at seven years of age, and how she had to learn to wait and serve her; how Wong Suk inherited a cloak from his red-haired boss, Roy Johnson, whom he rescued from the freezing cold when they worked together for the Canadian Pacific Railroad. At thirteen, Second Brother Jung hears of the 'legendary' tales of 'bad luck' that befell the drunk gambler Old Yuen, at the same time as he takes boxing lessons from Yuen's son, who fights like the 'Brown Bomber' (105, 111). When challenged by Frank Yuen to a fight, Jung remembers the heroic story of 'a great Chinese warrior in 1911,' Sun Yat-Sen, and feels his 'warrior arms grow stronger' (113). These examples show how biography, legend, history, and popular culture are conflated and influence Jung, as they do his sister. Choy does not rank these competing narratives in order of importance, or separate them into Chinese and Anglo categories. Rather, he reveals how children of immigrant parents are interpellated by the literature of their ethnic heritage and of their adopted country simultaneously. For example, even though census forms usually require a respondent to check only one language for 'mother tongue,' or ethnic origin, one does not grow up learning to be Chinese first, and then gradually becomes Canadian or American second. Instead, the second-generation children of Chinese immigrants grow up as both Canadian and ethnically Chinese. The hyphenated identity of Asian North Americans is a complex, fluid, and constantly shifting state.[7]

Traditionally, a strong belief in fate or the supernatural is seen as another characteristic that often distinguishes the ethnic subject from other Americans or Canadians. Usually, this trait is associated with an older immigrant who is haunted by memories of the past, or teachings of ancestors in the country of origin. Superstitious beliefs are contrasted with the progressivist, technologically oriented thinking of the adopted country. The reproduction of old ways of perceiving the world then constitutes an oppositional alterity for the younger generation, and for the readers. The effect of this device varies, and can create a sense of quaintness, Old World magic, or, at times, gentle mockery and derision. One reviewer of the novel notes that 'the seductive charm of this book hinges not so much on its varied storylines as on the mood of magic, superstition and fatedness that overhangs the narrative' (Naves Ii). Choy's use of this ethnic detail is similar to the way a filmmaker such as Zhang Yimou shows provincial China. What Rey Chow observes of Zhang applies to Choy: 'the ethnographer here is himself a "native" of the culture he is transcribing,' the 'articulation becomes in effect a culture's belated fascination with its own datedness, its own alterity' (*Primitive Passions* 145). The recreation of this quasi-mythic identity comes from the perspective of the modern observer who represents this otherness with some wonder.

What is significant about Choy's deployment of fate and superstition is that it is not confined to the older generation. Jung-Sum, Second Brother, says at one point, 'I believed in ghosts, like everyone else in Chinatown ... But there were good ghosts and bad ghosts, and you had to be careful not to insult the good ones nor be tempted by the bad ones. And you had to know a ghost when you saw one' (75). In a similar manner, it is young Sek-Lung, Third Brother, who becomes aware that Grandma's spirit is in the house after her death. He insists that 'Grandmama had never left me' (162), and sees her ghost many times. When other members of the family are aggravated, he thinks, 'I could not help it: my heart, my *eyes*, had not lied to me' (163). In this way, the division between the older and the younger generation, between the Old World and the New World, is minimized. Alterity becomes interiorized, as it is the young boy, the one who acknowledges his Chinese Canadian 'hyphenated reality,' who insists on the materiality and rationality of the spiritual experience.

Not surprisingly, however, it is Grandmother Poh-Poh herself who is endowed with the greatest powers of intuition and perception of the other world. At one point she shows her trembling fingers to her grandson and says, 'You see that, Little One? ... That is my body fighting with Death. He is in this room now' (148). Grandmother's life and spirit are symbolized by 'her precious jade carving, the small peony of white and light-red jade, her most lucky possession' (149). It is described almost as a living being as it 'seemed to pulse' and has a 'pink heart' with 'veins swirling out into the petals of the flower' (149). The semi-translucent carving suggests exquisite beauty, fragility, and rareness. It is also associated with passion and sexuality because it was given to Grandmother by her one-time lover, a young acrobat who taught her how to juggle. Blushing and laughing, she confesses that she had seen his white hair and white skin while he was bathing. Significantly, it is the pendant with the magical colour that holds 'the unravelling strands of her memory' (149). Shortly after she dies, Sekky finds the 'small, round' jade peony in his pocket and in his mind's eye sees 'Grandmama smile, and heard, softly, the pink centre beat like a beautiful, cramped heart' (151). Elements of the supernatural are intermingled with memory; ghosts are the real spirits of the past.

When she was alive, however, Grandmother's greatest talent was her ability to make old things new. In each of the three sections there is one moment of magical transformation, almost as glorious as a Joycean epiphany. These scenes are rendered in loving, lyrical detail, and, symbolically, they constitute the emblematic core of ethnicity for Wayson Choy. In the first section, Poh-Poh uses her skill in ribbon tying to make 'three small blooms for each of' Jook-Liang's tap-shoes (34). She twists and turns each end 'until the satin strips danced between her bony fingers' (32). Liang sees with amazement that she no longer has ordinary tap shoes: 'each of my tap-shoes was crowned with a perfectly delicate, perfectly brilliant bouquet of red pom-poms. Not even the silk-tasseled shoes of the First Concubine could have been lovelier' (35). With Poh-Poh's help, 'one China girl' can become Shirley Temple (34). This transformation of her dancing shoes is important because it serves to counter the unflattering image of herself that Liang sees: 'I looked again into the hall mirror, seeking Shirley Temple with her dimpled smile and perfect white-skin features. Bluntly reflected back at me was a broad sallow moon with slit dark eyes, topped by a helmet of black hair. I looked down. Jutting out from a too-large taffeta dress were two spindly legs matched by a pair of bony arms. Something cold clutched at my stomach, made me swallow' (43). Seeing and measuring herself through the screen of the other, Liang can see only the imperfections of her body, and the dominant culture's definition of beauty and loveliness. Looking at her reflection through the fantasy of Hollywood's lens, through white ideals of beauty, she, like Toni Morrison's Pecola from *The Bluest Eye*, finds her features wanting.[8] Yet the scene does not end in despair, as Liang is able to transcend the particularities of the visible into a world of self-actualized desire. In spite of Poh-Poh's discouraging remarks about a girl-child's uselessness and her dark warning about the coming of rain, the scene ends with a sense with Liang's uplifted spirits. She thinks, *'I'm not ugly,* ... I'm not useless' (43). Symbolically, just after she wishes for good weather, the clouds clear up: 'the light from the window brightened ..., the sitting room and hallway became brilliant, full of sun' (43). In the room, Liang exalts over her actual circumstances and is able to read her body differently. Ignoring both Hollywood's gaze and Poh-Poh's belittling ideologies about how a 'girl-child is *mo yung,'* or useless (32), she focuses on her special friend, old Wong Suk, her bandit prince. Their friendship and his encouragement enable her to forget her inadequacy: 'I thought of old Wong Suk leaning on his two canes. And I danced' (43). In spite of the visible markings on her body, her 'broad sallow moon' face and 'slit dark eyes' which does not conform to Hollywood ideals of beauty, she learns to find joy.

Similarly, in the second section, the adopted boy, Jung-Sum, is changed from someone who always felt like a misfit and an outsider to a boy who is strong and beloved by the family. The transformation occurs again through the help of Poh-Poh. Because he lost his mother and was taken from his abusive and drunk father, Jung-Sum feels particularly vulnerable and weak as a child. For his twelfth birthday, he is given an old topcoat which used to belong to his friend Frank Yuen's father. Grandmother cuts and stitches up the second-hand coat from Old Yuen to fit Jung-Sum. With the aid of some military-looking brass buttons, and the dry-cleaning skills of their friend, the charcoal coat metamorphoses and stiffens. When Jung tries it on, he is transformed into a man. With the coat on, he looks as grand as 'Generalissimo Chiang Kai-shek' (101). This reference aligns Jung with the national hero of Taiwan, whom mainlanders considered to be a rebel. He is not associated with old China but the breakaway independent island. Jung thinks: 'I felt intense heat embrace my shoulders, then curve over my back and drop upon my chest. I felt like a young warrior receiving the gift of his bright armour, a steely-grey coat born from fire and steam ... The coat felt and smelled like new' (101).

Both Liang's and Jung's transformations occur with the help of clothing – the tap shoes and the coat. Donning the right clothes allows the
children here to dream of themselves as famous, important people.
Clothing functions as a way of transformation in the same way that it
does in Chong's book, where Hing is shown in a photograph dressed as
a boy. In Choy's novel, clothing does not transform just one's external
appearance, but also the characters' actual perception of themselves. A
change in dress has the effect of changing the children's identities from
marked and disabled to positive and rejuvenated. This shift reinforces
the arguments I have been making about the important of the gaze in
the construction of identity, as the children see themselves from the
vantage point of others. As Kaja Silverman notes, 'Clothing and other
kinds of ornamentation make the human body culturally visible ... the
subject sees itself being seen, and that visual transaction is always
ideologically organized' ('Fragments' 145, 143). The characters' abilities
to imagine, adapt, and perceive are all embodied in, and signified
through, clothing.

In both these instances, Poh-Poh is able to recast an old or ordinary
thing into a marvel. This ability, a combination of natural gift and hard
work, is emblematic of ethnic immigrants' aptitude to adapt, to make
the best of what is available, and to give new life to old things. Significantly, the mode of transformation is that stereotypical emblem of the
Chinese North American – the Chinese laundry. Early Chinese settlers
opened laundries because they were not allowed to work at other kinds
of labour. Cleaning other people's clothes was difficult and demeaning
work.[9] But in this scene, the laundry machine becomes the means by
which the coat and, by association Jung, are reborn through fire and
water: 'Luxurious blasts of steam penetrated every fibre of the coat. The
machinery hissed and sang; the flames danced blue and red in a ring
beneath the water heater. The wool material stiffened "like new" in the
mix of chemicals and steam. The brass buttons began to gleam in the
sunlight pouring from the store window' (101). Through the author's
rich imagery, an ordinary cleaning machine becomes a powerful ve-
hicle of transformation, making an old discarded coat into a shiny new
garment. This is the valuable heritage that the grandchildren inherit
from the elders. Not only do they learn lessons of resilience, tenacity,
and frugality, but they learn to make the best use of whatever materials
and means they have to transform themselves into fighters.

Grandmother's pièce de résistance, however, is the wind chime that
she teaches Sekky to make. Sekky notes, 'Hers were not ordinary,

carelessly made chimes, such as those you now find in our Chinatown stores, whose rattling noises drive you mad. ... Each one that she made was created from a treasure trove of glass fragments and castaway costume jewellery' (145). While the family is embarrassed because Grandmama looks 'for these treasures wandering the back alleys' and 'peering into ... neighbours' garbage cans,' Sekky enjoys collecting the 'splendid junk: jangling pieces of broken vase, cranberry glass fragments embossed with leaves, discarded glass beads from Woolworth necklaces' (145-6). In working with the pieces of broken glass, she becomes an artist who attains immortality through art, in this case, her mosaic chime. Sekky observes: 'I became lost in the magic of her task: she dabbed a secret mixture of glue on one end and skilfully dropped the braided end of a silk thread into it ... the braiding would slowly, *very* slowly, unwind, fanning out like a prized fishtail. ... Each jam-sized pot of glue was treasured; each large cork stopper had been wrapped with a fragment of pink silk. ... Her hands worked on their own command, each hand racing with a life of its own: cutting, snapping, braiding, knotting' (148–9). Though the making of wind chimes is not a well-known art form, it is an apt emblem of Grandmother's skill. It requires perseverance, grace, patience, and entails a focus on detail. She creates splendour from the small and domestic, not the large canvas of Western artists. In her hands, useless refuse becomes a thing of beauty, a work of sweetness, music, and light. It is an apt metaphor for the invention and creativity of ethnic Canadians.

Her story, however, is not the main interest of the book. Rather, Choy's three-part structure illustrates differences between growing up female and growing up male in Chinese Canadian culture through the perspective of the various child narrators. The stories reveal the ways in which race, gender, and the familial and social hierarchy contribute to the formation of ethnic subjectivity. Judith Butler argues that 'the social regulation of race' is not simply 'another, fully separable, domain of power from sexual difference or sexuality,' but that the 'symbolic – that register of regulatory ideality – is also and always a racial industry,' the 'reiterated practice or *racializing* interpellations' (*Bodies* 18). In other words, in order to become speaking subjects, individuals must necessarily take up positions within an already established gendered and racialized symbolic order. The difficulties presented by this structure, which, as poststructuralists have pointed out, is essentially a dualistic and hierarchical one, are best illustrated in the *Bildung* of Liang, Only Sister, and Jung, Second Brother.

The stories of Jook-Liang and, to a lesser extent, Stepmother are particularly revealing about female racialized subjectivity. As young children, both Liang and Stepmother are denigrated by their relatives for being girls, and thought to be useless to the Chinese family. Stepmother's story is a muted one. She is doubly silenced by her patriarchal household and by the structure of the book, which does not afford her space to tell her version of the story. She functions mostly as a maternal figure in the novel, and never transcends what Marianne Hirsch calls the 'object status,' because as a mother 'she must always remain the object in her child's process of subject-formation; she is never fully a subject' (Hirsch 12). Her background is scantily and rather incidentally given by her daughter, Liang, who recounts that her mother came to Canada 'with no education, with a village dialect as poor as she was' (13). Orphaned at seven, she was eventually 'sold into Father's Canton merchant family' to be a concubine to Liang's father. Even after the death of the first wife, Stepmother's secondary status is maintained. Only at the very end of the novel does she speak out against the treatment of being called 'stepmother' by her own children, as decreed by Grandmother. Sekky describes her complaining of the fact that throughout her life, her '*own* two children – call [her]· *Step*mother,' in a manner 'as if pulled against her will' (235), rather than of her own volition. She has internalized the position of sacrificial and long-suffering woman, idealized in Chinese society.

Only once in the novel is there a hint that she has an interior subjectivity. This occurs during the preparations for her Mission friend Chen Suling's visit. The most sensitive of the children, Sekky, describes her 'sitting in Father's large wicker chair. She looked far away, and I knew she was thinking again of her girlhood in China and the family she had left behind, and the history that was hers, her ghost-whispering history' (136). Her isolation is emphasized by her remark that 'Suling is my only friend who knows *my* family stories,' which was spoken, according to Sekky, 'as if she were stranded on an island' (136). However, as Suling's visit never materializes, Stepmother's stories are never revealed. She suffers and endures much in silence. After receiving the package that gives notice of Suling's death, Stepmother 'closed up' her friend's 'thick book' and never mentions her name again. In a similar way, the death of her third baby is quickly passed over with little opportunity for her to show her grief. In typical Chinese manner, the family reacts with restraint and stoicism at the dead baby who was 'strangled by its cord' (97). Jung records the event in a matter-of-fact manner: 'Miscarriages and stillbirths were not uncommon in those days, and no one expected a safe delivery so soon after Stepmother had just had Sekky. Besides, the more practical *mahjong* ladies stressed, how could her man manage another mouth to feed?' (97). This scene reveals the extent to which the survival of the collective ethnic body depends on individual repression and sacrifice. The attitude of *que sera sera* is adopted by the community as a way of healing over what must have been a strong sense of loss. Looking at the bright side of things is one way in which immigrants manage to survive, and the fatalistic attitude enables Stepmother 'to accept that it was meant' (97).

Liang, who grows up with the same set of fatalistic, mythic, and patriarchal values, is able to resist internalizing many of the negative ideologies of being female. Partly, her subjectivity is constituted by successfully juxtaposing Chinese teachings about the devaluation of women with a more modern Canadian version of female selfhood. When Grandmother tells her, 'Jook-Liang, if you want a place in this world ... do not be born a girl-child,' she retorts, 'This is Canada ... not Old China' (31). Even at nine, however, she is quite aware of the unequal treatment of the sexes by Chinese Canadians: 'I recalled how Sekky had received twice the number of jade and gold bracelets that I had got as a baby, and how everyone at the baby banquet toasted his arrival' (31). What rescues her from the constant reminder of female worthlessness is Wong Suk, her 'one and only true friend' since she was five (38). Unlike Poh-Poh, who says that 'a beautiful girl-child from a poor family is even more useless than an ugly one from a rich family, unless you can sell either one for a jade bracelet or hard foreign currency' (42), Wong Suk sees Liang as 'his Shirley Temple princess' (38). Choy shows how competing ideologies from one's ethnic heritage and the surrounding American and Canadian culture intersect and continue to create sometimes constructive tensions in the gendered and racialized subject.

While as a female Liang experiences racial and gender prejudice, Second Brother Jung-Sum finds that he 'is an outsider in almost every way,' as one reviewer puts it (Horton 32). Unlike the other siblings, Jung is an adopted son, which adds another layer of otherness to his developing sense of self. In his section of the narrative, he struggles with his need to prove himself as a prizefighter and his growing awareness that he is attracted to other men. Even before he realizes that he has homoerotic tendencies, Poh-Poh mysteriously senses that he is different. She tells her friend that 'Jung-Sum is the moon,' which is

associated with 'the *yin* principle, the *female*' (82). While Liang fanta-
sizes about being Shirley Temple, Jung reads everything about Joe
Louis, and dreams of being a champion boxer. He uses his fists to prove
his machismo and to overcome his sense of not belonging. In a scene
that is reminiscent of the gladiatorial wrestling in D.H. Lawrence's
Women in Love, Jung's epiphanic moment occurs when he wills himself
to fight Frank Yuen, '*to win or die*' (116). At the crucial moment of their
struggle, Jung has an involuntary flashback of his father, who used to
beat him, and begins to cry.

> Frank Yuen, kneeling, bent forward and pressed my babbling head against
> his torn shirt. He began to rock me, and the slow rhythm of his rocking,
> back and forth, caught me off guard. I closed my eyes and moved with
> him, a child being cradled, back and forth. There was the smell of Frank's
> sweat and his tobacco; his rapid breathing sounded as loud and ragged as
> my own ... Frank's lips brushed my forehead, settled for a second, then
> lifted ...
>   As I, too, moved to get up, my whole body suddenly lit with an unbid-
> den, shuddering tension; a strange yearning awoke in me, a vivid longing
> rose relentlessly from the centre of my groin, sensuous and craving ... (117)

The scene, one of the most sensual in the novel, moves from fierce
combat, to tenderness, to sensuality. Choy adds a level of complexity to
his depiction of ethnic subjectivity through Jung and Frank, who are
both racially and sexually different from the normative culture, but
who find 'community,' in the positive sense that Bonnie TuSmith has
argued, albeit momentarily, in their embrace.[10] Frank Yuen's embrace
here functions in the way Wong Suk's did for Liang, and the way Poh-
Poh's embrace made 'the whole world seem ... perfect' for Sekky (146).
    The best example of ethnic confusion occurs in the third and longest
narrative in *The Jade Peony*, in that of Sek-Lung, Third Brother. This story
demonstrates the intricacies of being culturally different from the white
majority as a young boy in Canada in the 1940s. Sek-Lung remarks that
'words like *chink, nigger, bohunk, wop, jap* and *hymie* quickly infiltrated
my playground vocabulary' (186). He asks his mother if he is Chinese
or Canadian, but realizes that identity is not that simple: 'But even if I
was born in Vancouver, even if I should salute the Union Jack a hundred million times, even if I had the cleanest hands in all the Dominion
of Canada and prayed forever, I would still be *Chinese*' (135). One lesson
he soon learns is that being Asian on the West Coast at the onset of the

Second World War had crucial implications. Because his favourite pastime is playing at war and pretending that he is a pilot, he inevitably echoes the hatred of the Japanese that was prevalent at the time. He notes that the schoolchildren had 'begun to turn away from the Japanese boys and girls in the schoolyard. In the older grades, there were already fights between gangs of "good guys" and "Japs"' (195). From the adults, he hears about Japanese atrocities in China: 'There were tales of incredible enemy cruelty. A cousin wrote from Shanghai how the Japanese army were burying people alive, women and children. Another wrote how she witnessed living people, tied to posts, being used for bayonet practice. There were even darker rumours: the Japanese had camps for medical experiments, there were special camps for women hostages' (195). He learns to demonize all Japanese: 'I absorbed Chinatown's hatred of the Japanese, the monsters with bloodied buck teeth, no necks, and thick Tojo glasses; I wanted to kill every one of them' (196). This passage demonstrates, in Werner Sollors's words, that ethnicity, 'that is, belonging and being perceived by others as belonging to an ethnic group,' is an 'invention' (xiii). While Sekky hates the Japanese fiercely, his own Asian features render him vulnerable to misidentification, so that at one point he and his friends resort to wearing a Chinese flag and a button saying, 'I AM CHINESE' (219). For many white Canadians, all non-Westerners are the other, and the finer distinctions between Asian groups are lost.

Through the tale within the tale of Sekky's babysitter, Meiying, Choy reminds us that individuals do not always absorb to the same degree their culture's communal identifications and beliefs. Sekky's belief that all Japanese people are monsters evolves when his seventeen-year-old babysitter, whom he adores because 'she did so many things so well' (207), takes him to watch her Japanese boyfriend, Kazuo, play baseball. Sekky's description of Kazuo upon first meeting him reveals his comic efforts to distinguish between people of Chinese and Japanese ancestry through physical appearance: 'He had a high forehead, deep black eyes like coal, thin lips; his hair was shiny with hair cream. He looked like a Chinese movie soldier, a Good Guy, in one of those films we saw at the China War Effort Fund Drive. But he was *Japanese*' (211). Sekky's assumptions about the team's skills also change: 'All the players became incredible jugglers, chanting in rhythm and catching, throwing, catching. When I thought they could not catch or throw a ball one split second faster, they gave a shout in unison and abruptly stopped. They were as good as the star players on the Chinese Students Soccer Team, passing the ball with their heads and feet, faster and faster and faster. For a moment I forgot I was watching the enemy' (212). These passages, humorously told from a child's point of view, stress how racial differences are socially and ideologically constructed and inculcated. Sekky's surprise that the enemy looks like a Chinese Good Guy, and that the Japanese team plays as well as his own, indicates the permeability of the boundaries between himself and what he considered to be other. In what Rey Chow calls the 'diasporic postcolonial space' (*Writing* 117), ethnic and racial differences are unstable and are always evolving. Cultural identities transform when they encounter other cultures, and the identities themselves depend to a great extent on the perceiver, as well as on the subjects in question. Ethnic identities are 'mirrored,' in Lacan's sense of the term, by representations in their environment that 'determine the way' that subject 'will eventually regard' himself or herself (Silverman, *Subject* 160).[11]

Finally, the characteristics of Chinese Canadians are constantly being questioned in the novel. Bonnie TuSmith has noted that Frank Chin and Maxine Hong Kingston, for example, are Chinese American writers from a specific area of Kwangtung province, and that they are not 'representative of other Asian American writers' or 'Chinese in China' (34). In contrast, the origins of the Chinese Canadians in Wayson Choy's works, specially Poh-Poh, are much trickier to categorize. Their specific ethnic origins are shown to be as flexible as the languages and dialects they know. Early on, Liang observes:

> Poh-Poh spoke her *Sze-yup*, Four County village dialect, to me and Jung, but not always to Kiam, the First Son. With him, she spoke Cantonese and a little Mandarin, which he was studying in the Mission Church basement. Whenever Stepmother was around, Poh-Poh used another but similar village dialect, in a more clipped fashion, as many adults do when they think you might be the village fool, too worthless or too young, or not from their district. The Old One had a wealth of dialects which thirty-five years of survival in China had taught her, and each dialect hinted at mixed shades of status and power, or the lack of both. (15–16)

Language, and the fine distinctions between dialects and tone, are here shown to be markers of rank and ability. One of the reasons Poh-Poh is able to maintain her little matriarchy within the household is due to her linguistic skill. Sekky notes that with her friend, Mrs Lim, Grandmama talked 'in private riddles and spoke in a servant dialect, using a kind of clipped and broken grammar they had in Old China. And this was only one dialect of the many Chinatown dialects they knew in common. Each dialect opened up another reality to them, another time and place they shared' (134). This comment supports the post-structuralists' arguments about the discursive construction of reality and its relation to power. Grandmama is able to exercise power within her domestic and social circle because of her ability to manipulate language. However, this skill has limitations in Canada, where the range of her ability is not appreciated by the English-speakers.

This polyglot ability is not transferred to the grandchildren, and the result is shown to be sometimes frustrating. Sekky confesses his ignorance:

> I knew just enough Chinese and English to speak to people, but not always to understand the finer points; worse, each language was mixed in with a half-dozen Chinatown dialects. I never possessed enough details, in either language, to understand how our family, how the countless cousins, in-laws, aunts and uncles, came to be related ...
>
> English words seemed more forthright to me, blunt, like road signs. Chinese words were awkward and messy, like quicksand. I preferred English, but there were no English words to match the Chinese perplexities. I sometimes wished that my skin would turn white, my hair go brown, my eyes widen and turn blue, and Mr. and Mrs. O'Connor next door would adopt me ... (133–4)

Sekky's wish to be WASP, one shared by many children of minority backgrounds, comes from a sense of frustration stemming from difference. But instead of reacting with nostalgia to the loss of old Chinese ways, Choy's work suggests a quiet acceptance of change. Like the pieces of broken glass that Grandmama collects and refashions into new and beautiful wind chimes, the protagonists will be shaped into exquisite and wondrous subjects in time. There are new skills and new pleasures to look forward to in the New World. To Sekky's sense of confusion about language, Grandmama merely responds by saying, 'Different roots, different flowers ... different brains' (134). Indeed, there is a hint that what gives happiness to the young children growing up in Canada is not the complexities of the past, but a sense of simplicity, or belonging, and the chance to start afresh.[12] At one point, Sekky describes his experiences at school with his favourite teacher, Miss E. Doyle. The passage can be seen as the book's comment about growing up in English Canada. It suggests that the nature of belonging is rather ambiguous:

> We were an unruly, untidy mixed bunch of immigrants and displaced persons, legal or otherwise, and it was her duty to take our varying fears and insecurities and mold us into some ideal collective functioning together as a military unit with one purpose: to conquer the King's English, to belong at last to a country that she envisioned including all of us ...
>
> At recess, our dialects and accents conflicted, our clothes, heights and handicaps betrayed us, our skin colours and backgrounds clashed, but inside Miss E. Doyle's tightly disciplined kingdom we were all – lions or lambs – equals.
>
> We had glimpsed Paradise. (180, 184)

In Choy's view, paradise is possible, as long as one dutifully learns the King's English, and overlooks the various signs that indicate our ethnicity.

PART III

INVISIBLE MINORITIES IN ASIAN AMERICA

7

'Never Again Be the Yvonne of Yesterday': Personal and Collective Loss in Cecilia Brainard's *When the Rainbow Goddess Wept*

Filipino American author Cecilia Manguerra Brainard notes that her novel *When the Rainbow Goddess Wept* (1994) is about the 'collective wounding that Filipinos experienced' in the Second World War.[1] This wounding is one that has remained relatively obscure. She writes in the preface to the Philippine edition of the novel: 'Sometimes I think people have forgotten that War. Except the Japanese. They still talk about Nagasaki and Hiroshima. Unlike Filipinos, the Japanese are very good at immortalizing injustices done to them' (*Song* 3). Unlike my earlier chapters, which situate the politics of the visible on ethnic minorities or visible subjects in North America at the level of individuals, in this chapter, issues of power and abjection occur at the level of the community or group. Filipino North Americans have historically been less vocal, less visible, and less conspicuous as a group than Chinese or Japanese North Americans. Brainard's first novel, set during the Japanese occupation of the Philippines in 1941–4, attempts to give voice to this group and represent a past that largely exists in oral narratives and in memory. Using the form of historiographic fiction, Brainard bears witness to traumas experienced during the Second World War from the perspective of the colonized. Brainard points out that 'the book is fiction, it is not a historical document ... it has fanciful elements. But the novel is my way of documenting the triumph of the Filipino spirit over foreign oppression' (*Song* 3). One of the characteristics of postmodern fiction highlighted by Hutcheon is that it 'reinstalls historical contexts as significant and even determining, but in so doing, it problematizes the entire notion of historical knowledge' (*Poetics* 89). Like Denise

Chong's rewriting of Canadian history by her focus on the plight of Chinese Canadians, Brainard enables us to heal our cultural amnesia and see fuller and more localized, personal versions of stories about General MacArthur and the 'Death March' than have been circulated in North America.[2]

Narrated through the first-person voice of a girl of eight named Yvonne, *When the Rainbow Goddess Wept* documents the destructive effects of war upon the psyche, spirit, and bodies of the heroine, and her immediate family, as well as the Filipino people in general. It also describes Yvonne's journey from the age of innocence to that of experience. At the same time, the novel documents symbolically the loss of the Edenic pre-war Philippines (Casper, *Song* 253). As the war draws to a close, Yvonne, who is turning eleven, gets her first period, and studies herself in the mirror. She thinks: 'A knowledge filtered into my brain that I was different, that I had changed, that I would never again be the Yvonne of yesterday, of last year, of the past. I stood on some threshold, and where it led, I did not know' (203). Emblematically, this scene is suggestive of the Philippines as a nation, poised to begin a new destiny in the post-liberation, neocolonial era. However, just as Yvonne tries 'to smile bravely even as a lump of fear formed and caught' in her throat (203), Filipino people are shown to similarly be placed in a situation where it is no longer possible to return to the simplicity of an earlier world. Like Yvonne, Filipinos have been scarred by the colonial powers of the Spaniards, the Americans, and finally, the Japanese. Yet the novel is also careful to point out the dangers of cultural nationalism by showing the complex interstices between citizenship, gender, age, and economic power. As Yvonne's father explains to her: 'There are good and bad Americans, just as there are good and bad Filipinos ... I believe there are good Japanese' (51).

Like Filipino Australian Arlene Chai's *The Last Time I Saw Mother*, Brainard's novel depicts the personal, familial, and collective losses of Filipinos through imperialism and wars.[3] Like Chong's and Choy's works, this novel highlights the important links between the individual and the broader society and culture by its insistence on the impact of historical events on the life of the young protagonist. Because Brainard cannot access a historically trouble-free past, the heroic and mythic qualities of the Filipino people are suggested through a series of interspersed folk tales and stories told by the storyteller, Laydan, whose role is later taken over by Yvonne. These stories function to articulate a desire for a pure ancestral origin, and to suggest a longing, albeit sometimes idealized, for a romantic past before the advent of Euro-American colonialization. Problems in the war-torn years are suggestively linked to, and contrasted with, legendary tales of heroic valour and struggle. As a kind of Bildungsroman, the novel reveals the ways in which one girl adapts to the series of irrevocable injuries sustained by her people and their land. At the same time, different ways of resistance are suggested by Brainard both through references to mythical forms of heroism and descriptions of the guerilla warfare carried out by Filipinos during the war. In this way, the historical and the legendary, the actual and the fictive, dreams and disillusionment are shown to influence and construct the identity of the young Yvonne, who, by the end of the narrative, learns that she can survive and triumph over the devastating impact of cultural and political imperialism, the loss of childhood innocence, war, and dispossession. Viewed in a larger context, we can read the novel as Brainard's testament to the strength and endurance of Filipinos, who have overcome economic, cultural, and colonial violence in the last three centuries.

When the Rainbow Goddess Wept is structured as a descent from Eden. War is likened to a kind of purgatory, where one is dislocated, temporarily deprived of basic necessities, and rendered homeless. Subsequently, after the war, the characters ascend to an intermediate stage of what could be seen as earthly reality, where the task of reconstruction and rebuilding then takes place. Yvonne's memories of her youth before the war are carefree and prelapsarian, while the war years are compared to a state of hellish limbo. At the beginning of the novel, for instance, the society in Ubec, a fictional city Brainard constructs based on her native Cebu, is depicted in idyllic terms. Yvonne's fourth-grade teacher lectures her class about the Virgin Mary, who was 'spotless, perfect,' and tells her of the need to avoid 'concupiscence' (4). The innocent Yvonne, who associates the word with 'kissing and things like that,' decides, 'for good measure,' to include 'concupiscence in [her] list of sins' at her confession (4). This rather humorous view of sexuality is darkened during the occupation when she learns of the destructive and violent consequences of brutality and desire.

In another scene, her father, a professor at the University of Ubec, tells Yvonne and her cousin of the time before European colonialization: 'In olden days, Ubecans traded with Siamese, Chinese, and Borneans. The people lived in huts along the shoreline' (8). While there is not much commentary offered here, Brainard implicitly contrasts this state of people living in 'huts' with the more structured configuration brought

by the Europeans. With the arrival of Magellan in 1521 came the Spaniards, and 'they built that fort and the old church,' Yvonne notes (8).
More than four hundred years later, the Filipinos are still struggling to
free themselves of the political, cultural, and religious influences of
their conquerors. The 'fort' and the 'old church' still exert power over
the people. And, as Yvonne's mother comments wryly, 'Spaniards,
British, Americans – they come to Ubec ... You'd think Ubec was the
wealthiest city on earth instead of a sleepy seaside place' (14). Brainard's
opening pages remind us that Filipinos today live the way they do
because they have inherited Euro-American legal and socio-economic
structures, as well as their religion, due to the imperialist forms of
expansion of the past. As Robert Young points out, 'the globalization of
the imperial capitalist powers, of a single integrated economic and
colonial system, the imposition of a unitary time on the world, was
achieved at the price of the dislocation of its peoples and cultures' (4).

This Euro-American inheritance and dislocation of native ways is
depicted ambiguously at the outset. Life in the sleepy seaside town of
Ubec is a rather comfortable hybrid of Asian and Western cultures. One
of Yvonne's favourite pastimes is going to the Royal Theatre, which
showed 'two-year old Hollywood and Tagalog films' as well as hosting
the annual performance of the 'Chinese Acrobatic Troupe' (15–16). Celebrations and festivities are similarly an integration of native traditions
and Christian influences. On Christmas eve, Yvonne's family attend a
'mass' that was 'long' and 'tedious,' but which ended with a Filipino
'*media noche* banquet – ham, roasted pig, blood soup, fish rellenos,
sansrivals, leche flan' (23). There is a quality of nostalgia in Brainard's
description of the Christmas celebrations at this point. The festivities
are linked to a kind of Lacanian plenitude and childhood fulfilment:
'Papa got the bowl full of candies and coins for the traditional *sabwag*.
He instructed Esperanza and me to get ready, then he threw the coins
and candies on the floor. We scrambled for them and my cousin boasted
that she had more' (23). However, this sense of satisfaction, linked to a
kind of Lacanian imaginary stage, is shattered by the first signs of war
(see *Écrits*, chapter 3). As the children chew their nougats under star
lanterns out on the verandah, they see the sky turning 'bright red like a
brilliant sunset' (23). It is not a display of nature, but a fire set on
purpose to destroy the store of the local Japanese couple, friends of
Yvonne's family, who are now suspected of being spies. The harmony
and relative comfort of pre-war existence disappear with the onset of
war. The fire kills the Japanese couple and their baby, Sumi. Christmas

is no longer the joyful occasion that it was. As Yvonne notes, 'I stared at the Jesus in our belen. He was in His crib; Sumi wasn't. Then the tears formed and blurred my vision of the nativity set' (24).

War makes daily life in Ubec an impossibility. In order to highlight the sense of loss during the war years, Brainard depicts a number of typical Filipino pastimes and favourite foods. These scenes denote how traditional cultural practices shape the identity of her characters and delineate the particularities of Filipino life. At one point, Yvonne accompanies her grandfather to a cockfight, where there were 'almost a thousand rowdy people' (36). Here she witnesses the gambling, the betting, and the ensuing bloody fight between a 'large muscular Rhode Island Red' and 'a little native rooster of multi-colored feathers' (36). Although the aggressive Red with his 'razor-sharp spur' seemed destined to win, the 'puny little chicken with the uncertain gaze' is the one that eventually emerges victorious by thrusting his 'metal spur deep into the large rooster' (36). Yvonne winces at 'the sight of blood' and has to 'check' her 'rising nausea' (37). The scene foreshadows the bloodshed that is yet to come, and which will become a part of Yvonne's world. In its own way, it is a light-hearted but significant comment on the warring forces. Here the puny native rooster wins over the stronger imported Red, which suggests that cunning, skill, and the instinct for survival, here related to Filipinos, are more important than power and size.

In another pre-war scene, Yvonne's father decides to make a typical Filipino dessert that he boasts will be 'the most delicious leche flan in all of Ubec' (37). While Yvonne's mother protests that 'it's not time to cook' because 'Corregidor and Bataan are doomed,'[4] Papa nevertheless takes the time to select 'six brown eggs', 'holding each one up in the sunlight and peering through them before cracking them,' mixing them with milk, sugar, and Napoleon brandy (38). Brainard describes the preparation in loving detail: 'Holding the mold over the fire, he carmelized the sugar, swirling the golden brown liquid so it coated the bottom and sides of the mold' (38). Such attention to food seems extravagant and out of place in a novel about war, but the scene functions as a vivid contrast to the later depictions of wartime deprivation, when Mama complains that there is nothing but mongo beans, 'fish and rice' in the house (157). Linda Brown and Kay Mussell note that 'foodways bind individuals together, define the limits of the group's out-reach and identity, distinguish in-group from out-group, serve as a medium of inter-group communication, celebrate cultural cohesion, and provide a context for performance of group rituals' (5). The exquisite rendering of the cooking scene highlights Filipinos' love of sweets, their zest for life, and their normally leisurely attitude to living.

Upon leaving Ubec, Yvonne symbolically leaves behind the sweetness and paradisal scenes of her childhood years. In her journey to the countryside of Mindanao, where her family take refuge during the Japanese occupation, Yvonne learns at first hand of death, cruelty, loss, and the necessity of compromise. At first, the news about the horror of war comes merely as a third-hand report. The family learn, for example, the grim news about the 'survivors of the Death March' in the city: 'They were in pretty bad shape. They're lucky they managed to escape. They said the Japanese bayoneted those who couldn't walk; there was hardly any food. And the women, well, the Japanese soldiers raped them' (44). Shortly after this, however, war and death come much closer to Yvonne's family. As they are making their way through the jungle on horseback, Yvonne's pregnant mother goes into labour and is forced to give birth crouching behind some bushes while Japanese soldiers ride past. Instead of a new sibling she had been expecting excitedly, Yvonne only sees briefly a 'blue prune-faced infant' wrapped in some cloth (56). The baby dies and is buried in a makeshift grave under some rocks in the jungle. Similarly traumatic is the discovery of the massacre of their friend Doc Mendez's family. The doctor, who had been assisting a young woman in labour in another mountain, comes home to discover that his wife and his three children have been 'hacked to pieces' by the Japanese (59). In his grief, the doctor prays helplessly: 'So why me, God? Why my family? Jesusa was a good woman, God. All she wanted was to help the people ... And the children, they never harmed anyone ... Why did You have to take them like that?' (70).

In a very short time, Yvonne is plunged from an untroubled, carefree world into one of hellish horror. The scenes parallel the experience of thousands of Filipinos at the time who likewise experienced directly the inhuman atrocities under the Japanese. Most of these are undocumented and remain only as tales or oral narratives. Brainard's record of these stories parallels the work of other minority writers like Joy Kogawa in *Obasan* and Toni Morrison in *Beloved* who write in an attempt to 'rememory' what has been done to their community in the past. This effort is dependent not only upon historical documentation, but also imaginative and emotional engagement. Satya Mohanty's comments about Morrison apply equally well to Brainard: 'Morrison indicates in several ways why historical memory might be available to human subjects only if we expand our notion of personal experience to refer to ways of both feeling and knowing, and to include collectives as well as individual selves. The braiding and fusing of voices and emotions makes possible the new knowledge we seek about our postcolonial condition' (222). Brainard recognizes that what we call identity, in particular racial identity, is inextricably linked to experience that is located in history. *When the Rainbow Goddess Wept* is important as a representation of the individual and collective experiences of Filipinos during the Second World War from the perspective of the colonized people themselves. Like other postcolonial writers, Brainard partici- pates in the effort to 'help change the way the colonized world was seen, to tell their own stories, to wage a battle of the mind with colonial- ism by re-educating readers' (Boehmer 189).[5]

One way to alleviate the horror of the experience for Brainard's heroine as well as for her readers is through the use of folk tales. At crucial moments in the narrative, Brainard interrupts the realist histori- cal diegesis with a legendary or mythical one. A Japanese soldier comes to the family's yard at one point when the men are away and demands food. He points to the chicken and asks Yvonne's mother to catch it for him. The mother refuses to cooperate and 'stood there, with feet astride, left hand on her hip, right hand gripping the machete, head thrown back' (72). Later, as Yvonne recounts the incident to her father, she compares her mother to 'Bongkatolan the Woman Warrior' (89). Bongkatolan, the 'woman warrior with dark hair reaching her ankles,' who 'equalled the finest men warriors,' is reputed to have 'killed a dozen men, thus enabling her and her brother to escape' (72). Her story is linked to that of the Ilianon tribe, who were driven into exile and then given a land 'which would have everything they desired' (73).[6] The story of the promised land comes at a moment when the Japanese seem to be triumphing over the Filipinos. It functions to balance the sense of despair and loss in the main narrative, and it renders the mother's actions significant.

In another instance, Yvonne associates the plight of her friend Nida with one of the stories that 'sustained' her spirit. During their journey by boat to Taytayan, Yvonne is given to carry in her wicker basket a 'brick-sized gold bullion' that is intended to be used to finance the resistance. On the boat, however, a Japanese soldier begins to randomly inspect bags. To prevent the discovery, Nida offers herself sexually to the soldier, 'laughing coquettishly,' and whispering 'in his ear' (102). Yvonne observes the 'Nida's eyes lit up as she ran her tongue over her lips. Right before my eyes, she seemed to undergo a transformation as she thrust out her chest' (102). They and the gold arrive safely, but the unfortunate result of the escapade is that Nida becomes pregnant. In despair she thinks, 'Every time I will look at the baby's face, I would just remember that – that savage ... The smell of him made me want to throw up' (113). For Yvonne, one way of coping with the tragic consequences is through remembering Laydan's stories: 'That afternoon, Nida and her problem made me imagine she was the Maiden of Monawon under the evil clutches of Deathless Man' (123). Yvonne then proceeds to narrate how the legendary hero Tuwaang saves the maiden by smashing the flute that contains the soul of the Deathless Man. This juxtaposition of the actual and the mythic occurs repeatedly in the novel. The legends evoke the heroism and spirit of another age. Through them, native values and Filipino resistance and identity are recreated and recalled. While the narratives do not actually alter the casualties and deaths suffered at the hands of warring Japanese, American, and Filipino soldiers, they serve to sustain and empower the girl through the period of adjustment. In this way, Brainard can be said to be participating in what Epifanio San Juan, Jr, calls 'alter/native national allegory,' which is 'born in the conjuncture of what is desired and what is exigent' (*Allegories* 59, 62).

Through this incident, Yvonne also learns to reassess the teachings of the nuns at her convent. While they had categorically condemned 'concupiscence' as bad and virginal perfection as good, Yvonne has to take a more mature and qualified view of Nida's situation. She ruminates on how 'Nida did what she did on the boat and got pregnant ... It was too bad. I remembered the colorful bargirls at Slapsy Maxie's Bar. Everyone in Ubec knew that some of the girls had two-headed bastards – who their fathers were, one could only speculate. Well, Nida was just like those girls. And yet I liked Nida. She had been kind to her tubercular mother; she had saved us from the Japanese on the boat. She did a bad thing to do good. Nida was bad and good together' (120). As part of Yvonne's progress from innocence to experience, she learns that the binary notions of good and evil depend very much on context. Here, the definition of a good woman, though inextricably linked to notions of delicacy and chastity by her Catholic teachers, is much more flexible than what she had been taught. Being good and doing good sometimes meant that one had to be a bad woman. Yvonne learns to negotiate between the dichotomous teachings taught by figures of authority, and reinterprets the facts, an act reminiscent of reinscription and retelling.

Through these incidents, Brainard's heroine participates in the act of witnessing, giving a testimonial to those who survived the trauma of the Japanese occupation of the Philippines during the Second World War.

Whereas, for the most part, the Japanese people in the book are portrayed as cruel imperialists, Brainard does make distinctions between the individual and the group. Like Wayson Choy, who shows the consequences of war hysteria on Japanese Canadians, Brainard also includes vignettes that reveal the human side of the Japanese. Collectively, the Japanese soldiers are figured as the enemy, but in various subnarratives they are depicted as everyday people caught in the confusion of war. At one point in the novel, Yvonne's father becomes responsible for a Japanese prisoner of war. The man is 'around forty years old with a serious face and gentle eyes' (81). When he finds out that Yvonne's father is a professor, he tells them that he also teaches English, and that he has a daughter who is eleven: 'Akemi loves pine trees. She says they sing when the wind blows. And rivers – ah, how she loves rivers' (81). Upon hearing this information, Yvonne begins to 'feel sorry' for the Japanese soldier. She starts to imagine 'Akemi in a kimono with cherry blossoms' that night (82). This little vignette not only humanizes the enemy, but also gives the readers an idea of the emotional costs of war. Because he tries to escape, Yvonne's father is forced to shoot the Japanese soldier. After the act, he says to his wife with great sadness: 'What makes me happy is seeing my students' eyes flood with understanding. That is what I understand. I don't understand fighting and hurting and killing. I've killed a man, Angeling' (83). Scenes like this reveal the traumatic effects of war on the psyche. No matter if one has won a battle or not, the effects are ultimately that of loss and debilitation. It is around this point that Yvonne's family 'all sank into a lethargy,' feeling 'a sense of hopelessness that the war would never end, that [they] would never resume the lives' they had had (108). Yvonne notes that 'because we had seen some of the terrible possibilities in Mindanao ... we were no longer ignorant. It was as if we had eaten from the tree of knowledge; and now, although wiser, we had lost our innocence' (108).

The loss of innocence affects more than just the young heroine. *When the Rainbow Goddess Wept* also narrates a collective disenchantment and feeling of disappointment of Filipinos towards America and Americans. Historically, Filipinos have had a love/hate attitude towards the United States. As William Pomeroy points out, 'the arrival of a U.S.

army of conquest coincided with the breaking-up of the Spanish colonial system' at the end of the nineteenth century (16). Expecting to establish the Philippine Republic after the surrender of the Spanish garrison, Filipinos had to then engage in a large-scale war from 1899 to 1902 against U.S. colonial forces. It is estimated that over two hundred thousand Filipinos died as a direct result of U.S. military conquest.[7] Subsequently, attitudes toward the American colonial power varied according to social position and class. Many middle-class and wealthy businesspeople surrendered and collaborated with the U.S. government by 1901, while guerrilla radicals who wanted self-government continued their struggle for independence until as late as 1912. The U.S. Comission Government of William Taft implemented laws that made revolutionary opposition to foreign domination a criminal activity, and those apprehended were imprisoned or given the death penalty. In *When the Rainbow Goddess Wept*, this turn-of-the-century war against the United States is remembered only by Grandfather Lolo Peping, who reminds his family of American treachery: 'The thing with Americans is they watch out for themselves first. Don't believe all that malarkey about brotherhood and equality ... Keep in mind that the Americans lied to us ... They said they'd help us get rid of the Spaniards, that America would honor Philippine Independence, and ... They betrayed us!' (19).

Grandfather tells them that in the island of Samar at the turn of the century, 'the Americans, who took over the town, arrested and imprisoned all men over eighteen years old' (19). When the prisoners refused to work and rebelled, 'the Americans methodically tortured and killed the civilians. They burned houses, destroyed crops and livestock until at last they ferreted out the rebels. Then they killed them all' (19). These stories of cruelty, though set in the past, parallel those of the atrocities of the Japanese soldiers, thereby linking the two colonial powers. Against this background, one reads of the American commitment to aid Filipinos during the Second World War. When the Japanese forces invaded the country, General MacArthur, along with the USAFE, departed in early 1942 with the promise that he would return. Pomeroy notes that 'in truth, U.S. colonial and military strategy was not based on protecting and upholding the interests of the Filipino people but on preserving U.S. colonial interests which Filipinos were expected to defend' (107). There was actually very little serious effort to provide for the defence and the security of the Philippines.

Much of the events of *When the Rainbow Goddess Wept* take place during this time when the Filipinos had to struggle on their own against the Japanese, who were engaged in their 'Holy War for Asian Liberation,' but had their own views of dominating Asia (see Friend, *Blue-Eyed Enemy* 3). Pomeroy notes that 'over 40 years of U.S. occupation and indoctrination had had their effect. Most Filipinos as a result were sympathetic to the U.S. and looked to the victory and re-arrival of U.S. forces' (107). Compared to the Americans, the Japanese appeared harsh and ruthless. Consequently, Filipinos, unlike other colonized peoples such as Indonesians, looked to their colonizers as liberators rather than as conquerors by the end of the Second World War. In the novel, however, Brainard is careful to delineate a range of attitudes towards Americans through characters of different age groups and social positions. Yvonne's mother exemplifies the view of many Filipinos. She 'survived on the illusion that everything was temporary. MacArthur and the Americans would return. The Philippines would be liberated, and we would resume our lives in Ubec' (75).

Yvonne's father, a middle-class man who, like Brainard's father, had been schooled in the United States, is initially sympathetic towards Americans and American ways.[8] When he tells his daughter about his experiences in America, she views it as a kind of exotic place from a fairy tale. Yvonne reads a book that mentions 'snowflakes and oranges' and remembers that Papa had said 'snow was like powdered sugar, and oranges looked like large mandarins' (82). Having heard anecdotes of his having to wear heavy coats in the winter, she 'wrapped a bandanna' around her head and ears, 'pretending there was snow all around' (82). This play-acting scene is familiar to many colonial people in tropical climates who grow up educated with Euro-American books and culture. Snow and America exist as dreamscapes of desire for Yvonne and other Filipinos. For North American readers, the passage works as a kind of reverse exoticism, a defamiliarization of the everyday world of Western society, as Yvonne hears of 'strange' foods like 'broccoli' (46) and places like the Smythe River where there were 'pines and enormous Redwood trees' (50). However, these innocent references to American ways become more ominous in the light of what John Tomlinson calls the 'threat of cultural imperialism to national identity' (88). Though Tomlinson notes that national cultures are 'conceptually problematic' (68), because 'most nations ... are not homogeneous cultural entities' (73), he does acknowledge that there is a '*real* cultural threat' (75) in the expansion of certain facets of the American way of life.

In *When the Rainbow Goddess Wept*, this threat is articulated by a friend of the family, Gil Alvarez, who tells Yvonne's father that he had defied his family by opening his mind to American ways in his younger days. He says: 'I believed in democracy, in their educational system. I was one of the first to discard our native barong shirts for American tailored suites, even though I sweltered in them. Pilar ... filled our house with Stateside products. Everything was Made in America. We watched Hollywood movies and read *Life* magazine' (140). Lately, however, Gil Alvarez has begun to question his position and his sense of identity. As he explains, 'I've just realized that for all the American clothes and American canned goods, and all the American magazines and books I have crammed into my head, I am not an American. I am a Filipino ... The books that my children studied in school, the ones mentioning snow and apples, are destructive – we do not have snow and apples in the Philippines. We Filipinos have lost ourselves by saturating our brain with all this snow and apples and American ideas' (141). The loss of Philippine cultural identity due to American global expansion is a problem that the nation still struggles with today. Much of the media and many writers and intellectuals communicate in English, the language in which they were educated, rather than the native Tagalog or other dialects. The loss of a shared native language has meant a concomitant loss of native expressions, literary traditions, and even a sense of self. For this reason, a number of critics have pointed out the need to return to an oral and folk tradition that 'views the world as a living text, a text full of meanings.'[9] Brainard's novel participates in this effort to recarve a Filipino identity, and impart a sense of historical importance to personal experience.

On this subject, Edward Said points out, 'granted that American expansionism is principally economic, it is still highly dependent and moves together with, upon, cultural ideas and ideologies about America itself, ceaselessly reiterated in public' (*Culture* 289). Said explains that the 'twinning of power and legitimacy, one force obtaining in the world of direct domination, the other in the cultural sphere, is a characteristic of classical imperial hegemony. Where it differs in the American century is the quantum leap in the reach of cultural authority, thanks in large measure to the unprecedented growth in the apparatus for the diffusion and control of information' (*Culture* 291). Critic San Juan, Jr, goes as far as to say that 'We Filipinos don't have any real identification of ourselves as belonging to a nation because that nation of all the classes and sectors in the Philippines is non-existent; that organic embodiment of the national popular will has not yet come into being, was in fact aborted and suppressed by U.S. military power when it was being born during the revolution of 1896–1898, a culmination of three centuries of revolts against Spanish rule' (*Allegories* 11). In 1951, five years after the declaration of independence from the United States, Claro M. Recto pointed out that the 'crisis of nationalism' (399) was created by the 'fact that many of our countrymen have assiduously cultivated a servile mentality' (400). He urged Filipinos to rely on 'native resourcefulness, patience, resiliency, good nature and good sense' rather than being 'spoon-fed' (401): 'We are not Americans, and those of us who pretend to be Americans risk only the ridicule and laughter of their so-called brothers behind their backs. We could not in fact become Americans, even if we wanted to, to the discomfiture of some of our countrymen, and I suggest therefore that we cease thinking of ourselves as some sort of second-hand citizens of the United States' (398).

Though Brainard's novel does not deal with the Americanization of the Filipino people in depth, Gil Alvarez's observations do make an impression on the other characters and on young Yvonne. In the novel, Alvarez echoes Recto's sentiments when he says, 'Americans don't consider Filipinos their equal ... At best they treat Filipinos like second-rate citizens' (122). He recalls seeing a sign in front of a restaurant in California that read, 'NO FILIPINOS OR DOGS ALLOWED' (141). While Yvonne's father is at first reluctant to adopt an anti-American stance because of his own positive experience in the United States, towards the end of the novel and near the end of the Japanese occupation, he does change his mind about Americans. After his friend Alvarez dies, tortured as a prisoner by an American who has run amok, Yvonne notices that her father's attitude has become less tolerant: 'My father lost faith in Americans. He had lived with them; he had known them and loved them. But now he realized that a lot of what Gil Alvarez had said about Americans was true. And my father realized ... that Filipinos must shape their destiny, that they were responsible for their future, that America (for all her verbal good intentions) watched out for herself and her citizens first of all, even if this meant using other countries and peoples' (198). This disillusioned and, ultimately, more mature and independent view influences the heroine, and is meant to parallel the growth of the Philippines as a nation. Loss of faith in America is accompanied by a stronger sense of cultural identity and empowerment.

As a result, rather than waiting for MacArthur to return, Yvonne's father 'and other men continued with the guerrilla warfare with an intensity that had been lacking before' (198). Brainard describes details

of the Filipino resistance during the occupation – women pulling together their 'guerrilla notes' to buy a black sow that produces 'little
black piglets,' which they then use to barter for 'food and necessities,'
and men developing 'aggressive plans' to 'slow down the Japanese'
(149). In their own island, 'the guerrilleros liberated towns until three-
quarters of the island of Ubec was in guerrilla hands' (200–1). These
examples are small triumphs, rather than grand victories, but they
reveal the strength and resilience of Filipinos under seige. In addition to
these instances of resistance and cooperation, Brainard also has Yvonne
recall the folk tale about the Ilianon people being led to the promised
land of Nalandangan. This story, involving a fierce and conquering
tribe of the Magindanaos who invade and destroy the life of 'tranquility
and plenty' of the Ilianon people, is invoked again in order to reassure
Filipinos that there is still hope, and that peace and freedom will be
restored (203). It reiterates a promise of justice, and expresses a desire
for a way of life based on a harmonious interaction with nature, which
prevailed before the advent of war and imperial aggression.

Shortly after retelling this comforting tale, Yvonne and her family
return to Ubec, where they, like the Ilianon tribe, discover that almost
everything has been destroyed in their once Edenic homeland. Yvonne
recounts that though they knew in their minds that Ubec was devas-
tated, in their hearts, they believed that they 'would be going home to
the Ubec [they] had always known' (208). However, the church, the
theatre, and 'most of the houses were destroyed,' and people had 'lost
parents, brothers, and sisters' (208). In short, the paradisal life Brainard
had outlined at the beginning of the novel no longer exists. Nevertheless, instead of despair, the book ends with a positive note. Yvonne's
father places the destruction in the context of history, thereby lessening
the present-day catastrophe: 'He told us of how Ubec came to be, and
how it would stand long after we were all gone. ... this war was merely
a part of Ubec's rich and long history. Ubec would rebuild the buildings
by the wharves, fix up the old churches whose walls had enormous
holes in them. And people would replace the stone statues of heroes on
the plaza grounds ... Ubec would grow like a mollusk, growing in
layers outward, with the new growth approaching the hills and mountains' (209). As her father speaks, Yvonne is able to envision a more
optimistic future: 'I saw people living in Ubec centuries before me and
centuries after me – an endless parade of humanity through time. And I
knew that invaders could not really destroy Ubec, could never destroy
its people' (209).

In addition to this vision, Yvonne also finds her place in society at this time through her identity as a storyteller. On the last page of the novel, she looks up to the sky and sees the epic singer, Laydan, who has passed away. Yvonne reiterates the promise never to forget her stories. As Leonard Casper notes, 'like Laydan, Yvonne has *become* the spine and flesh of her people. They are her song. She is the future; the past recreated, recovered; her song is the spirit of healing, the resilience of tribal/national memory that will not let essences die' (*Song* 254). In spite of the loss of her homeland as she knew it, or perhaps because of it, Yvonne is able to discover a part of herself that she had not known before – her strength of spirit and her talent as a storyteller. It is through this art that Yvonne, and Brainard herself, articulates the forgotten tales and histories, the important and heroic struggles, the pain and aspirations of the Filipino people during the war. Brainard's novel allows us to see Filipinos and Filipino Americans not simply as the conquered and the dispossessed, but as people with powers of resilience and resistance. In this way, she, like the other authors in this study, makes visible what has been obscured by largely American hegemonic versions of the past.

8

'Thrumming Songs of Ecstasy': Female Voices in Hiromi Goto's *Chorus of Mushrooms*

All the poets know that: whatever is thinkable is real ... So, urgently and anxiously, I look for a scene in which a type of exchange would be produced that would be different, a kind of desire that wouldn't be in collusion with the old story of death. This desire would invent Love, it alone would not use the word love to cover up its opposite ... On the contrary, there would have to be a recognition of each other ... each would take the risk of *other*, of difference, without feeling threatened by the existence of an otherness, rather, delighting to increase through the unknown that is there to discover, to respect, to favor, to cherish.

Hélène Cixous and Catherine Clément, 'Sorties'

Hiromi Goto's *Chorus of Mushrooms* is a novel that celebrates women's voices, storytelling, and female creativity. Like a number of the works in this study, it is a postmodern novel, a metafictive work that exhibits an awareness of the text as a narrative.[1] At once a 'Japanese folk legend,' a 'love story' (back cover), a 'personal myth' (acknowledgments) and a 'true story' (1), *Chorus of Mushrooms* sings of the power of female imagination, strength, force, and desire through a number female voices and perspectives. It attempts to rewrite what Hélène Cixous calls the '*once upon a time*' story, to subvert authority and the 'stability of the masculine structure that passed itself off as eternal-natural' (Cixous and Clément 65) through its fragmentary structure, its narrative voices, and its recurring motifs. At the same time, it participates in the politics of the visible by mobilizing a number of stereotypes – of the Oriental woman, of the aged, and of the docile Japanese Canadian, in particular.

In the chapter on *The Jade Peony*, I looked at the way the three-part structure of the novel provided different and complementary versions of the same story – that of the development of ethnic subjectivity in Canada in the early half of the twentieth century. In this chapter, I similarly begin my examination of *Chorus of Mushrooms* with a discussion of the use of multiple perspectives. Unlike Choy's book, however, Goto's first novel uses a form of narration that is disruptive, disconnected, and layered, calling into question the reader's assumptions about literary conventions, power, position, and origin. Goto's book goes further than Choy's in its questioning of authority and voice. At the same time, much like in the work of others such as Shum and Chong, Goto affirms and claims a space for those marked figures, the gendered and racialized others in Canadian society. By highlighting the matrilineal relationship of grandmother to daughter and granddaughter, for example, Goto reconfigures traditional views of love, desire, and heterosocial and familial bonding that are prevalent in Western culture. In addition, through the use of motifs and images such as mushrooms and various insects, women, particularly the Japanese Canadian protagonists, are shown to be figures of endurance, imagination, and power.

Of her work, Goto has stated, 'It can be said that I write about Japanese Canadian issues with a racial and feminist slant' ('Translating' 112). She feels uncomfortable with reacting to 'the imbalances of living in a primarily white culture' and would rather 'act' than react ('Translating 112). She says, 'in writing, I can empower my reaction as a simultaneous resistance/empowered celebration. Language, the site of colonization, becomes an instrument I use to try to dismantle it' ('Translating' 112). As I see it, Goto's fiction functions as a way of asserting subjectivity, in the same way that Traise Yamamoto says that through their writing, 'Japanese immigrant and Japanese American women assume a selfhood that has often been denied them' (4). Yamamoto argues that Japanese American women need to claim 'the self as a functional totality when it is fragmented into identificatory categories defined less by an underlying humanity and more by a taxonomy of difference' (4). Goto's playful use of language, whether it is shown in her refusal to translate Japanese phrases, as noted by Mark Libin, or in her rewriting of folk tales, as discussed by Guy Beauregard, reveals her attempts to rescript Japanese Canadian female subjectivity and to challenge what Cixous calls the 'old story' of otherness.

In *Articulate Silences*, King-Kok Cheung emphasizes that there are *'different* manifestations of both speech and silence' (19–20). For Cheung, 'language can liberate, but it can also coerce, distort, and regulate' (*Articulate Silences* 20). Conversely, she argues that silence, which usually signifies voicelessness in Western culture, can also be 'enabling,' and silences are 'the very antitheses of passivity' (*Articulate Silences* 20). While Goto's novel can be seen as a rewriting of Joy Kogawa's *Obasan*, as a number of critics have noted (see Libin 137 and Beauregard 47), it does not simply reverse the paradigm of speech and silence so prevalent in that better-known novel. Mark Libin points out that Goto's protagonist 'Obachan is a whirlwind of words, as opposed to the hauntingly silent Obasan of Kogawa's novel' (137), but what is of greater significance is the way in which silence is broken. Female desire and female creativity are expressed not primarily through official public discourse in *Chorus of Mushrooms*, but through myriad forms, including poetry, metaphor, cooking, eating, sex, songs, stories, and chants. The 'thrumming songs of ecstasy' ripple outward for those who choose 'to listen' because 'you know you can change the story' (70, 220).

Goto's novel is told through a 'chorus' of voices: italicized fragmentary conversations between Murasaki and her unnamed lover; Obachan Naoe's monologues and recollections; a third-person narrator; and Murasaki's accounts. Imbedded in these narratives are myths and stories from Japan; Obachan Naoe's name printed in Japanese characters; an illustration of a postcard; signs from a grocery store; a shopping list; three newspaper clippings; and an essay. The multiple narrators and the fictional documents create a rich multilayered perspective, which has the effect in the novel of what Mikhail Bakhtin calls 'heteroglossia.' Bakhtin notes that the novel incorporates different kinds of languages and belief systems, including those of 'generic, professional, class-and-interest group (the language of the nobleman, the farmer, the merchant, the peasant); tendentious, everyday (the languages of rumour, of society chatter, servants' language) and so forth, but these languages are ... kept primarily within the limits of the literary written and conversational language' (*Dialogic Imagination* 311). Through the incorporation of other people's languages, the author distances herself from that discourse, presents it objectively, yet is able to reveal its power, shortcomings, or consequences.

Through the structure of multiple perspectives, the echoing and ironic use of everyday discourse in North American culture, and the representation of women through non-traditional acts of heroism and imagery,

Chorus of Mushrooms challenges the invisibility, the effacement, and the silencing of Asian Canadians, particularly Japanese Canadian women. So much of Japanese Canadian history and culture is haunted by the internment and dispersal of Japanese Canadians during the Second World War that it is almost impossible to think or write about Japanese Canadians without this association.[2] When Goto reinscribes the birthmarks on her body, she not only reworks stereotypes of the Asian woman as Chong and Shum do, but she also retrieves and at the same time exorcizes this history, which has left its mark on Japanese Canadians. She critiques the whole fabric of society with her insistence that we understand the ideological effects of stories that are familiar to us, making us hear them in different ways. By playing with the genres of myth, fantasy, and the novel,[3] she makes us aware of the importance of voice and perspective. Whose myths and values are being reproduced in society depends on who is doing the telling and who is in control. She confronts the abjection and otherness of minorities, the aged, and women by refuting traditional expectations of them and transgressing narrative conventions and literary boundaries. Her motifs of reawakening and rebirth reformulate Japanese Canadians' subjectivity – from a psyche based on the historical burden of suffering, betrayal, and survival to one that acknowledges the past, but finds possibilities in fantasy, boldness, and beauty.

Goto's narrative approach is different from that of other Asian American or Asian Canadian writers like Amy Tan or Wayson Choy who also self-consciously play with narrative form. Both *The Joy Luck Club* and *The Jade Peony* use multiple narrators, but in conventional ways: the narrators take their turns in telling their version of the story. Whereas in Tan's novel, the older generation of Chinese women seem to possess the insight and wisdom of the East that the Asian American women of the younger generation do not, in Goto's novel, there is no such dichotomy between generations. In Choy's novel, though the narratives of the three siblings are interrelated, they are nevertheless presented in separate distinct sections. In Goto's novel, the demarcation between storyteller and listener is less clear. There is more of a postmodern play of story and form as fragments, as pieces to be constructed into a whole by the reader. At one point in the novel, Murasaki asks Obachan Naoe to tell her a story: 'You're supposed to be the one telling stories to me. You know, the grandmother telling stories of the past to the avidly listening grandchild and all that' (172). But Obachan refuses to claim the authority of the Old World storyteller, and instead says, 'And don't you think stories are shared. That there is a partnership in the telling and listening, that it is of equal importance?' (172).

What Obachan says about sharing is indicative of the process and structure of Goto's novel as a whole. She tells Murasaki: 'We must both be able to tell. We must both be able to listen. If the positions become static, there can never be stories. Stories grow out of stories grow out of stories. Listening becomes telling, telling listening' (172). In this manner, what is stressed is a dialogic exchange, a constant crossing between two or more people in which both sides are respected. Stories are told against a background of normal literary expectations and are questioned, often reassessed. In the novel, the official account of events is often inaccurate and must be supplemented by other narratives. Obachan's departure, which we know was deliberate and planned through Obachan, is reported in the local newspaper as a 'missing person's' case. The article depicts Obachan as an elderly immigrant who is liable to get lost in the blizzard-like snow conditions. One constable predicts that 'an elderly woman isn't likely to survive a single night during weather like we've been experiencing' (88). Murasaki, who at first doesn't know what happened, speculates about her and makes up stories: 'She went back to Japan,' and 'She went ape-shit and was raving' (88). Murasaki observes, 'I found out then, that everybody, including me, was always looking for a story. That the story could be anything' (89). This incident shows how events can be misread and misinterpreted, and the importance of location and identity in the construction of truth. Obachan's age, her sex, and her ethnicity cause people to imagine or expect certain endings. The unpredictability of the resulting adventure is the reason why we ought not trust just one account, one story, or one voice of authority, but instead must judge all the evidence for ourselves.

Other examples reveal the ways in which the novel is dialogized. In his well-known study of discourse in the novel, Bakhtin notes that 'the novel permits the incorporation of various genres, both artistic (inserted short stories, lyrical songs, poems, dramatic scenes, etc.) and extra-artistic (everyday, rhetorical, scholarly, religious genres and others)' (*Dialogic Imagination* 320). All these genres 'enter the novel,' bringing 'into it their own languages' (Bakhtin, *Dialogic Imagination* 321). The languages 'may be either directly intentional or treated completely as objects, that is, deprived of any authorial intentions' (Bakhtin, *Dialogic Imagination* 321). For Bakhtin, these languages 'stratify the linguistic unity of the novel and further intensify its speech diversity in fresh ways' (*Dialogic Imagination* 321). More importantly, the incorporation of various forms 'permit languages to be used in ways that are indirect, conditional, distanced' (Bakhtin, *Dialogic Imagination* 323). In Goto's novel, double-voiced discourse functions in a number of ways. As Bakhtin notes, heteroglossia, 'serving to express authorial intentions but in a refracted way,' constitutes a 'special type of double-voiced discourse' and 'serves two speakers at the same time and expresses simultaneously two different intentions: the direct intention of the character who is speaking, and the refracted intention of the author' (*Dialogic Imagination* 324). Initially, this discourse mocks in a playful manner our expectations of the novel and the story, and questions our assumptions about the difference between reality and fantasy. Secondly, and more seriously, the incorporation of various genres and voices in Goto's novel results in an ironic view of racist attitudes and discourses in Canada. Thirdly, Goto challenges our society's views of the aged by incorporating truisms and commonplace beliefs about the elderly. All these discourses are 'internally dialogized,' and as Bakhtin notes, the result is 'a concentrated dialogue of two voices, two world views, to languages' (*Dialogic Imagination* 324–5).

An example of how Goto plays with readers' expectations with the novelistic discourse occurs in the opening pages. Goto prefaces her narrative with a conversation between Murasaki and her lover that serves as a metacommentary on the novel. The lover asks her to tell a 'true story' about Murasaki's Obachan (1). Aware that people want not the truth, but only what they want to hear, Murasaki answers, 'It's like people want to hear a story, and then, after they're done with it, they can stick the story back to where it came from' (1). Yet, despite her frustrations about its efficacy, she agrees, 'Here's a true story' (2). Paradoxically, she starts her story with '*mukashi, mukashi, omukashi*,' which means, 'in ancient times, in ancient times, in very very ancient times.' This phrase, like 'once upon a time,' signals the beginning of a fairy tale or a myth, rather than a 'true story' or history.[4] At the same time, Goto insists repeatedly through the voices of Murasaki and Obachan Naoe on the difficulty of distinguishing between 'true' and made-up stories. Unapologetic about her imperfect Japanese and her understanding of her grandmother, Murasaki tells her lover, 'I'm making up the truth as I go along' (12). For her part, Obachan Naoe wants to tell stories that are different from those of her parents: 'Funny how parents tell teaching stories yet they never bother to taste the words they utter. How the words are coated with honey and nectar but the flesh inside is weak and hollow. Let me tell a different story' (7). For both characters, the truth about the past is not enough to set us free. If necessary, one has to make up the story, the past, and the truth in order to create the desired result, 'an immigrant story with a happy ending' (212). As Linda Hutcheon notes, 'Of course, the past once existed. But we can *know* it today only through its documents, its traces in the present. If our knowledge of the past is something constructed (or even re-constructed), its meaning cannot be eternal and is certainly not unchangeable. It is this realization of the potential for change that postmodern fiction can exploit and expose' (*Canadian Postmodern* 22). The various inserted discourses about stories, the truth, and the past reveal Goto's concern not so much with accuracy, but with representation and the power of representation. Whose version of the truth gets told is perhaps more important than the question of what is truth.

Other inserted 'extra-artistic' discourses in the novel call into question the way we use language to classify and categorize. For example, Murasaki's shopping experience in the 'ethnicChinesericenoodle-Tofupattiesexoticvegetable section of Safeway' (90) demonstrates the doubly marginalized positions of Japanese Canadians in Canada. Something as innocent as signs in a supermarket become significant here. What Murasaki recognizes as *hakusai* leaves is labelled 'suey choy' in Chinese at the grocery store according to Canadian shopping conventions. The naming may not change the sweetness of the vegetable, but it does give an indication of place and position of the ethnic subject. In Canada, while all Asians occupy a minority position vis-à-vis the dominant white culture, these inserted signs suggest that there are fine distinctions and hierarchies among us. Chinese food and Chinese names have become more widely accepted in Canadian mainstream culture than Japanese food. What Murasaki humorously calls 'vegetable politics' may be linked to various socio-historical differences between Chinese and Japanese Canadians and their degrees of assimilation and acceptance by the dominant culture. Japanese Canadians, unlike Chinese Canadians, experienced internment and the relocation of families during the Second World War. After the war, some Japanese families shortened their polysyllabic names in order to blend in with the Chinese and assimilate better. Consequently, their communities have been scattered and displaced. Even today, there are still more Chinatowns than there are Japantowns in North America. Thus, innocent signs at a supermarket are indirect, daily reminders of the tenuous position of Japanese culture in Canada in the past and today.

Other inserted discourses provide similar ironic commentaries on normative and racist assumptions in Canada. Murasaki recollects her Sunday school experience where she and her fellow students sing, 'Red and Yellow, Black and White / They are precious in His sight / Jesus loves the little children of the world!' (59). While the teacher assures them that 'everybody is the same,' the pictures that accompany the song show 'Indians with feathers and black boys with curly hair wearing only shorts and yellow people with skinny eyes. And a blond girl with long eyelashes with a normal dress on' (59). The pictures belie the lyrics of the song as, in Murasaki's view, the only 'normal' one is the blond girl. The other children all signal difference while whiteness is not seen as a racialized identity. As Mary Maynard notes of such instances of liberal pluralism, 'In such pluralism difference tends to be treated as existing all on one plane or on the same level. All forms of diversity are lumped together as examples of difference, implying that they are similar phenomena with similar explanations ... Under pluralism, differences in access to resources or life chances etc. become largely explicable in terms of personal culpability or luck' (128–9). Murasaki observes that 'Jesus must be pretty blind if he thought everybody was the same. Because they weren't' (59). The insertion of the song juxtaposed with her observation creates a dialogic tension in this instance that has an ironic effect.

The most important feature of the novel is its use of multiple narrators and the fragmented narrative. Goto chooses to tell the story in a number of voices, or dialogically, to supplement Murasaki's story with that of Obachan Naoe's, as well as with those various inserted discourses. One of the effects of this multilayered perspective is a polyphony of voices. Voices that traditionally been othered, exoticized, and silenced are expressed. We hear of Obachan's past, about her unhappy marriage and her longings. Of her daughter she thinks: 'This Western food has changed you and you've grown more opaque even as your heart has brittled. Silver-edged and thin as paper. I love you still. You are my daughter, after, all, and this you cannot change' (13). This chorus of voices that together narrates the stories of issei, nisei, and sansei Japanese Canadian women is a strategy to combat Orientalist discourse where Asian American and Asian Canadian women are often 'cast in an undifferentiated pool of Asian women whose (assumed or enforced) foreignness and physical exoticism promise a range of delights: Lotus Blossom, China Doll, Madame Butterfly, Geisha Girl, Suzy Wong, Dragon Lady' (Yamamoto 65). As Traise Yamamoto notes,

'whether delicately or dangerously sexual, such images are all inflec-
tions of the same trope and reveal the extent to which the Asian American woman's body is invested in an orientalist economy of sexual
power and fantasy' (65). In the novel, Murasaki's first boyfriend, Hank,
typifies this view, as he asks her if she could do 'special things' with
him, like 'Oriental sex' (122). When Murasaki questions him about this,
he says, 'You know. The Oriental kinky stuff. Like on "Shogun"' (122).
Murasaki's initial reaction is one of anger. But later, she recollects the
scene and playfully repeats the question, 'Do you want to have Oriental
sex?' to her current lover. They both confess to ignorance about 'Oriental sex' but agree to 'make it up together' (123). This decision to 'make it
up together' is more in keeping with the kind of 'radical transformation
of behaviours' that Cixous talks about (Cixous and Clément 83). Cixous
calls for a way to imagine 'difference or inequality' leading to 'desire
without negativity, without one of the partner's succumbing.' Cixous
promotes relationships where 'we would recognize each other in a type
of exchange in which each one would keep the *other* alive and different'
(Cixous and Clément 79). Reimagining otherness so that it is no longer
infused with derogatory associations is one of the central concerns of
Chorus of Mushrooms.

Rewriting female, especially Asian women's, sexuality is another of
the crucial issues of the novel. Goto challenges the stereotype for two
reasons. Firstly, as we have noted, the Asian woman is 'orientalized' to
embody, on the one hand, the ideal femininity of 'submissiveness,
subservience, obedience, passivity and domesticity,' and on the other
hand, an excessive other who is 'exotic and sexy,' 'more sexually available than her other American sisters' (Uchida 162). Yamamoto notes
that 'While Asian American men have been routinely portrayed as
asexual (either as bestially crazed warmongers or spectacled geeks), the
female Asian body seemingly cannot be racially marked without hy-
persexual encoding. That is, engendering of the Asian body is always
inscripted through the sexual, either in terms of lack or excess' (73).
Yamamoto observes that 'it is perhaps for this reason that direct,
explicit mention of sexuality and the body has been until recently
largely absent from the writings of Asian American women' (74). In
Chorus of Mushrooms, the Asian female body is deliberately and lovingly delineated, but in terms that are neither orientalized nor exoticized.
Goto answers Hollywood and popular representations of the Asian
woman with a bold and original figure – that of an old woman whose
sexuality awakens after many years of lying dormant. In addition, the

novel is filled with scenes of sensuality between mother and daughter, and grandmother and granddaughter; and with hedonistic scenes of consumption.

Secondly, reworking representations of the Asian woman is consequential for Goto, who is Japanese Canadian and aware of her literary predecessors. Since the early 1980s, the most influential Japanese Canadian, and possibly Japanese North American, text has been Joy Kogawa's *Obasan*. In *Obasan* female sexuality is repressed, unspoken, and troubled.[5] The heroine, Naomi Nakane, calls herself an 'old maid' and describes her personality as 'tense' at the beginning of the novel (Kogawa 7). When questioned by her impertinent student Sigmund about being 'in love,' Naomi is evasive, and acknowledges that at thirty-six she is a 'spinster' and 'an old maid' (Kogawa 8). As a child, she is molested by the man who lived next door, Old Man Gower, who forbids her to tell her mother. Naomi grows up withdrawn and silent: 'If I speak, I will split open and spill out' (Kogawa 63). Critics have noted that Naomi's 'resignation is ultimately complicit with social amnesia' (Cheung, *Articulate Silences* 143). King-Kok Cheung notes that 'Naomi's evasions, which fall readily into a pattern explored in psychology as "posttraumatic stress disorder," are shared by many actual victims of sexual and political abuse' (*Articulate Silences* 143). Her Obasan is similarly detached and unable to express herself: 'the language of her grief is silence' (Kogawa 14). Even Aunt Emily, the crusader and 'word warrior,' is an 'old maid' (Kogawa 32, 8). Thus, because of what they have suffered socially and politically, the women in Kogawa's *Obasan* all tend to lead problematic, damaged sexual lives.[6]

In *Chorus of Mushrooms*, Hiromi Goto reconfigures Japanese Canadian female subjectivity by giving her heroines not only the power of speech, but also the possibility of enacting their desires. The liberation does not just happen to Murasaki, who represents the sansei, but self-empowerment also occurs with the figure of Obachan, who is one of the issei. While they lead very different lives, the two women are linked in the narrative as they both embark on journeys of discoveries: 'Two women take up two different roads, two different journeys at different times' (200). Obachan Naoe's rejuvenation starts while she is on the mushroom farm. Already an eighty-five-year-old woman, Obachan, who has been married and divorced, feels that having sat for twenty years in her rocking chair is long enough and decides to do something about it. In contrast to youth, she feels that old age is the time for speech: 'When I was young and beautiful, my lips were an ornament upon my face. Now my face is crumpled with care and seams adorn my cheeks. My mouth bursts wide and the words rush out, a torrent of noise and scatters' (24). Along with the 'torrent of noise,' she wishes for sexual emancipation. She herself sees the humour is being so old and being 'horny as a musk-drenched cat' (39). Her attempts at masturbation are viewed by her daughter Keiko as the acts of a 'senile' woman (40), but they reverse traditional expectations of the aged. On the topic of aging, feminist philosopher Luce Irigaray has observed that a woman's life is particularly 'irreversible' because it is marked by irreversible events and stages such as puberty, 'losing her virginity, becoming pregnant, being pregnant, childbirth, breast-feeding' ('How Old Are You?' 114–15). Each of these events may repeat, but happen differently, and change women's bodies and spirits so that 'female sexuality ... is more related to becoming, more attuned to the time of the universe' ('How Old Are You?' 115). For this reason, Irigaray says, 'What is often defined as the end of a woman's life is for her just as much an opportunity to have more time for social, cultural, and political life' ('How Old Are You?' 115). She urges women to 'become virgins, to relieve our bodies and souls of cultural and familial fetters ... it's not always a matter of gaining something more but one of being capable of something less. Feeling more free vis-à-vis your fears, fantasies about others, freeing yourself from useless knowledge, possessions, and obligations' ('How Old Are You?' 117). Obachan Naoe follows her fantasies at the moment when most people think it is too late to do so.

On the mushroom farm, Obachan Naoe experiences a sensual awakening that Irigaray would call an experience of becoming, perhaps becoming a virgin. Described in quasi-mythic terms, Obachan's rejuvenation is a physical and a spiritual one. She is like the epic hero being strengthened as she soaks in the moisture of the fungus:

> for the first time in decades, moisture filtered into her body ... her sallow cheeks shone a little more roundly and the loose skin where she once had breasts began to rise like bread, like *manto*. Her skin, so dry, slowly filed, cell by cell, like a starving plant, the mushroom moisture filling her hollow body. The wet tinkling into her brittleness. Blood stirring, restless. Like silk threads, they wound through her. Old chicken arms grew longer, filling with supple strength, her buttocks, curving, swelling, with flesh and longing. She could hear her body filling, the rippling murmur of muscles and bones, squeak of hair growing long and smooth, long enough to sweep the soft skin of her back. Her yellow parchment skin growing taut, glowing coolly like newborn silkworms. (84–5)

Instead of fighting dragons, however, Obachan's first adventure in her newly restored body consists of awakening her dormant sexuality: 'She stroked her breasts, the soft skin of her nipples, pinched gently the skin puckering with sudden ache ... The soft wet mud kisses on her cheek, inner arms, the skin beneath her knees. Along her inner thighs' (85–6). Her self-exploration leads her to a heightened state of eroticism and freedom to a place 'beyond the painful register of human sound, the unheard chorus of mushrooms' (86).

The awakening is the first act of her resolution to leave the security of her family and the prairie farm where all the dust 'is familiar' (4). Putting her own needs first rather than that of her daughter and grand-daughter, she thinks: 'There are things I haven't experienced yet. Moments of joy I haven't allowed myself to live. I don't want to die before I've ever fallen into my flesh or laughed myself silly' (76). Her departure is compared to an insect that sheds a layer of itself: 'I must leave this chair like a husk, leave like a newly formed cicada. A silk moth' (77). Goto compares Obachan's metamorphosis to that of a silk moth. The comparison is significant partly because the silkworm produces something precious and beautiful, but also because of the intensive and highly specialized care needed to nurse the silkworm from egg to worm to cocoon stage. As a girl, Obachan is not able to finish her education because the family does not have 'enough money' (22). She is sent to work at a silk farm where she nurses the worms, 'fed them, changed their sheets of mulberry leaves, fed them, sorted them, fed them' (23). In 'this nursery of extravagance' no one talks, 'each woman, each girl keeping the unwritten silence, and the only sound thousands upon thousands upon thousands of minuscule jaws munching in ferocious appetite' (23). The work initially has a disturbing psycho-sexual impact on Naoe because she says, 'each night I dreamt my body was covered with squirming, munching, defecating worms, wriggling into my nose, my ears my eyesmymouth' (23). But Naoe grows to like them, comparing them to infants: 'hairless, cream white and soft as the skin on a baby's neck' (23). The narrative is an account of female sacrifice and gendered labour. Here, the pseudo 'maternal' work and nurturing capacities of young women are perversely used for commercial purposes. The work, though not difficult, entails a kind of suppression on the part of the workers. The women keep silent and all their energies are devoted to the nourishing of the tiny worms.

When, at the age of eighty-five, Obachan compares her transformation to that of a silk moth, she is implicitly rejecting the caregiver role, the moth being the object on which attention is lavished. She likens herself to the precious thing that produces beauty and wonder, the spinner of the silk thread. No longer willing to keep silent and remain in the background, she is the one with the 'ferocious appetite' whose needs must be met. The comparison to the cicada works in a similar fashion. Like the silk moth, the cicada lives through a period of obscurity and silence, but bursts into life at the end of the 'long pupa stage' (157). The cicada exemplifies another story of liberation after years of repression. According to Murasaki: 'After seven years of silence and darkness, they dig out from the soil and climb the bark of a tree ... in the morning there is nothing but a dry husk. The cicadas with newly patterned brittle wings fly off to other trees where they sit in the sun and shriek their songs, as long as there is light. They have only seven days to find a mate and complete their cycle so they shriek and hum and rattle and saw, with their bellows in their chest. They never shut up' (157). Cicadas are also associated with Obachan Naoe's childhood in Japan, where she grew up with her brother Shige. As children Naoe and Shige sat and watched the cicadas as they 'welcomed the heat with their newly brittled wings. They clung to the bark of trees and cried and shrilled in thrumming songs of ecstasy. The songs rippling outward on the sweat-moistened air around them' (70). Like Obachan Naoe, cicadas enjoy a brief moment of glory and ecstasy after spending many years underground. Cicadas are 'strong fliers that spend their time high in the trees, so they are rarely seen or captured.' Though small in size, their sounds are 'among the loudest produced by any insects' (University of Michigan web site). The association with this extraordinary insect that transforms itself so radically evokes certain themes in the novel – that of giving voice and song to the voiceless, that of exhilaration and celebration after repression and exile.

Obachan 'sings' and reveals her creativity and power in more ways than one. After she leaves the farm, she initiates sex with Tengu, the truck driver who picks her up, to her great pleasure. Their initial sexual encounter takes place in a bathtub, again reminiscent of a baptism or renewal into a new life. On the road, when they are stopped by the policemen for a spot check, Obachan is asked to walk a straight line. Instead of obeying him, she performs a marvellous act like a 'world class gymnast' (145). She flings into a side aerial. 'Graceful and weightless,' she spins so fast that her body's 'a blur and there is no ground, no sky' (144). This spinning reminds one of the spinning of the cocoon by a silkworm. Both acts are feats of wonder produced by those who may look insignificant and small. Towards the end of the novel, Obachan

Naoe becomes the star of the Calgary Stampede. Transgressing traditional expectations that come with her age, with her racialized and gendered body, Obachan Naoe enthrals the crowd by riding as 'The Purple Mask,' the mysterious bullrider who 'gives bullriding a whole new meaning' (217). Although this is performance before a crowd, Obachan's bullriding is also a kind of self-fulfilment. When she rides, she no longer hears the crowd or the rodeo announcer, but seeks the place where she and the bull 'can move as one' (218). She rides until she finds the space where she and the bull 'are pure as light as sound. Where stars turn liquid and you can taste sweet nectar in your mouth' (219). The moment is described as a culmination of spiritual and physical pleasure: 'Heat of the bull between your legs, riding on a crest of power. Tension and pleasure as fine as a silken thread. The moment of such sweet purity, it brings tears to your throat, your eyes. Makes your lips tremble' (219). In the moment of ecstasy, we forget that it is an eighty-five-year-old Japanese Canadian woman who has brought us and herself to this height.

The female figure in the novel who does not easily fit into this feminist liberatory paradigm is Keiko, Murasaki's mother. Keiko has deliberately 'forsaken' her identity, as Naoe observes (13). She has 'converted from rice and *daikon* to weiners and beans' (13). Keiko and her husband's story is that of successful assimilation, or cultural invisibility. As Murasaki's father explains: 'When we moved to Canada, your Mom and I, we decided it would be best for our children if we let them slip in with everybody else. Sure, we couldn't change the colour of their hair, or the shape of their face, but we could make sure they didn't stand out. That they could be as Canadian as everyone around them' (207). The father and mother stop speaking Japanese, and he becomes as silent as the 'mushrooms in the quiet of the dark' (207). Keiko believes that 'if you live in Canada, you should live like a Canadian,' and she puts all things Japanese behind her (189). It is only when Obachan leaves the house that she is falls sick, becoming aware of the cultural void in her life. Murasaki sees the illness as a 'nervous breakdown' (127), but Keiko's condition – staying in bed for days, never opening the curtains, and never turning on the lights – align her with the mushrooms and insects. Like the cicadas and silkworms, she, too, is growing in silence and darkness, preparing for the moment of transformation and deliverance.

As in *The Kitchen God's Wife*, the transformation is brought about through food. Murasaki learns to cook Japanese food with the help of a cookbook, treating her parents to miso soup and *tonkatsu*. Becoming familiar once again with their food and their culture, suggested by their name, Tonkatsu, Murasaki says that she and her parents 'forgave each other for all our shortcomings' at this meal taken 'between night and dawn' (153). This epiphany is followed by many other scenes featuring Japanese food. The period is described by Murasaki as 'a chrysalis time' for Keiko and her (153). Keiko's words slowly comes back, and she begins to laugh and 'poke holes into the words she said out loud' (153). The insect metaphor suggests an eventual freedom from the silence and darkness of Canadian assimilatory culture.

Even before Keiko's transformation, there are a number of scenes in the novel that are less dramatic but also redefine female desire. These are the scenes where mother and daughter achieve a kind of quiet contentment or rapture through seemingly everyday and domestic, but traditionally feminized, tasks. One such scene is the cleaning of ears with the *mimikaki*, a 'long slender piece of wood' or bamboo (155). This is a traditional task and performed by mothers on their children (see 26). When Murasaki's mother performs this task on her daughter, Murasaki finds herself reacting involuntarily. Smelling the scent of her mother's clothes, Murasaki says: 'My eyes shut on their own accord and my body limped' (155). The actual cleaning of the ears, an act of female bonding, is described in sensual terms:

> Anticipatory shudder of fear or longing or I don't know what. The thrill of bamboo piercing fragile tissue, tearing through tender flesh, but the longing for the first touch, the unknown. I hovered in that delicate place between anticipation and intense pleasure, teetering between fear and longing, hovered above the delicate skin over my closed eyes, a pinpoint of light yet heavy as golden honey ... The sensation was incredible. My mouth watered with delight, my toes curled in exquisite pleasure. (156)

Murasaki is able to hear sounds she 'had never heard before' (157) after her ears are cleaned, but what is remarkable in the scene are the sensations and eroticism evoked in the daughter by the maternal act.

In a similar manner, even though there is a language barrier between Obachan Naoe and her daughter Keiko, they are still able to communicate through touch and their bodies. One event that Obachan looks forward to in her old age is 'hair day' (41), which, like the cleaning of the ears, is a feminized, domestic task, but similarly depicted in sensual terms. Goto transforms the ordinary and everyday event of washing hair into a loving scene of bonding between two women:

> I close my eyes, the pleasure of touch magnified when I feel without my
> eyes.
>   Keiko's soft, middle-aged belly leans into my shoulder. Warm and soft,
> like *manto*, I feel my stringy muscles loosen their hold on my bones. Her
> belly absorbs my pain ... Keiko's fingers in my hair, through my hair, on
> the tired skin of my head. Ahhhhhhhh. She rubs small powerful circles
> with her fingers and thumbs, the tension rising up, off my head, floating
> upward like angels to heaven. (42)

The description of hair washing goes on for more than two pages, and
at the end, Obachan remarks that her hair glows like 'filaments from a
silk worm' (44). Through this act performed by her daughter, Obachan's
body is transformed, as the silkworm transforms itself into a precious
and beautiful material.

In depicting these female scenes of tenderness and pleasure, Goto
represents the Japanese Canadian female body in fresh new ways.
Cixous has remarked that woman 'has not been able to live in her
"own" house, her very body' because she has been told that 'hers is the
dark region' (Cixous and Clément 68). She laments that 'we have internalized this fear of the dark' (Cixous and Clément 68). Women 'haven't
gone exploring in their house. Their sex still frightens them. Their
bodies, which they haven't dared enjoy, have been colonized. Woman is
disgusted by woman and fears her' (Cixous and Clément 68). For a
woman of Asian descent, another added complication is that she has
been either hypersexualized by Western and mass culture, or rendered
a creature of passivity and docility by Orientalist discourse and Asian
patriarchal teachings. She has also been rendered silent and invisible by
pressures to assimilate into North American white society. Sexuality
and the exploration of the female body and female pleasure have until
recently not been a topic about which much was written. Goto's novel,
then, explores Asian North American woman's libidinal gratification in
a non-exoticized and non-orientalized manner. Her female characters
are not afraid of, or disgusted with, their own bodies, as Cixous has
noted of women. They find ways of enjoying these quiet moments of
languor and sensuality.

Through these unconventional scenes of ecstasy, Goto rescripts female desire, subjectivity, and pleasure. What is noteworthy in each of
these instances is that self-fulfilment, though achieved through the

body, rarely comes about through the typical heterosexual coupling. Obachan Naoe's moments of bliss do not always depend on the presence of a man. She achieves happiness in doing things herself, like bullriding, which is an activity that is normally associated with men, or else she enjoys the pampering and care of other women. In addition, by delineating the astonishing feats performed by Obachan Naoe, Goto pushes the limits of several types of boundaries in her work. As a narrative, *Chorus of Mushrooms* borrows from genres such as the legend, myth, and folk tale, as well as the postmodern magic realist novel, at the same time as it stands as an immigrant *Bildung*. Goto also confounds traditional expectations of what women, especially old and Asian women, can accomplish. In this way, she is reconfiguring Asian Canadian identity as well as the Canadian ethnic or immigrant story. As Obachan Naoe says to Tengu, 'I have been sitting safe for so long – If I don't move against that grain, I will certainly be stuck there forever' (145). *Chorus of Mushrooms* moves against the grain in its insistence of difference, its celebration of female power, voice, and *jouissance*. Its differently aged and multi-abled characters challenge and reconstitute the Orientalist gaze so that we, like Obachan Naoe, do not get 'stuck there forever.'

9

'On the Fence That Was Never Finished': Borderline Filipino Existence in Bino Realuyo's *The Umbrella Country*

In an essay entitled '"A Better Tomorrow"? The Struggle for Global Visibility,' Aihwa Ong writes: 'No longer confined to the borderzones of managed cultural encounters, powerful Asian subjects now circulate in the stratosphere of Western society ... By moving "out of place," affluent Asian newcomers upset the ethno-racial hierarchy that has disciplined Asian Americans as a docile minority' (179). Ong's essay, largely focusing on overseas Chinese, especially Chinese investors and professionals, is optimistic, forward looking, and energetic. When we apply her statements to Filipinos, however, these generalizations about the economic achievements of Asian Americans sound rather hollow and become somewhat ironic. Though Filipinos in the United States total close to 2.1 million, as E. San Juan, Jr, notes, most of the new immigrants – professionals and skilled workers – are still assigned 'a subordinate and tokenized status in the class and ethnic hierarchy' (*Philippine Temptation* 101). Because of historical specificities such as the neocolonial position of the Philippines and the influence of American culture on the Filipino imagination (San Juan, Jr, *Philippine Temptation* 102), Filipinos in the diaspora still remain invisible and at the border zones of culture.

In this chapter, I use the notion of borders/boarders as a way of looking at the liminal existence of Filipinos in the diaspora. Being located at the borders is Realuyo's way of expressing what I have been calling invisibility. In his well-known essay 'Filipinos in the United States and Their Literature of Exile,' first published in 1992, Oscar Campomanes argues that 'an exilic sensibility ... informs both the identity politics and the cultural production' of Filipino Americans (51). While I agree that 'motifs of departure, nostalgia, incompletion, rootlessness, leave taking, and dispossession recur with force' in writing by Filipinos in the United States (Campomanes 51), my view is that a number of recent works reveal a much more complex construction of the Filipino subject. Using Bino Realuyo's novel *The Umbrella Country* as an example, I argue that Filipinos in the diaspora are no longer simply torn between their home country and America, between the Old World and the New World, or between positions of exile and return. Instead, in addition to these struggles, the Filipino subject is also faced with competing struggles over identity based on sexuality, gender, economic status, region of origin, age, and religion. Realuyo's *The Umbrella Country* is an excellent text to discuss in this context because it features protagonists who exist at the borders, those who do not quite fit into conventional or normative cultural categories. The book, which has a chapter about 'female boarders,' depicts the lives of those who are not at home, who 'left as soon as they found a better place to stay' (64). These protagonists, like Gringo, who squats 'on the fence that was never finished' (187), are constantly struggling with their borderline, invisible positions. They are Filipinos in their homeland, yet they are already Americans; they are children, yet they have seen too much to be innocent; they are boys 'who think they're girls' (58). And they live in a country where the sun beats down so hard you have to hide under an umbrella.

In this novel, set during the years of martial law in the 1970s,[1] borders of all kinds are particularly important because they serve as demarcations of one's political and social identity. When Ferdinand Marcos signed Proclamation No. 1081 in 1972, placing the country under his rule, he cited rebel factions, seditious Communists, and Muslim extremists as the reasons for his decision. In reality, many other groups, such as students, workers, and peasants, had become fed up with the government and had organized a series of protests in the late 1960s 'in response to increasing awareness of the internal inequalities, corruption in government, and external domination of the country's economic and political affairs that had continued since the country's colonial period' (Zwick). What the martial law decree did, however, was enable the military to classify ordinary Filipinos into seditious or loyal citizens. By suspending the writ of habeas corpus, Marcos created a climate of uncertainty, fear, and suspicion, where friends and neighbours could, and did, end up erecting borders between themselves for the purposes of political and physical survival.

Though the work is not overtly political, several aspects of the novel reveal the intense scrutiny and surveillance under which ordinary citizens were placed at this time. Characters in the novel are often under each other's gaze; neighbours peer into other families' lives and homes; and children grow up knowing their parents' secrets. Privacy in such an overcrowded country is a precious commodity that only the rich can afford. Gringo sleeps in a room 'too small for four people' where rows of cabinets were used as partitions (22). The family's common bedroom is a permeable space through which waft kitchen smells and other reminders of the world outside. From his side of the room, Gringo remembers the 'lingering smell of food,' and notes that 'We always slept with noises of the streets – yells of boys selling salted eggs and fried pork rinds in wicker baskets they carried over their heads' (22). The street sounds, the market, and even politics are all part of the bedroom. Family members are reminded of the political situation, of the nightly curfew, as 'voices disappeared, and it became so quiet sometimes that the snapping of leaves from tamarind tress could easily be heard' (23). There is little of the traditional North American divide between outside and inside, between private and public, between the individual and the community.

The permeability of space and the ease with which boundaries are crossed can be interpreted positively as a sign of the strength of the family or community versus the individual. But in Lacanian psychoanalytic terms, the lack of distinction between self and other is a characteristic of the pre-Oedipal stage, where the child is dependent upon the (m)other, and has not yet recognized 'his own image in a mirror' (*Écrits* 1). According to Lacan, the mirror stage is a necessary part of identification, separation, and maturation. As Elizabeth Grosz points out, 'only at this moment does it become capable of distinguishing itself from the "outside" world, and thus of locating itself *in* the world' (*Jacques Lacan* 35). In Realuyo's novel, the characters are suspended in this perpetual stage of confused recognition/misrecognition (Grosz, *Jacques Lacan* 39). The demarcation between the self and the other, between the developing country, the Philippines, and its father and protector, the United States, is never clear. Viewed through the lens of psychoanalysis, the novel is much more than a simple *Bildung*; it also depicts the arrested growth of the Filipinos, and the difficulty in separating the Filipino subject from the colonizing American.

The lack of boundary and privacy occurs both within the home and in the larger community. Early in the novel, Gringo's entire poor neighbourhood, signified by the reference to 'a multitude of eyes' (7), comes out to watch Daddy Groovie install plastic gutters in his house. Groovie, whose name, like his gutters, was 'made in the States' (6), is the prototype of the Filipino who is seduced by American advertising into believing that anything made stateside is better than anything made locally. Even though he was born and raised in the Philippines, Groovie's thinking has been largely shaped by the culture of the West. Comically and somewhat predictably, this same big crowd comes out a week later to witness the deterioration of the stateside product, which has melted in the heat. The scene where Groovie climbs up the ladder to fix the gutters is narrated as a social comedy. Neighbours like Mr Sing-sing and 'Mrs.-from-across-the-street' become the audience for the show, and all have their opinions about imported gutters (11). The simple task of repairing one's home, normally a private domestic chore, becomes a public spectacle. To add to the comedy, Groovie's shorts fall down while he is on the job, revealing his 'dark cratered moons' (14). Thus are one's private parts – in this case, Groovie's buttocks – open to public, or universal, scrutiny. The exposure does not hinder Groovie. The narrator notes that 'to live in our street was to have a skin as thick as rubber slippers' (15). Shame, Gringo learns, 'had only made people miserable, hungry ... what was important was that we did what we had to do to fill our empty stomachs with food, to keep our lives going' (15). In this case, the permeability of boundaries between the domestic and the public becomes a part of daily living, a matter-of-fact condition, accepted by those whose socio-economic situation permits no space for false modesty or fastidiousness.

The re-enactment of 'Miss Unibers' by the children of the neighbour-hood is another example of the permeability of boundaries. This time it is between private fantasies and mass- media representations, between the performance and the constitution of gender identity. The children in Gringo and Pipo's group adapt and recreate the Miss Universe pageant as their 'game of the season' (30). Because the contestants in Gringo's game are both girls and boys, the community pageant becomes a kind of Bakhtinian carnival that, as Stallybrass and White note, 'is both a populist utopian vision of the world seen from below and a festive critique, through the inversion of hierarchy, of the "high" culture' (7). Though a Miss Universe pageant, hosted then by Bob Barker,[2] is not exactly what one would classify as 'high' culture, it is an important international event, bringing tourism and global attention to the host country as well as to the winning beauty queen. Nhi T. Lieu remarks that 'beauty contests may appear frivolous and trivial, but as a cultural practice they stage complex struggles over power and representation' (127). This struggle is re-enacted by the children as they vie to win their version of the 'Miss Unibers' title.

The seriousness of the contest for the 'reigning queen' is enormous, both for the children and for those who put on the beauty contests. Gringo notes that the whole city is transformed by the arrival of the Miss Universe pageant in the Philippines: 'neighbors were talking about how the streets were cleared of beggars, how walls were built to hide the slum areas not far away ... how men and women were hired to clean the streets in red-and-white uniforms and to flash welcoming smiles, how we should all keep clean and stay around the block because somebody might come and pick us up in thinking that we were children of the streets' (38). Holding the Miss Universe pageant in the Philippines for the first time, Filipinos are challenged to perform the characteristic for which they are most famous, their hospitality. They are encouraged by the government not only to welcome visitors, but to self-consciously put on a public face of agreeableness. Gringo notes that Sergio Putita was smiling every day because 'people were asked to smile at foreign visitors to the city' (39). The city temporarily becomes a theatre or a stage, where 'everybody was acting unusual' (39). Even the weather is expected to put on a performance: 'helicopters had been regularly circling the skies that month' (39). They were 'trying to blow away the clouds so it won't rain again, especially during Miss Universe' (40). Here, the boundary between representation and reality has deliberately been obfuscated. Manila, its residents, the weather, all must conform to the tourist brochures of the city as the perfect tropical haven. The climate must be warm but not wet; the people friendly and helpful; the streets clean and free of beggars. In anticipation of the great amount of publicity generated by the pageant, authorities attempt to manipulate not only the city's looks, but people's attitude, clothing, and behaviour. Not complying – in this case, not wearing clean clothes – could lead to questioning, or detention, or worse.

This failure to distinguish between fantasy and reality, between the image and the substance, is mirrored in the games of the children. For them, the Miss Universe pageant becomes a public enactment of private fantasies of power, beauty, glamour, adoration, and wealth. They watch Miss Spain, who has run away with the 'glittering crown' (42), copying her 'big-teeth smile' and 'studying her walk, her hairdos, her glowing eyes, her gait ... A whole city of children held in her spell' (42). All the people in the neighbourhood are transfixed by the television:

'we all watched attentively and nervously, wanting more than anything to fall all over her knees' (42). For many Filipinos, more than half of whom live below the poverty line (see Leonard Davis, chapter 3), a beauty pageant sustains the Cinderella fantasy of 'rags to riches' and fame. The seeming ease in which an unknown young woman, a commoner like themselves, becomes a worldwide celebrity simply through her looks creates a phantasmagoric desire in viewers from the very young to the very old. In addition, an international beauty pageant is inextricably linked with the American dream, with escape from poverty and obscurity. Being beautiful and desirable, particularly by white folks, *mga putî*, is one of the imagined ways in which a Filipina could get to the United States.

For Gringo, his brother, and Sergio Putita, the participants in the Miss Universe Pageant are not only enactments of economic and social success, but they also provide lessons in gender behaviour. Judith Butler's notion that 'gender is instituted through the stylization of the body and, hence, must be understood as the mundane way in which bodily gestures, movements, and enactments of various kinds constitute the illusion of an abiding gendered self' ('Performative Acts' 402) is useful to our understanding of the formation of gender identity in the novel. The boys take the performance of gender in the Miss Universe pageant seriously. Sergio Putita 'watched so closely that his mouth began to bubble' (42). Pipo studies Miss Spain's bodily gestures in order to recreate them. For him, the contest is so important that 'he skipped dinner to prepare for our next Miss Unibers' for several nights (46). For the boys who are experiencing the trials of adolescence and puberty and are being constantly reminded of their masculinity, the 'Miss Unibers' game becomes a place of relative freedom and transgression. Because it is a neighbourhood game, it becomes a site where boys like Gringo and Sergio Putita can play out their fantasies of femininity without being chastised. In fact, they are actually applauded for their exaggerated and makeshift performance of femininity.

What the children learn, though, is that a performance and a display of femininity, however good, does not mean that one becomes woman in society. One cannot simply take on the gender identity of one's choice, as Daddy Groovie constantly reminds his son. Patriarchal society has rigid prescriptions of gender differences. Groovie says to Pipo, 'look at your father, *lalaking-lalaki*, real man, real man, look at these arms, see those, scars, scars, only a man would have those, look at you, you're growing up to be a girl, you know? Miss Unibers? Miss Unibers?

That's for girls! Boys don't dress up and become Miss Unibers! You *idioto!'* (57). Yet in spite of the fact that the children's Miss Unibers game, like the Bakhtinian carnival, is not intrinsically radical, but a 'licensed release,' it is still a site of what Stallybrass and White call 'symbolic inversion and transgression' (18). It is an 'act of expressive behaviour which inverts, contradicts, abrogates, or in some fashion presents an alternative to commonly held cultural codes, values and norms' (Babcock, qtd in Stallybrass and White 17). The Miss Unibers game and the re-enactment of 'certain scenes from the Stations of the Cross, especially on Mondays following the Virgen Maria procession in the street' (85) by Sergio Putita and Pipo expose and question the limitations and expectations of the cultural and religious institutions that they parody.

Daddy Groovie, who punishes Pipo for his *bakla,* or feminine behaviour, himself fails to distinguish between male identity and the performance of hypermasculinity. Groovie does not see any boundaries between acting and identity, between the show and the substance. In a chapter titled 'Hallowed by Thy Name' that highlights the links between Groovie as a father figure and the authority of religion, Realuyo exhibits the cultural constructedness and dangers of hypermasculinity. Groovie's attempts to teach Pipo how to be a man and his own irresponsible behaviour as a man reveal the inadequacy and the superficiality of the ideal. For Groovie, maleness is as much an image as it is an attitude. He tells Pipo: 'Oy, Pipo, straighten your back ... like that, no, don't bend your back, your hands, don't swish, keep your blood flowing through your wrist ... don't bend your arm, keep it down, like this, see? that's the way men are, always ready to blow' (51). He assumes that all males perform masculinity for women: 'that behind, keep it tight all the time, girls like it tight like that, you see?' (51). Daddy Groovie wants Pipo to be like Jun, who acts like all the other Juniors: 'they walked with that same macho strut, as if their balls were hanging too low, too heavy ... they talked the same, in a way that never really made sense; and ran the same way, legs spread so far apart that they went in opposite directions' (52). Groovie is conscious of the male subject as spectacle. His idea of masculinity is in keeping with some of the qualities Richard Dyer associates with male pin-ups: 'muscularity,' the 'symbolic association of male power and the phallus,' and 'masculinity-as-activity' (Dyer 269). It is a masculinity produced by films, magazines, and advertisements. Dyer notes that these images of men, 'founded on such multiple instabilities are such a strain' (276). He

explains: 'Looked at but pretending not to be, still yet asserting movement, phallic but weedy – there is seldom anything easy about such
imagery. And the real trap at the heart of these instabilities is that it is
precisely *straining* that is held to be the great good, what makes a man a
man' (276). In Realuyo's novel, the strain of performing masculinity
and demonstrating 'what makes a man a man' is illustrated in Daddy
Groovie's fits of uncontrollable violence. Through his dealings with his
wife and children, Groovie shows just how difficult keeping up the
image of the real man can be.

Groovie is the one character in the novel who self-consciously and
outrageously flaunts his masculinity abroad and at home. He demonstrates the excesses that this masculine identity brings, yet he wants his
sons to be a real man like himself. Unable to control his job, his country's
politics, and the restrictions imposed by martial law, he takes out his
frustrations on his family. The feeling of impotence outside his home is
turned inward into domestic aggression and violence. At one point,
having lost yet another construction job, he gets drunk and finds 'a
reason to whip [Pipo] on the legs with his *yantok*' (61). It is at this point
of drunken violence that he takes the name Daddy Groovie. To him, it is
a 'Stateside name' (61), but it is in a foreign language and 'hard to say'
for the rest of the family (62). Through this moniker, Realuyo makes
clear the likeness of the father figure to the imperialist United States.
Like a father, America is supposed to be a benevolent protector of the
Philippines, but, like Daddy Groovie, America abuses its powers and
mistreats those who rely on it.

America's encroachment on Philippine borders of identity, culture,
and economic life is revealed in the novel mainly through Groovie.
Groovie's vision of 'Nuyork. Tall buildings. Good food' (18) echoes that
of many dreams of impoverished Filipinos. As Theodore Friend notes,
'For many Filipinos the United States continues to have an almost
magical power as benefactor and exploiter. In popular mentality many
Filipinos ascribe to America a nearly limitless capacity to shape and
resolve, for good or for evil, Philippine destiny' ('Philippine-American'
3). For Daddy Groovie, America is an other that represents all that is
positive. It is that place of wonder and possibilities. Once in America,
Groovie writes to tell his children of the many opportunities there:
'Many jobs here for those who aren't very picky' (190). He writes, 'so
many places here to go. So many things to buy. So much food here'
(190). But even for those who have not reached America, products from
America have already entered into the daily lives and discourse of

Filipinos. Among the things Gringo mentions in his home are 'Mazola Cooking Oil' (99), a 'General Electric fan' (160), a Singer sewing machine (166), and Prell (99).[3] As Friend notes, 'The fact remains that the United States, with a gross domestic product more than eighty times as great as that of the Philippines, and with a trade volume forty times as great, will influence the Philippines heavily without planning, without trying, without even wanting to do so' ('Philippine-American' 18).

These and other U.S. products that cross Philippine borders easily not only make it difficult for economic nationalism, but also help create a mentality of self-loathing and apathy. Things in the Philippines seem barely adequate compared with the United States. As Gringo notes,

> Everybody seemed to be complaining more, finding it difficult to cope. Prices were going up too fast. Bread was shrinking in size.
> That was when the States filled people's faces, blinked in everybody's eyes. And when they got tired of brownouts, the heat, the mosquitoes, the States appeared in every word they spoke. (193)

People start talking about the 'food in California,' the 'Balikbayan box, full of fruitcake,' shoes that are 'PX Goods. Stateside *yan*' (193). Because few people can afford to travel to the United States, or are able to move there, commodities become fetishized substitutes for their unfulfilled dreams of America. Friends and neighbours ask Gringo's family about their father: 'When is he going to send me my Samsonite? ... When is he going to send me Yardley and Ivory? Also, I want some Stateside Colgate, what do you call it there, Crest?' (193). The situation is akin to what Frantz Fanon describes of the effects of colonialism in Africa: 'Culture, extracted from the past to be displayed in all its splendour, is not necessarily that of his own country ... The efforts of the native to rehabilitate himself and to escape from the claws of colonialism are logically inscribed from the same point of view as that of colonialism' (38). Here, commodities from the States have replaced indigenous products and culture. Stateside goods have also become the currency for expressing neighbourly and familial love or concern. Filipinos no longer value their traditional ways and goods, but see themselves through their colonizer's eyes.

In contrast to Daddy Groovie, who is enamoured of, and associated with, stateside products, Gringo's mother represents local Filipino culture and its resilient spirit. She is the one member of the family who refuses to leave the Philippines for America at the end of the novel.

From the start, Gringo notes, 'I always felt she was never interested in the idea of going to the States' (18). Mommy Estrella is depicted as a Christ-like figure, associated frequently with fish, blood, rain, and patience. '*Paciencia,*' she tells Ninang Rola, as she 'chopped the fins off the fish' (106). In the chapter titled 'Sangre,' Mommy Estrella cuts her finger with a kitchen knife and then goes outside in the rain, where she embraces the outpouring of nature: 'she slowly lifted her hands and opened her palms as if trying to catch the drops. I couldn't see her bloody finger anymore, I was looking at her head, the way she moved it back so that her face was directly facing the sky ... The heavy rain weighted down her clothes but she ignored it' (110). Mommy Estrella is represented here as a Christ-like figure with her outstretched arms. She embodies the patient suffering of the Filipino people. This wounding that she attempts to wash off with falling rain is only one of many that she receives in the course of the novel. She suffers through Groovie's lovemaking, 'the silent screams muffled by Daddy Groovie's hands' (26). Afterwards, Gringo notices 'bruise spots on her back, so fresh, so soft. Light lines of old scars, perhaps taking the shape of Daddy Groovie's hands' (26). In the novel, Groovie is the male aggressor associated with America, while Mommy Estrella, the winner of Miss Tanso, a star who has been repeatedly raped and brutalized, stands in for the Philippines.

Unlike Groovie, Estrella understands Philippine culture and teaches the boys to appreciate it. Knowledgeable about traditional healing practices, she 'pounded Mayana leaves to soak in water and wore them on her wounds' (199). Before they leave for America, she takes them to Luneta Park and tells them: 'Look around you. Take as much of this air in. Leave it inside your body for a minute. This country smells differently' (273). She also shows them how to make *dinuguan*, a stew made up from pig ears, tripe, blood, and other 'pig parts, peppers, onions, garlic,' vinegar, and coconut milk (277). It is her sense of belonging to the Philippines, as well as her desire to live her own life, that makes her unable to cross national boarders as easily as Groovie does.[4]

The relationship between Groovie and Estrella is important because, like that between the United States and the Philippines, it is characterized from the start by violence. Here the domestic situation sheds light on the political and the parallels reveal the hazy boundaries between the two worlds. According to the character Ninang Rola's accounts of the past, Groovie, who was then called Germano, 'looked Stateside in his nice suit.' He 'looked like Elvis' and took her to the 'Hollywood nightclub' (116, 123). Significantly, he is frequently represented through

American cultural images and icons. Realuyo has remarked that in Philippine society, Hollywood is like 'an altar of gods and goddesses' (Realuyo web site). After a night of dancing, aspiring to be 'just like in the Elvis movies' (123), Groovie conquers Estrella, not through seduction, but by drugging her, raping her, and getting her pregnant. Ever since the rape, Estrella has had to endure his bouts of drunkenness, his beatings, his physical and verbal abuse. She works silently in front of the sewing machine, keeping the family together, while he hangs around with his friends, dreaming of his American life. Unable to retaliate against his male power, just as the Philippines is unable to fight American cultural and economic encroachment, 'her weapon had always been her silence' (168).

The rapacious and abusive relationship between Groovie and Estrella mirrors the political and economic relationship between the United States and the Philippines. Neferti Tadiar has argued that 'the economies and political relations of nations are libidinally configured, that is, they are grasped and effected in terms of sexuality' (219). Tadiar points out that because of the 'tremendous difference between them in national wealth and global power,' the special relationship between the Philippines and the United States is no marriage, and the Philippines 'is no wife; she is, rather, the mistress of the United States. Feminized in this relationship of debt and dependence, the Philippines produces the surplus pleasure (wealth) that the United States extracts from her bodily (manual) labor' (223–4). Tadiar says, the 'mode of relations between the Philippines and the United States operates according to a fantasy of relations between masculine and feminine ideals that has become dominant in economically advanced nations – a sexual masquerade in which the Philippines serves as a feminine ideal for the United States, servicing his power the way Philippine prostitutes service U.S. military men, symbols of U.S. national (masculine) strength' (227).

In the novel, Estrella is not only feminized and disempowered through her silence and her stoic acceptance of Groovie's brutality, she is also constantly depicted as engaged in domestic, female labour. After a particularly ferocious beating, she puts all her energies into working. It is as if only through labour can her body heal itself:

As she gathered the clothes, separated the white from the color, and soaked all of them in water, the mounds on her face subsided, the cuts on her shoulders healed ... From the time she woke up in the morning, she would be in the kitchen cooking, measuring water in the rice with her fingers, scrubbing pots later until all the stains and grease were gone, only to use them and darken them again. She never rested. She just kept on moving. Her hands were either soaked in Tide lather or inside a fish's stomach pulling guts out ... Mommy seemed like she was just there and her body was disconnected from all her thoughts. (177–8)

Disconnected from her dreams and desires, Estrella, like many Filipinas, becomes pure labour material. As Tadiar puts it, 'the depletion of natural resources and destruction of the productive capacity of out-moded economic forms, especially those that have been female domi-nated, have forced the transformation of an already feminized labor force into the semiprocessed products that await final processing for the realization of surplus value. In this sense, women are the last abundant resource of the nation – they are like the surplus products they themselves sell for subsistence, now sold themselves by their own feminized nation' (235).[5]

Other women in the novel similarly exist in a liminal space. Though they are not physically abused, they exist in marginal conditions, living in temporary homes, without security. Ninang Rola lives as an unmar-ried relation of Estrella in the household, and though she exerts much power in the family, she is ordered to leave by Groovie in one of his drunken fits. Similarly, the two other women we see in the novel are *queridas* or other women. They board with Gringo's family because they are mistresses to men who already have wives and families else-where. As Rola notes, 'they're in hiding, always running from the real wives' (65). In fact, Rola observes, times have changed, 'just about everyone is a *querida*, so sad' (66). Rola's comments remind us of the high percentage of Filipinas who act as bar waitresses, hostesses, prosti-tutes, mail-order brides, and domestics not only in the Philippines, but in Japan, Hong Kong, the Middle East, Europe, and North America too (see Tadiar 230, 234–9). They are all *queridas* in the sense that they live outside the conventional structures of the nuclear family. Like the board-ers in Realuyo's novel, they live at the borderline of society and culture, frequently hiding from authorities, constantly moving, and surviving only by becoming 'thick-skinned' social outcast (67).

The depiction of these *queridas* as marginal beings is starker than the surrealistic representations of mistresses in Jessica Hagedorn's *Dogeaters*. In that better-known Filipino novel, also set during the Marcos era, women like Lolita Luna are also others, mistresses to men who have wives, but they are often depicted with rich and powerful men (*Dogeaters*

95–7). There is a wider range of women and subject positions in Hagedorn's novel. Some lead lives with a measure of freedom, excitement, and glamour. Though they do not all lead happy lives, they have relationships with generals, with men who drive fast cars, or those who hold political power. In contrast, Realuyo's novel depicts a set of characters who live on the cusp of starvation. He writes about those who are so poor they have little time to do anything else but worry about 'putting food on the table' (Realuyo, 'Conversation' 303). When they die, their deaths do not make the news. They do not frequent nightclubs, and they are not connected with the rich, or with the President or his entourage. They live with 'a company of rats' in the city and do not have enough money to travel in their own islands. As Gringo observes: 'we stayed here, in the sun, where water was scarce because we never had money to go anywhere. I knew I lived in a country of countless islands, but I was born in the heart of smog so I hardly saw the sea' (135). Until they finally leave Manila for America, Gringo's family stay close to their asphalt neighbourhood, confined by the curfew and the heat, and surrounded by the 'steady parade of dust, dirt, and people' (3). They are characters who are in many ways in the in-between state of being and non-being, of existence and oblivion.

Of all the scenes in the novel, the one that most overtly deals with the crossing of boundaries is in the chapter entitled 'Curfew.' In this chapter, Gringo, who still sits on 'the unfinished concrete-block fence' watching people (206), embarks on a jaunt with Boy Spit and sees the lives of those who live beyond his circumscribed neighbourhood. Though he was not exactly innocent before, he witnesses scenes that take him beyond the borders of his daily social and sexual milieu. He transgresses several boundaries: he breaks the curfew rule; and he leaves the familiar asphalt streets to go to the 'overgrowth of grass' (221) beyond the railways and encounters the sights and smells of one of Manila's shantytowns. Here in the 'makeshift street,' there 'was no curfew' (226). The squatter area is so poor that residents are indifferent to the police. Boy Spit says, 'We're so used to them. Here, we break all rules' (230). Gringo describes the place as a 'giant sewer' (226). He says, 'I could smell each image that I saw: rotting food, piles of month-old garbage, the schools of flies' (226). He is taken to the cave where he sees a circle of boys performing a sexualized ritual. They are in 'a circle joined together by arms ... Their belts unbuckled. Pants almost down' (232–3). What shocks him most is his discovery that the boy in the middle of the circle is his brother Pipo. After breaking so many interdictions and borders, he discovers that the boundaries have already been broken in his own home by his brother.

What is significant about this scene, which takes place during the curfew, is that it highlights a number of marginal and borderline positions that complicate the trajectory of the *Bildung* or the immigration narrative. Of the work, Realuyo says, 'I don't want the book to be read only as a coming-of-age story of the two brothers. I think there is much more in the novel than watching Gringo and Pipo deal with their lives. I am also trying to explore the strange and very complex nature of family bonds amid poverty and sometimes violent circumstances, while telling the quiet story of the Philippines during its most turbulent period' ('Conversation' 305). The cave scene reveals the dark side of the coming-of-age and immigrant stories. It shows how subjectivity entails the multiple intersection of gender and sexual identity, economic situation, class, age, and politics. By defying curfew rules as well as parental and religious injunctions, and by transgressing heterosexual codes of behaviour, these boys reject the culture's normative prescriptions of behaviour.

The scene also continues the novel's motif of the blurring of boundaries. The heart of darkness that Gringo discovers here is that those acts of violence, those horrific and unnameable fantasies of his childhood that he associated with Boy Manicure, take place not just in the broader world but also within the confines of his family. The ultimate transgressive act in the novel is not just a political or legal one, but a psychosexual one as well. The perpetrator is not someone whom one reads about in the newspapers, it is Gringo's own brother. What Gringo learns is that the enemy is not without but within, a theme that we have seen repeatedly in the violence of the father against his family, paralleled by U.S. cultural and military aggression against her ex-colony.

Yet the circle scene has a utopic element about it. The children in the circle form a community that exists outside the borders of society. In spite of the fact that many of them come from impoverished homes and difficult familial situations, they are able to find a moment where they fulfil their desires. The circle, like the 'Miss Unibers' pageant, exists alongside, but outside of, the regulated normative world. It defies martial law and order, and heteronormative gender codes of behaviour. The children, who are in many ways outside Filipino culture and society, find a place and time of their own, creating a surreal world of energy, potency, and enchantment. They have survived their borderline existence.

Through these various intersecting problems represented in a novel about immigration, Realuyo shows the otherness at the edge of the Western other. Global borders, east and west, north and south, are only some of the many demarcations of identity, subjectivity, and selfhood. Within those large categories are others that render diasporic or ethnic subjects marginal and invisible even in their own community. Asian subjects who move 'out of place' may find themselves in other border zones that entail constant balancing on unfinished fences.

Afterword

Asian American and Asian Canadian authors deal with the psychic, social, and historical damage of being named and categorized as a racial other and as a marked subject through a series of negotiations, accommodations, and acts of resistance. Many of the authors examined in this study aim to get beyond the screen of the visible in order to locate and reconstitute a self and/or a community that has been displaced or rendered invisible. They perform the important task of witnessing, which, as Kelly Oliver notes, 'works to ameliorate the trauma particular to othered subjectivity' (7). In her book *Witnessing: Beyond Recognition*, Oliver attempts to redefine our current understanding of how we gain subjectivity. Instead of viewing subjectivity as a process of recognition – the recognition conferred on others by the dominant group, a process we have been discussing in this book – Oliver proposes a new subjectivity that 'is founded on the ability to respond to, and address, others' (15). Crucial to her redefinition of subjectivity is the process of witnessing, both in the sense of 'eyewitness testimony' and 'bearing witness' to something that cannot be seen (16). She asks, 'how can we witness and bear witness to oppression, domination, subordination, enslavement, and torture in ways that open up the possibility of a more humane and ethical future beyond violence?' (18).

I bring up Oliver's philosophical reflections at this point because the new vision that she articulates is contiguous with the desires, albeit merely implied in some cases, of many of the Asian North American authors in this work. Oliver's vision is not the alienating gaze described by Sartre or Lacan, but one that is 'enabling because of the interconnection between the senses and the elements that make vision possible' (202). Influenced by Merleau-Ponty, Oliver sees vision as one 'part of a sensory system that includes what we take to be more proximal senses like touch, taste, or smell' (202). By not privileging vision alone, which implies distance between subject and object, philosophers like Merleau-Ponty, Irigaray, and Lévinas are able to challenge the traditional separation of the senses that serves as the basis for the separation of the sensible and the intelligible, the mind and the body, objective theoretical knowledge and subjective personal feeling, the visible and the invisible (Oliver 210–12). What is needed is another way of looking that does not rip open, pry, or penetrate the other, but that 'touches the unseen substrate of the visible' (Oliver 215). What is needed is the texture or fabric of vision.

In her poetic conclusion, Oliver suggests that 'If we reconceive of recognition from a notion of vision that emphasizes the fullness of space and the connections – interdependence even – between the visible world and vision, between the seer and the seen, then we begin to move away from the Hegelian struggle for recognition and toward an acknowledgement of otherness ... Vision itself becomes a process, a becoming, rather than the sovereign of recognition' (221).[1] These notions of interdependence, communication, communion, the circulation of energy, the process of relationships between bodies in the world, as highlighted by Oliver, are fruitful ways of rearticulating some of the issues I have been accentuating in this book. Writers like Denise Chong, Bino Realuyo, and Cecilia Brainard ask us to see personal experience, myth, and national history in relation to each other. Bienvenido Santos, Mina Shum, and Hiromi Goto point out the destructive effects of the gaze that fixes and pierces. In their own ways, Shirley Lim, Amy Tan, and Wayson Choy represent their worlds for us with sensual and sensory details, with articles and items that enable us to see the grain of life beyond the surface of the visual.

Much of the focus of this book has been on how the daily rituals and textures of life – such things as food, clothing, household objects, domestic space, and the relationships between parents and children – are used to construct and delimit identities for Asian North Americans that are different from those prescribed or imagined by the dominant culture. Another motif I traced is that of storytelling, and the creation and preservation of ethnic difference through myth, history, and collective memory. By attending to these elements of Asian North Americans rather than just the visual markings of our bodies – our black hair, facial features, and accents – we see and enable others to see beyond the screen and move away from the spectre of the Oriental. What lies beyond the visible is still very much in a process of becoming, as Asian North American subjects are still shaping hybrid identities, interacting with other cultures and ethnicities in our community, and coming to terms with varied forms of sexual, gendered, spiritual, and religious experiences in a rapidly shifting transnational society. Though hyphenated, we are still viewed in our contemporary society as racially different from whites. And while this difference has more often been worn as a hair shirt rather than a mantle of privilege in the past, we are still not willing to discard it completely. Some of the features that have been fetishized as Asian in North America have become signifiers or selling points for some Asian Americans in the media world and the movie industry.[2] But for many Asian North Americans, including most of the authors in this study, these 'Asian' markers of difference are regarded with mixed feelings of pride, pain, vexation, and nostalgia. They attempt to catalogue, to narrate their experiences of otherness in order to record, to memorialize, and to discursively transform and reclaim not only the past, but also their significance in identity formation in the present moment.

I began this book by pointing out how birthmarks and our physical appearance mark us as Asian North American subjects. I end with the hope that the reading, telling, and witnessing of these stories by those who have been marked in the past will lead to a re-evaluation and a re-imagination of relationships between us all. As Kelly Oliver remarks, 'Relations with others do not have to be hostile alien encounters. Instead, they can be loving adventures, the advent of something new. Difference does not have to be threatening; it can be exciting, the source of the meaning of life' (224).

Notes

Introduction

1 There have been a number of studies that deal with representations of Asians in the media, in history, and in American culture. Robert G. Lee points out that, historically, there were six images of the Oriental in popular culture in *Orientals*; Darrell Hamamoto examines problems in the representation of Asian Americans on TV in *Monitored Peril*; Gina Marchetti studies how Hollywood has dealt with fears of yellow peril in *Romance and the 'Yellow Peril'*; and Josephine Lee outlines some of the stereotypes of Asian Americans in theatrical performance in the first chapter of *Performing Asian America*. See also works by Said, Wong ('Ethnicizing Gender'), Uchida, Ma (*Deathly Embrace*), and others.

2 Palumbo-Liu points out that in an essay written in 1928, Robert E. Park insisted that 'racial difference is determined not by mental nature, but by a *physical* sign' (*Asian/American*, 86). Aside from the face, Park argued that 'one striking difference between Oriental and Occidental people is that the former are more conscious, more conventional, in their behaviour than we' (R.E. Park, *Race and Culture* 250, qtd in Palumbo-Liu, *Asian/American* 88).

3 Clairol hair colour products have expanded greatly into the Asian market in the last decade. Recent popular women's magazines in Japan, Taiwan, Hong Kong, and Singapore feature Asian models who sport brown or reddish bronze-coloured hair.

4 Enoch Padolsky, referring to a short story by Jewish Canadian writer Matt Cohen, notes that 'in an earlier Canadian racial terminology, "visible minority" meant dress and appearance and not just pigmentation' (26).

5 Sau-ling Wong *Reading* has noted that the term Asian American 'expresses a political conviction and agenda: it is based on the assumption that regardless of individual origin, background, and desire for self-identification, Asian Americans have been subjected to certain collective experiences that must be acknowledged and resisted' (6).

6 A number of factors have created differences between race in Canada and the United States. Enoch Padolsky points, for example, to Canada's dual *'Official Languages Act*, official Canadian multiculturalism ... a growing openness to Aboriginal self-government,' and the relatively small and new community of blacks in Canada as compared to the United States (23–4).

7 In the last decade, black intellectuals like Paul Gilroy have been influential in attempting to move away from the Manichaeism of fixed black and white identities in their work.

8 Smaro Kamboureli makes a similar observation about the ambivalent effect of multiculturalism. 'The Multiculturalism Act (also known as Bill C-93) recognizes the cultural diversity that constitutes Canada, but it does so by practising a sedative politics, a politics that attempts to recognize ethnic differences, but only in a contained fashion, in order to manage them' (82).

9 In his chapter 'Race, Nation, Migrancy, and Sex,' Palumbo-Liu looks at the willingness of contemporary minority individuals to use plastic surgery to transform their features. The implication is that the body is linked to the psyche: 'the morphing of physical form anticipates the revision of the psyche within, and the way that transformed body will be viewed by others' (*Asian/American* 95).

10 Michael Banton points out that 'the Linnaean classificatory enterprise depended upon the assumption that the various sets of individuals to be classified were stable, for how could they be classified if they were changing?' (5). This instability also creates problems in today's society when we speak of racial categories (see Appiah).

11 Abdul JanMohamed notes that 'the perception of racial difference is, in the first place, influenced by economic motives ... Africans were perceived in a more of less neutral and benign manner before the slave trade developed; however, once the triangular trade became established, Africans were newly characterized as the epitome of evil and barbarity' (80).

12 According to Michael Omi and Howard Winant, this stage was followed by two others. One began around the 1920s, when race difference came to be seen in cultural and social terms, along with biological ones. Ethnicity displaced race as a sign of difference. Later, after the cultural and radical movements of the 1960s, came a resurgence and transformation of notions

of difference concerning people of colour. Omi and Winant characterize this third phase as the class- and nation-based paradigms for understanding race (14–51).

13 This kind of classification is similar to what European botanists, influenced by Linnean typologies, did with the plants that they 'discovered' in India and Africa. As Sara Mills notes, 'the plants were ... no longer seen in terms of their original classification system, which often related to their use in medicine, their food-value, their relation to other elements within an eco-system and their position within a cosmological and symbolic system, but rather they were seen out of context in terms of the similarity or dissimilarity of their morphology (plant structure) to European plant species' (53).

14 Name of sender withheld.

15 I am not suggesting that the situation depicted in Ellison's novel is the same as that experienced by Asian Americans today as I am aware of the cultural and socio-historical differences between African and Asian Americans.

16 On the issue of race, Michael Omi and Howard Winant present a cogent argument about the need to rethink racial categories. They argue that a critical 'process-oriented theory of race' must meet three requirements. It must apply to 'contemporary political relationships' in an 'increasingly global context' and 'across historical time' (204).

17 Kamboureli was discussing the effect of the Multiculturalism Act on ethnic subjects at this point.

18 Among other things, Said's monumental *Orientalism* is a study of how visuality operates in our culture. Rey Chow discusses the spectacle of 'being Chinese' in *Primitive Passions,* especially Part I.

19 On the women's part, the reasons most often cited for becoming a mail-order bride or a sex worker are poverty and the desire to help their family financially (see Philippine Women Centre 57).

20 In her introduction to *Charlie Chan Is Dead*, Jessica Hagedorn outlines some stereotypes of the Oriental: 'The slit-eyed, bucktooth Jap ... The inscrutable, wily Chinese detective ... The childlike, indolent Filipino houseboy ... The sexless, hairless Asian male. The servile, oversexed Asian female. The Geisha. The sultry, sarong-clad South Seas maiden. The serpentine, cunning Dragon Lady ... Dogeater ... Gooks ... Passive Japanese Americans' (xxii). She argues that characters like Charlie Chan, Fu Manchu, Madame Butterfly, and others created by American popular culture, are now 'dead' and replaced by more complex figures in recent works by Asian Americans (*Charlie Chan*).

21 I am using the term 'experience' in a way that takes into account the relationship between discourse, cognition, and reality. Joan Wallach Scott
notes the importance of 'focussing on processes of identity production and
insisting on the discursive nature of "experience" and on the politics of its
construction. Experience is at once always already an interpretation *and*
something that needs to be interpreted' (400).

22 In Hawaii, plantation managers wanted a stable labour force and so
requested a small number of women because they thought a feminine
presence would have a salutary effect on the men (Sucheng Chan, *Asian
Americans* 104).

23 An article in the Victoria *Colonist* of 18 June 1905 warned that if British
Columbia did not endeavour to keep Orientals out of the province, the
whites would be ousted out of existence because 'the Chinese, or the
Japanese, through an evolutionary process which has been in progress for
centuries is now, as we find him a marvellous human machine, competent
to perform the maximum of labour on the minimum of sustenance. He
does not require to maintain a home as white men do; does not spend one
50th part of what the meanest white labourer considers absolutely necessary for clothing; lives in a hovel where a white man would sicken and die
– and with it all performs ... unskilled labourious tasks quite as efficiently
as a white man, and, given the training, is equally proficient at duties
requiring the exercise of some skill' (qtd in Adachi 65).

24 For a comparative study of Filipina domestic workers in Los Angeles and
Rome, see Parreñas.

25 This figure includes those who have identified themselves as black, Arab/
West Asian, and Latin American.

26 A number of chapters in Fong's book are sub-headed 'Visibility and Invisibility,' but he does not always elaborate on the metaphor. In most cases,
Fong attempts to debunk myths that have developed in the media about
Asian Americans in various fields such as work, education, the media,
family, etc.

27 Yamamoto notes that 'the inaugural moment of alienation is one marked
by the perception of physical difference' (93). Her point highlights what
I call the politics of visibility. But in her chapter titled 'In/Visible Difference,' Yamamoto focuses on the face, in particular, the Oriental eye (94).
Eyes certainly set apart most Chinese, Japanese, Koreans, Vietnamese, and
others from Europeans, but they are not necessarily the primary markers
of difference for Filipinos or South Asians.

28 Frankenberg points out that Jewish Americans, Italian Americans, and

Latinos have, at different times and from varying political standpoints, been viewed as both 'white' and 'non-white' (11).

29 Using the same terms, but in a different way, Frankenberg points out that 'whiteness' refers 'to a set of cultural practices that are usually unmarked and unnamed' (1).

30 Though she does not deal with Asian American subjects in particular, Mary Jacobus also uses Freudian melancholia to discuss the effects of racial and ethnic othering (see *Psychoanalysis and the Scene of Reading*).

31 Filipinos use the term 'TNT,' which refers to a kind of hide-and-seek, to designate those who are in the United States without papers and have to hide from immigration authorities.

32 In *Race and Resistance*, Viet Thanh Nguyen argues that Asian American academics and intellectuals have tended to valorize works by Asian Americans that show resistance rather than accommodation and assimilation. Nguyen notes the 'ideological heterogeneity of a diverse Asian American population, and the willingness of a considerable portion of that population to participate in and perpetuate such commodification and the social and economic practices that lead to it' (24).

33 In *Obasan*, Aunt Emily tells Naomi of 'one fellow who changed his name to Wong and passed for Chinese' (187).

34 Many studies on Asian American literature include Asian Canadian Joy Kogawa. For example, see books by Sau-ling Wong, King-Kok Cheung, and Traise Yamamoto. Other writers, such as Edith Maud and Winnifred Eaton and Bharati Mukherjee, have been claimed by Canadian as well as American scholars.

35 For essays on Chinese Australians, see Wenche Ommundsen.

36 In Canada, South Asian writing has been studied separately, or as an integral part of postcolonial literature (see Goellnicht, 'Long Labour' 13–14). In the United States, South Asians from countries as diverse as Bangladesh, Bhutan, India, the Maldives, Nepal, Pakistan, and Sri Lanka have been claiming and making use of the term 'Asian American,' particularly since the 1980s (see Shankar and Srikanth, introduction).

37 As with other critics, my choice of texts may have initially been influenced by my own ethnic background. As a third-generation Chinese who was born in the Philippines and who is now a Canadian, I was particularly attracted to narratives by Filipinos and Chinese Canadians.

38 In Canada, Asian Canadian authors are not usually studied alongside Asian American authors but are more often subsued under broader categories of ethnic, ethnic minority, postcolonial, or multicultural litera-

ture, or writing about race (see Seiler; Kamboureli; Mukherjee; and Hutcheon and Richmond). There are a number of scholars who are working on, or currently completing works on, Asian North American authors, for example, Don Goellnicht, Guy Beauregard, Marie Lo, and Rita Wong, among others.

39 For example, see Patricia Chu and Rachel Lee. Exceptions to this are the works of Filipino American critics such as E. San Juan, Jr, and Oscar Campomanes.

40 Maxine Hong Kingston's *The Woman Warrior* is a work that defies generic classification; it can be read as both novel and autobiography. Sidonie Smith notes that the five narratives in *The Woman Warrior* 'are decidedly five confrontations with the fictions of self-representation and with the autobiographical possibilities embedded in cultural fictions, specifically as they interpenetrate one another in the autobiography a woman would write' (151).

1 Writing Historiographic Autoethnography: Denise Chong's *The Concubine's Children*

1 Chong. Reading and lecture at Wilfrid Laurier University, Waterloo, Ontario. 20 November 1995.

2 In her study of Confucianism in *The Concubine's Children*, Ellen Quigley notes that the book 'appears outside Western epistemologies and systems of autobiographical representation that categorize the proper "I"/eye within the gaze of an individual and proper-tied identity' (237). In her article, Nancy Lee sees Chong's biography as a supplement to textbooks on Canadian history.

3 Lien Chao emphasizes Chong's writing 'as a process of breaking through the historical silence which has enclosed both her family and the Chinese community' (105). My chapter, written largely before I read her work, begins with issues of history, but is more concerned with the problematic representation of the ethnic and gendered other.

4 These were some of the qualities ascribed to prostitutes, particularly in the late nineteenth and early twentieth centuries (see Bell, chapter 3). In this period, Chinese prostitutes were considered to be more injurious to the community than 'white abandoned women,' and they were depicted in newspapers as 'syphilis-infected' and luring young white men into corruption (Peter Li 75).

5 Collins argues that 'women of color have performed motherwork that challenges social constructions of work and family as separate spheres, of

male and female gender roles as similarly dichotomized, and of the search for autonomy as the guiding human quest' (59).

6 I am using Lacan's notion of the gaze and stressing the importance of the scopic drive in the formation of subjectivity. But 'returning the gaze' is also a phrase used by Himani Bannerji to talk about how minority authors empower themselves and attempt to shift the centre (see Bannerji's introduction to *Returning the Gaze*).

7 Teresa Zackodnik's essay, which studies the use of photographs in Chong's book, was published after I had written my chapter. We approach the narrative from different angles, but some of our observations are similar. She notes, 'Chong comes to see these family photographs as performative – "recording" a self more desired than "actual" – and her text as another layer in that performance, one that draws together a family divided by geography and custom' (51).

8 Denise Chong confirmed that Penguin Books chose the photograph that was to grace the cover of the book in a conversation I had with her on 16 November 1999 at Wilfrid Laurier University.

9 Being in between cultures is a common theme in Asian American literatures (see Amy Ling and Misha Berson).

10 Chow was referring to Zhang Yimou's films about rural and feudal China.

2 A Filipino Prufrock in an Alien Land: Bienvenido Santos's *The Man Who (Thought He) Looked Like Robert Taylor*

1 In attempting to determine what 'Filipino American' means, N.V.M Gonzalez notes that because of the history of American colonization of the Philippines, 'in the United States ... Philippine-born or not, the Filipino straddles, perforce, two cultures and two histories' (65).

2 In his pioneering essay on Filipino literature in the United States, Oscar Campomanes argues that 'motifs of departure, nostalgia, incompletion, rootlessness, leave taking, and dispossession recur with force in most writing produced by Filipinos in the United States and by Filipino Americans, with the Philippines as either the original or terminal reference point' (51). While some of these motifs are present in *The Man Who (Thought He) Looked Like Robert Taylor*, I hesitate to categorize the novel as fitting into what Campomanes calls a 'literature of exile and emergence rather than a literature of immigration and settlement' (51) as this particular novel by Santos is precisely about the difficulties of immigration and settlement.

3 Donald Goellnicht has made a similar point about Chinese men: 'the restrictive and exclusionary laws instituted by the dominant white culture

against the Chinese had emasculated these immigrant men, forcing them into "feminine" subject positions of powerlessness and silence, into "bachelor" Chinatowns devoid of women and into "feminized" jobs that could not be filled by women' ('Tang Ao' 192).

4 Monica and Alipio's story is published in Santos's collection of short stories, *Scent of Apples*, as 'Immigration Blues' (3–20).

3 Rescripting Hollywood: Performativity and Ethnic Identity in Mina Shum's *Double Happiness*

1 Filipina domestic workers were formally recruited to Hong Kong and women constitute a majority (83.3 per cent) of Filipino migrants there (see Parreñas 2, 38). The number of domestic workers was estimated at between 130,000 and 150,000 by the mid-1990s (Parreñas 39).

2 These interruptions are not unlike those in films like Martin Scorsese's *Taxi Driver* (1976) and Woody Allen's *Manhattan* (1979), as some of my graduate students point out. I am grateful to Ellen Vincer for bringing up these parallels.

3 Bakhtin used the term 'heteroglossia' to discuss how a novel could incorporate a number of voices, sometimes serving 'two speakers at the same time and express[ing] simultaneously two different intentions' (*Dialogic Imagination* 324). I argue that Shum is also attempting to use such double-voiced techniques in her narrative.

4 Jacques Derrida uses spectralization to describe 'the incarnation of an ideational or phantomatic form in an aphysical body that is then taken on as the real body of a living and finite being' (as paraphrased by Cheah 146).

5 I am thinking of the novels of Ann Radcliffe, where rapacious and tyrannical father figures abound. In *The Mysteries of Udolpho* (1794), for example, Montoni refuses to let Emily leave his castle and go back to France, while the priest and father figure Dorriforth, in Elizabeth Inchbald's *A Simple Story* (1791), banishes his wife, Miss Milner, and her daughter when they displease him.

4 To Make Sense of Differences: Communities, Texts, and Bodies in Shirley Geok-lin Lim's *Among the White Moon Faces*

1 The term 'peranakan' is used among ethnic Chinese in Indonesia, Malaysia, and Singapore to 'refer to the native-born Chinese who have gradually lost their mother tongue and cultural characteristics. *Peranakans* may

speak the indigenous language of the host country (or a creolized version of it), observe some very old Chinese customs and ceremonies as well as acquiring indigenous ones, and are regarded by both the unassimilated Chinese migrants ... and the indigenous people as belonging to neither group' (Wu 160).

2 Rugg says, 'When I view the list of names representing the war dead on the facade of the country courthouse in a certain town in Tennessee, I am "remembering" men who died long before my own birth, and additionally (because some of the names are listed under the heading "Colored"), I remember something of our sad history that the makers of the memorial might not have intended' (25).

5 'Some Memories Live Only on Your Tongue': Recalling Tastes, Reclaiming Desire in Amy Tan's *The Kitchen God's Wife*

1 This structure is also found in Tan's more recent works such as *The Bone-setter's Daughter*, where Luling Young's stories from old China are juxtaposed with her daughter Ruth's contemporary life in San Francisco.

2 Sau-Ling Cynthia Wong notes of the structure of this novel in comparison to *The Joy Luck Club* that 'the daughter's role is ancillary. The staggered framework has given way to a sandwiching of the mother's tale, which forms the bulk of the novel, between two thin slices of the daughter's life. The daughter's presence, its countervailing function almost reduced to irrelevance, is now little more than a conduit for the True Word from mother, a pretext for Winnie's outpouring' ('Sugar Sisterhood,' 197). Another critic, Yuan-Yuan, emphasizes the imaginary aspects of China, as it is a 'semiotic space of recollection,' and 'is reconfigured into a variety of discourses: myth, legend, history, and fantasy' (353).

3 Homi Bhabha notes that: ' Hybridity is the sign of the productivity of colonial power, its shifting forces and fixities ... Hybridity is the revaluation of the assumption of colonial identity through the repetition of discriminatory identity effects ... For the colonial hybrid is the articulation of the ambivalent space where the rite of power is enacted on the site of desire, making its objects at once disciplinary and disseminatory – or, in my mixed metaphor, a negative transparency' (112).

4 Sigmund Freud used the term 'overdetermined' to refer to those hysterical symptoms that he traced to infantile sexual scenes (108). I employ the term to suggest the same psychic phenomenon – that certain actions have exaggerated importance because of their link to childhood psyche and emotional development.

5 The first chapter of Sau-ling Wong's *Reading Asian American Literature* discusses alimentary motifs. Although Wong looks at certain scenes in *The Joy Luck Club*, she mentions *The Kitchen God's Wife* only in passing.

6 I have studied the means by which cooking and food are problematically linked to the exoticization of the Old World in recent films by Asian directors (see Ty, 'Exoticism Repositioned').

7 Wong plays with the meaning of assimilation: 'Instead of *assimilating to* the dominant society – that is, allowing the circumstances controlled by those in power to overwhelm them – the experts in "eating bitterness" *assimilate* even the most unpromising material for their own sustenance. Thus is the external transformed into the internal, the alien overcome, and life, continuity, ensured' (*Reading* 77).

8 Rey Chow notes that 'primitive passions emerge not simply because of the love of what is past or old; they are not simply feelings of nostalgia. Rather, they involve a *coeval, co-temporal* structure of representation at moments of cultural crisis' (*Primitive Passions* 43).

9 In contemporary China as in old China, sons are still prized highly over daughters. Sons are believed to be the ones who will support their parents in old age. As one woman notes, 'No sons is bad. There is nobody to take care of them when they are sick. Nobody to bring them food or boil water for them. That is a bad thing' (Wolf 196).

10 Wolf observes that Chinese women 'have always been judged by their accomplishments in the home ... their self-image and that held by their kin and friends will continue to be tied to their domestic roles' (219).

6 'Each Story Brief and Sad and Marvellous': Multiple Voices in Wayson Choy's *The Jade Peony*

1 In his study of *The Joy Luck Club*, Stephen Souris uses the term 'multiple monologue narratives' to situate Tan's novel in the context of other novels such as Woolf's *The Waves* and Faulkner's *The Sound and the Fury, As I Lay Dying*, and *Absalom, Absalom!* as novels that employ a decentred, multi-perspectival form (99).

2 In her study of the use of the short-story cycle by Asian Americans and Asian Canadians, Rocío Davis looks at *The Jade Peony* with a different focus. For her, 'the three novellas develop central motifs to create one overreaching presence: Chinatown itself' (200).

3 In an interview with Glenn Deer, Wayson Choy said, 'I really wanted to write a book about survivors. I wanted to write a book about people who were decent and who survived' (41).

4 Looking at *The Jade Peony* and the question of 'Chineseness,' Christopher Lee notes that 'Choy interrogates the process of becoming Chinese, linking ethnic identity formation with various power structures such as the family and the Chinese community-at-large' (19). Our points about the complexities of ethnic identification are similar, but I explore representations of ethnicity rather than the construction of Chineseness. Lee's essay focuses mainly on the third part of the book while I look at the all three sections.

5 Though Aijaz Ahmad has criticized Jameson's generalizations, the point about the conflation of the private and the public world is still perceived to be true for non-white writers.

6 The term originated with Frank Chin, who sees food pornography as an exploitation of the exotic aspects of one's ethnic foodways through exaggeration (see Wong, *Reading* 55).

7 Maria Ng notes that one of the ways in which Choy attempts to 'illustrate the complexity of Chinese Canadianness' is through the use of 'character naming and dialogue ... Choy does not hesitate to flesh out his story with both hard-to-pronounce and hard-to-remember names. His prose is also made (intentionally?) awkward by a mixture of transliteration and unidiomatic English' (174, 180–1).

8 I bring up the example of this well-known African American novel to show similarities in the construction of racialized subjectivity in North America. In her comparative study of Asian American and African American texts, Anne Anlin Cheng points out that 'to propose that the minority may have been profoundly affected by racial fantasies is not to lock him/her back into the stereotypes but to perform the more important task of unraveling the deeper identificatory operations – and seductions – produced by those projections. The "truth" of "Asian Americanness" or "African Americanness" has always been and will continue to be a site of contestation for both those raced subjects as well as for whites' (106).

9 Several stories in Judy Fong Bates's collection are set in Chinese laundries in small towns in Ontario.

10 TuSmith points out that there is a 'myth of individualism and a parallel myth of community in the broad American culture,' but that the first myth is usually considered romantic and heroic. Ethnic writers, however, 'have an alternative vision.' They identify much more strongly with their ethnic cultural community (22).

11 Silverman notes that 'social norms play an important role in the mirror stage, and that the child's identity is from the very beginning culturally mediated' (*Subject* 160).

12 While the setting of this scene pre-dates the multicultural policies of the

1970s, Choy, like many other Canadians, is very much a product and supporter of these liberal policies that stress the harmonious cointeraction and cohabitation of various races and ethnicities. That this harmony entails a loss or repression of the language, culture, and religion of those who are not English, French, or Christian has only recently become a topic of open discussion by Choy and others. In a recent lecture, he talked about growing up as a 'banana,' white on the inside, but yellow on the outside, and related it to similar experiences of Native children, who were McIntosh apples, red on the outside and white on the inside, and also to Caribbean Canadians, who were Oreo cookies, black on the outside and white on the inside (reading and lecture, Wilfrid Laurier University, 18 November 2002).

7 'Never Again Be the Yvonne of Yesterday': Personal and Collective Loss in Cecilia Brainard's *When the Rainbow Goddess Wept*

1 Cecilia Manguerra Brainard, *Song of Yvonne* (Quezon City: New Day Publishers, 1991), was subsequently reissued as *When the Rainbow Goddess Wept* (New York: Dutton, 1994). Unless otherwise noted, quotations in the body of the essay will be from the American edition.
2 Hollywood movies about the involvement of the Philippines in the Second World War include *Bataan* (1943), starring Robert Taylor and directed by Tay Garnett, and *Corregidor* (1943), starring Otto Kruger and Elissa Landi and directed by William Nigh. In accounts of the Philippines and the Second World War in American history, the heroism of American soldiers and the role played by General Douglas MacArthur are usually highlighted. For example, see William Manchester, *American Caesar*, and the accounts found in the U.S. Army Center for Military History. Brainard brings in the local perspective from residents of Cebu.
3 In Chai's novel, the hardships endured by Filipinos during the Japanese occupation are also related in flashbacks or through stories told by the mother to her daughter. There are similar accounts of Japanese cruelty in the narratives.
4 Shortly after the Japanese attacked Pearl Harbor, they destroyed American air power on the ground at Clark Field. Philippine-American land forces yielded to the much smaller Japanese expeditionary force and were rapidly driven back to Bataan and Corregidor, where they managed to hold out for six months. See Theodore Friend, 'Philippine-American Tensions in History' (13).

5 Boehmer was writing about Chinua Achebe at this point.
6 In *Song of Yvonne*, this desire is expressed as 'balete trees and bamboos lining the river banks, tigbaws laden with golden flowers rippling under the hot sun, betel nut groves in nearby valleys' (63).
7 See Pomeroy, *The Philippines* (2). Others report a much higher figure. Mark Twain was amazed at the report that 'thirty thousand American soldiers killed a million Filipinos' and commented, 'It seems a pity that the historian let that get out; it is really a most embarrassing circumstance,' as paraphrased by Epifanio San Juan, Jr ('Postcolonial Theory' 32).
8 In an essay titled 'Someday I'll Visit Valparaiso,' Brainard writes that her father was in engineering classes at Valparaiso University' (7).
9 For example, see Consolacíon Alaras, 'The Concept of English Studies in the Philippines' (22).

8 'Thrumming Songs of Ecstasy': Female Voices in Hiromi Goto's *Chorus of Mushrooms*

1 Linda Hutcheon has noted that 'postmodern texts tend to make very self-conscious their writing, their reading, and the various contexts in which both acts take place,' which can 'make problematic such issues at gender, authority, facts, and subjectivity' (*Canadian Postmodern*, 17–18).
2 Goto herself was born in Japan in 1966 and immigrated to Canada with her family at the age of three. Unlike Kogawa, whose family experienced internment, Goto was part of the post-1965 wave of immigrants.
3 In her later works, Goto similarly plays with myths and fantasies. Her book for children, *The Water of Possibility*, and her second novel, *The Kappa Child*, both use myth and fantasy, and the figure of the kappa, a Japanese water sprite.
4 Libin notes that 'the repeated invocation of this formalized opening phrase demonstrates the impossibility of a singular beginning' (127).
5 A number of critics have noted Naomi's difficulty with self-expression (see, for example, Goellnicht, 'Father Land,' Manina Jones, and Ty, 'Struggling with the Powerful (M)Other').
6 Interestingly, another Japanese Canadian novel, *The Electrical Field* by Kerri Sakamoto, similarly depicts protagonists with troubled sexual lives. Sakamoto's characters are also trying to pick up the pieces of their lives after the Japanese internment. Miss Saito, also a 'spinster,' is haunted by her childhood experiences and takes an unusual amount of interest in her

Japanese Canadian neighbours' private lives. The adulterous Chisako is found murdered, while Miss Saito's young friend, Sachi, frequently has inexplicable self-inflicted cuts on her body.

9 'On the Fence That Was Never Finished': Borderline Filipino Existence in Bino Realuyo's *The Umbrella Country*

1 Evidence for a 1970s setting lies in the novel's mention of Miss Spain as the winner of the Miss Universe contest. Amparo Munoz from Spain won the title in 1974.
2 American television game show host, best known for *The Price Is Right*.
3 I would like to acknowledge the ideas of my students in my class of Fall 2000, 'Contemporary Asian Writers in the Diaspora.' In particular, Jennifer Bell and Carrie Villeneuve discussed the prevalence and use of stateside products in Realuyo's novel.
4 At the end of the novel, Mommy Estrella betrays the children by not going with them to America. Her domestic 'betrayal' paradoxically signals her loyalty to her motherland. In *Betrayal and Other Acts of Subversion*, Leslie Bow notes that 'ethnic and national affiliation are determined in part by conflicts over how sexuality is performed, potentially situating the female body as a register of international and domestic political struggle, as a site of national divisions and loyalties' (10).
5 For a study of how Filipino women are exported as mail-order brides, cheap transnational labour, and nurses, see Rolando Tolentino.

Afterword

1 I am being selective in what I choose to highlight from Oliver's text. In her concluding chapters, she also speaks of love, of the look of love, and of the loving eye (215, 219).
2 I am thinking, for example, of martial arts skills associated with Lucy Liu in *Charlie's Angels* and Jackie Chan in the *Rush Hour* movies.

Works Cited

Abao, Frances Jane. 'Retelling the Stories, Rewriting the Bildungsroman: Cecilia Manguerra Brainard's *When the Rainbow Goddess Wept.' Humanities Diliman* 3.1 (2001): (1–14).

Adachi, Ken. *The Enemy That Never Was: A History of Japanese Canadians* (1976). Introduction by Timothy Findley. Afterword by Roger Daniels. Toronto: McClelland and Stewart, 1991.

Ahmad, Aijaz. 'Jameson's Rhetoric of Otherness and the "National Allegory."' *Social Text* 17 (Fall 1987): 3–25.

Alaras, Consolacion R. 'The Concept of English Studies in the Philippines.' *Philippine Post-Colonial Studies: Essays on Language and Literature.* Ed. Cristina Pantoja Hidalgo and Priscelina Patajo-Legasto. Quezon City: University of the Philippines Press, 1993.

Anderson, Benedict. *Imagined Communities: Reflections on the Origin and Spread of Nationalism.* London: Verso, 1983, rpt. 7th impression, 1996.

Ang, Ien. 'On Not Speaking Chinese: Postmodern Ethnicity and the Politics of Diaspora.' *New Formations* 24 (1994): 1–18.

Appiah, Anthony. 'The Uncompleted Argument: Du Bois and the Illusion of Race.' *'Race,' Writing, and Difference.* Ed. Henry Louis Gates, Jr. Chicago: University of Chicago Press, 1986. 21–37.

Bakhtin, M.M. *The Dialogic Imagination: Four Essays.* Ed. Michael Holquist. Austin: University of Texas Press, 1981.

– *Rabelais and His World.* Trans. Helene Iswolsky. Cambridge, Mass.: MIT Press, 1968.

Bannerji, Himani. 'The Paradox of Diversity: The Construction of a Multicultural Canada and "Women of Color."' *Women's Studies International Forum* 23.5 (2000): 537–60.

Bannerji, Himani, ed. *Returning the Gaze: Essays on Racism, Feminism and Politics*. Toronto: Sister Vision Press, 1993.

Banton, Michael. *Racial Theories*. Cambridge: Cambridge University Press, 1987.

Barthes, Roland. *Camera Lucida*. Trans. Richard Howard. London: Jonathan Cape, 1981.

Bates, Judy Fong. *China Dog and Other Tales from a Chinese Laundry*. Toronto: Sister Vision, 1997.

Beauregard, Guy. 'The Emergence of "Asian Canadian Literature": Can Lit's Obscene Supplement?' *Essays on Canadian Writing* 67 (Spring 1999): 53–75. 23 pars.

– 'Hiromi Goto's *Chorus of Mushrooms* and the Politics of Writing Diaspora.' *West Coast Line* 29.3 (1995/96): 47–62.

Bell, Shannon. *Reading, Writing and Rewriting the Prostitute Body*. Bloomington: Indiana University Press, 1994.

Bergland, Betty Ann. 'Representing Ethnicity in Autobiography: Narratives of Opposition.' *Yearbook of English Studies* 24 (1994): 67–93.

Berson, Misha, ed. *Between Worlds: Contemporary Asian-American Plays*. New York: Theatre Communications Group, 1990.

Bhabha, Homi K. *The Location of Culture*. London & New York: Routledge, 1994.

Boehmer, Elleke. *Colonial and Postcolonial Literature: Migrant Metaphors*. Oxford: Oxford University Press, 1995.

Bottomley, Gillian. 'Culture, Ethnicity, and the Politics/Poetics of Representation.' *Diaspora* 1.3 (Fall 1991): 303–20.

Bourdieu, Pierre. *Photography: A Middle-brow Art*. Trans. Shaun Whiteside. Stanford: Stanford University Press, 1990.

Bow, Leslie. *Betrayal and Other Acts of Subversion: Feminism, Sexual Politics, Asian American Women's Literature*. Princeton: Princeton University Press, 2001.

Brainard, Cecilia Manguerra, ed. *Contemporary Fiction by Filipinos in America*. Manila: Anvil, 1997.

– 'Someday I'll Visit Valparaiso.' *Philippine Woman in America*. Quezon City: New Day, 1991.

– *Song of Yvonne*. Quezon City: New Day, 1991

– *When the Rainbow Goddess Wept*. New York: Dutton, 1994.

– *Woman with Horns and Other Stories*. Quezon City: New Day, 1987.

Brainard, Cecilia Manguerra, and Edmundo F. Litton, eds. *Journey of 100 Years: Reflections on the Centennial of Philippine Independence*. Santa Monica, Calif.: Philippine American Literary House, 1999.

Brennan, Teresa. *The Interpretation of the Flesh: Freud and Femininity*. London: Routledge, 1992.

Brown, Linda, and Kay Mussell. *Ethnic and Regional Foodways in the United States: The Performance of Group Identity*. Knoxville: University of Tennessee Press, 1984.

Bulosan, Carlos. *America Is in the Heart: A Personal History* (1946). Seattle: University of Washington Press, 1973.

Butler, Judith. *Bodies That Matter: On the Discursive Limits of 'Sex.'* New York: Routledge, 1993.

– 'Performative Acts and Gender Constitution: An Essay in Phenomenology and Feminist Theory.' *Writing on the Body: Female Embodiment and Feminist Theory*. Eds. Katie Conboy, Nadia Medina, and Sarah Stanbury. New York: Columbia University Press, 1997. 401–17.

Campomanes, Oscar. 'Filipinos in the United States and Their Literature of Exile.' *Reading the Literatures of Asian America*. Eds. Shirley Geok-lin Lim and Amy Ling. Philadelphia: Temple University Press, 1992. 49–78.

Casper, Leonard. 'Paperboat Novels: The Later Bienvenido N. Santos.' *Amerasia Journal* 13.1 (1986–7): 163–70.

– '*Song of Yvonne*: Possibilities of Humanities in an Age of Slaughter,' *Philippine Studies* 41/2nd Quarter (1993): 251–4.

Chai, Arlene. *The Last Time I Saw Mother*. New York: Fawcett Columbine, 1995.

Chan, Kenyon S. 'Rethinking the Asian American Studies Project: Bridging the Divide between "Campus" and "Community."' *Journal of Asian American Studies* 3.1 (February 2000): 17–36.

Chan, Sucheng. *Asian Americans: An Interpretive History*. New York: Twayne's Immigrant Heritage of America Series, 1991.

– 'The Exclusion of Chinese Women, 1870–1943.' *Entry Denied: Exclusion and the Chinese Community in America, 1882–1943*. Ed. Sucheng Chan. Philadelphia: Temple University Press, 1991. 94–146.

Chao, Lien. *Beyond Silence: Chinese Canadian Literature in English*. Toronto: Tsar, 1997.

Cheah, Pheng. 'Chinese Cosmopolitanism in Two Senses and Postcolonial National Memory.' *Cosmopolitan Geographies: New Locations in Literature and Culture*. Ed. Vinay Dharwadker. New York: Routledge, 2001. 133–69.

Cheng, Anne Anlin. *The Melancholy of Race: Psychoanalysis, Assimilation, and Hidden Grief*. New York: Oxford University Press, 2000.

Cheung, King-Kok. *Articulate Silences: Hisaye Yamamoto, Maxine Hong Kingston, Joy Kogawa*. Ithaca: Cornell University Press, 1993.

– '"Don't Tell": Imposed Silences in *The Color Purple* and *The Woman Warrior*.' *PMLA* 103.2 (1988): 162–74.

Cheung, King-Kok, ed. *An Interethnic Companion to Asian American Literature.* New York: Cambridge University Press, 1997.

Chong, Denise. 'Being Canadian' [The First Clifford Sifton Lecture, Vancouver]. *Globe and Mail.* 20 April 1995. A29.

– *The Concubine's Children.* Toronto: Penguin Books, 1994.

– 'The Fiction in Non-fiction' [excerpts from the Fifth Annual Merle Shain Memorial Lecture]. *Quill & Quire* 62.4 (April 1996): 11.

– Reading and lecture. Wilfrid Laurier University. 20 November 1995.

Chow, Rey. *Primitive Passions: Visuality, Sexuality, Ethnography, and Contemporary Chinese Cinema.* New York: Columbia University Press, 1995.

– *Woman and Chinese Modernity: The Politics of Reading between West and East.* Minneapolis: University of Minnesota Press, 1991.

– *Writing Diaspora: Tactics of Intervention in Contemporary Cultural Studies.* Bloomington: Indiana University Press, 1993.

Choy, Wayson. *The Jade Peony.* Vancouver: Douglas and McIntyre, 1995.

– *Paper Shadows: A Chinatown Childhood.* Toronto: Penguin, 1999.

Chu, Patricia. *Assimilating Asians: Gendered Strategies of Authorship in Asian America.* Durham, N.C.: Duke University Press, 2000.

Cixous, Hélène, and Catherine Clément. 'Sorties: Out and Out: Attacks/Ways Out/Forays.' *The Newly Born Woman.* Trans. Betsy Wing. Minneapolis: University of Minnesota Press, 1986.

Collins, Patricia Hill. 'Shifting the Center: Race, Class, and Feminist Theorizing about Motherhood.' *Representations of Motherhood.* Ed. Donna Bassin, Margaret Honey, and Meryle Mahrer Kaplan. New Haven: Yale University Press, 1994. 56–74.

Counihan, Carole, and Penny Van Esterik. *Food and Culture: A Reader.* New York and London: Routledge, 1997.

Davis, Leonard. *The Philippines: People, Poverty and Politics.* Houndmills and London: Macmillan, 1987.

Davis, Rocío G. *Transcultural Reinventions: Asian American and Asian Canadian Short-Story Cycles.* Toronto: TSAR, 2001.

De Lauretis, Teresa. *Alice Doesn't: Feminism, Semiotics, Cinema.* Bloomington: Indiana University Press, 1984.

De Van, Gilles. 'Fin de Siècle Exoticism and the Meaning of the Far Away.' Trans. William Ashbrook. *Opera Quarterly* 11.3 (1995): 77–84.

Deer, Glenn. 'Asian North America in Transit.' *Canadian Literature* 163 Asian Canadian Writing (Winter 1999): 5–15.

– 'An Interview with Wayson Choy.' *Canadian Literature* 163 Asian Canadian Writing (Winter 1999): 34–44.

Derrida, Jacques. *A Derrida Reader: Between the Blinds.* Ed. Peggy Kamuf. New York: Columbia University Press, 1991.

Double Happiness. Dir. Mina Shum. National Film Board, 1995.

Dyer, Richard. 'Don't Look Now: The Male Pin-Up.' *The Sexual Subject: A Screen Reader in Sexuality*. London and New York: Routledge, 1992. 265–76.

Eliot, T.S. 'The Love Song of J. Alfred Prufrock,' 'The Waste Land.' *Norton Anthology of English Literature: Major Authors*. 5th ed. Ed. M.H. Abrams. New York: Norton, 1987. 2504–7, 2511–26.

Ellison, Ralph. *Invisible Man*. New York: Random House, 1947.

Eng, David L. *Racial Castration: Managing Masculinity in Asian America*. Durham, N.C.: Duke University Press, 2001.

Espiritu, Yen Le. *Asian American Women and Men*. Thousand Oaks, Calif.: Sage Publications, 1997.

Fanon, Frantz. 'On National Culture.' *Colonial Discourse and Post-Colonial Theory: A Reader*. Ed. Patrick Williams and Laura Chrisman. New York: Columbia University Press, 1994. 36–52.

Flitterman-Lewis, Sandy. 'To Desire Differently: Feminism and the French Cinema.' *Film and Theory, An Anthology*. Ed. Robert Stam and Toby Miller. Malden, Mass: Blackwell, 2000.

Fong, Timothy P. *The Contemporary Asian American Experience: Beyond the Model Minority*. Upper Saddle River, N.J.: Prentice Hall, 1998.

Foucault, Michel. *The History of Sexuality: An Introduction*. Vol. 1. Trans. Robert Hurley. New York: Vintage, 1990.

– *Madness and Civilization: A History of Insanity in the Age of Reason* (1965). New York: Vintage, 1988.

– *The Order of Things: An Archaeology of the Human Sciences*. New York: Vintage, 1973.

Frankenberg, Ruth. *White Women, Race Matters: The Social Construction of Whiteness*. Minneapolis: University of Minnesota Press, 1993.

Freud, Sigmund. 'The Aetiology of Hysteria.' *The Freud Reader*. Ed. Peter Gay. New York: W.W. Norton, 1989. 96–111.

– 'Three Essays on the Theory of Sexuality.' Ed. Peter Gay. New York: W.W. Norton, 1989. 239–91.

Friend, Theodore. *The Blue-Eyed Enemy Japan against the West in Java and Luzon, 1942–1945*. Princeton: Princeton University Press, 1988.

– 'Philippine-American Tensions in History.' *Crisis in the Philippines: The Marcos Era and Beyond*. Ed. John Bresnan. Princeton: Princeton University Press, 1986. 3–29.

Gilroy, Paul. *There Ain't No Black in the Union Jack*. London: Hutchinson, 1987.

Goellnicht, Donald. 'Father Land and/or Mother Tongue: The Divided Female Subject in Kogawa's *Obasan* and Hong Kingston's *The Woman Warrior*.' *Redefining Autobiography in Twentieth-Century Women's Fiction*. Ed. Janice

Morgan, Colette T. Hall, and Carol L. Snyder. Foreword by Molly Hite. New York: Garland, 1991. 119–34.

– 'A Long Labour: The Protracted Birth of Asian Canadian Literature.' *Essays on Canadian Writing* 72 (Winter 2000): 1–41.

– 'Tang Ao in America: Male Subject Positions in *China Men*.' *Reading the Literatures of Asian America*. Ed. Shirley Geok-lin Lim and Amy Ling. Philadelphia: Temple University Press, 1992. 191–212.

Gonzalez, N.V.M., and Oscar V. Campomanes. 'Filipino American Literature.' *An Interethnic Companion to Asian American Literature*. Ed. King-Kok Cheung. New York: Cambridge University Press, 1997. 62–124.

Gordon, Richard. *Bataan, Corregidor, and the Death March: In Retrospect*. 14 January 2003. http://home.pacbell.net/fbaldie/In_Retrospect.html.

Goto, Hiromi. 'Alien Texts, Alien Seductions: The Context of Colour Full Writing.' *Literary Pluralities*. Ed. Christl Verduyn. Peterborough, Ont.: Broadview Press, 1998. 263–9.

– *Chorus of Mushrooms*. Edmonton: NeWest Press, 1994.

– *The Kappa Child*. Calgary: Red Deer Press, 2001.

– 'Translating the Self: Moving Between Cultures.' *West Coast Line*. 22 (30/2) (Fall 1996): 111–13.

– *The Water of Possibility*. Regina, Sask.: Coteau Books, 2001.

Grene, Nicholas. 'Shavian History.' *George Bernard Shaw: Modern Critical Views*. Ed. Harold Bloom. New York: Chelsea House Publishers, 1987. 233–50.

Grosz, Elizabeth. 'The Body of Signification.' *Abjection, Melancholia and Love: The Work of Julia Kristeva*. Ed. John Fletcher and Andrew Benjamin. New York: Routledge, 1990. 80–103.

– *Jacques Lacan: A Feminist Introduction*. London and New York: Routledge, 1990.

– 'Voyeurism/Exhibitionism/The Gaze.' *Feminism and Psychoanalysis: A Critical Dictionary*. Ed. Elizabeth Wright. Oxford: Basil Blackwell, 1992. 447–50.

Gunew, Sneja. 'The Melting Pot of Assimilation: Cannibalizing the Multicultural Body.' *Transnational Asia Pacific: Gender, Culture, and the Public Sphere*. Ed. Shirley Geok-lin Lim, Larry E. Smith, and Wimal Dissanayake. Urbana: University of Illinois Press, 1999. 145–58.

Hagedorn, Jessica, ed. *Charlie Chan Is Dead: An Anthology of Contemporary Asian American Fiction*. New York: Penguin, 1993.

– *Dogeaters*. New York: Penguin, 1990.

Hall, Stuart. 'New Ethnicities.' *'Race,' Culture and Difference*. Ed. James Donald and Ali Rattansi. London: Sage, 1992.

Hamamoto, Darrell Y. *Monitored Peril: Asian Americans and the Politics of TV Representation.* Minneapolis: University of Minnesota Press, 1994.

Harvey, Monique. 'Achieving Double Happiness: An Interview with Mina Shum.' *The Peak.* http://www.peak.sfu.ca/the-peak/95–2/issue12/dblhap.html.

Heilbrun, Carolyn. *Writing a Woman's Life.* New York: Norton, 1988.

Hinz, Evelyn J. 'Mimesis: The Dramatic Lineage of Auto/Biography.' *Essays on Life Writing: From Genre to Critical Practice.* Ed. Marlene Kadar. Toronto: University of Toronto Press, 1992.

Hirsch, Marianne. *The Mother/Daughter Plot: Narrative, Psychoanalysis, Feminism.* Bloomington: Indiana University Press, 1989.

Horton, Jerry. Review of *The Jade Peony. Quill & Quire* 62.1 (Jan. 1996): 32.

Hutcheon, Linda. *The Canadian Postmodern: A Study of Contemporary English-Canadian Fiction.* Toronto: Oxford University Press, 1988.

– *A Poetics of Postmodernism: History, Theory, Fiction.* New York: Routledge, 1988.

Hutcheon, Linda, and Marion Richmond, eds. *Other Solitudes: Canadian Multicultural Fictions.* Toronto: Oxford University Press, 1990.

Inchbald, Elizabeth. *A Simple Story.* Ed. J.M.S. Tompkins, with an introduction by Jane Spencer. Oxford: World's Classics, 1988.

Irigaray, Luce. *Elemental Passions.* Trans. Joanne Collie and Judith Still. New York: Routledge, 1992.

– 'How Old Are You?' *Je, tu, nous: Toward a Culture of Difference.* Trans. Alison Martin. New York: Routledge, 1993. 113–17.

– *Speculum of the Other Woman.* Trans. Gillian C. Gill. Ithaca: Cornell University Press, 1985.

Jacobus, Mary. *Psychoanalysis and the Scene of Reading.* Oxford: Oxford University Press, 1999.

Jameson, Fredric. *The Political Unconscious: Narrative as a Socially-Symbolic Act.* Ithaca: Cornell University Press, 1981.

– 'Third World Literature in the Era of Multinational Capitalism.' *Social Text* 15 (Fall 1986). 64–88.

JanMohamed, Abdul R. 'The Economy of Manichean Allegory: The Function of Racial Difference in Colonialist Literature.' *'Race,' Writing, and Difference.* Ed. Henry Louis Gates, Jr. Chicago: University of Chicago Press, 1986. 78–106.

Jeffords, Susan. *The Remasculinization of America.* Bloomington: Indiana University Press, 1989.

Johnson, Brian D. 'A Bold and Blissful Leap of Faith.' *Maclean's* (31 July 1995): 42–4.

Jones, Manina. *That Art of Difference: 'Documentary-Collage' and English-Canadian Writing*. Toronto: University of Toronto Press, 1993.

Kamboureli, Smaro. *Scandalous Bodies: Diasporic Literature in English Canada*. Toronto: Oxford University Press, 2000.

Kaplan, E. Ann. *Looking for the Other: Feminism, Film, and the Imperial Gaze*. New York: Routledge, 1997.

Kellner, Douglas. *Media Culture: Cultural Studies, Identity and Politics between the Modern and Postmodern*. London and New York: Routledge, 1995.

Kim, Elaine. '"Such opposite creatures": Men and Women in Asian American Literature.' *Michigan Quarterly Review* 29 (1990): 68–93.

Kingston, Maxine Hong. *The Woman Warrior: Memoirs of a Girlhood among Ghosts*. New York: Vintage, 1977.

Kogawa, Joy. *Obasan*. Toronto: Penguin, 1981.

Kondo, Dorinne. *About Face: Performing Race in Fashion and Theater*. New York: Routledge, 1997.

Kristeva, Julia. *The Kristeva Reader*. Ed. Toril Moi. New York: Columbia University Press, 1986.

– *Powers of Horror: An Essay on Abjection*. Trans. Leon Roudiez. New York: Columbia University Press, 1982.

Lacan, Jacques. *Écrits: A Selection*. Trans. Alan Sheridan. New York: W.W. Norton, 1977.

– *The Four Fundamental Concepts of Psycho-Analysis*. Ed. Jacques-Alain Miller. Trans Alan Sheridan. New York: W.W. Norton, 1977.

Lee, Christopher. 'Engaging Chineseness in Wayson Choy's *The Jade Peony*.' *Canadian Literature* 163 Asian Canadian Writing (Winter 1999): 18–33.

Lee, Josephine. *Performing Asian America: Race and Ethnicity on the Contemporary Stage*. Philadelphia: Temple University Press, 1997.

Lee, Nancy. 'Telling Them Our Stories: Chinese-Canadian Biography as a Historical Genre.' *The Chinese in America: A History from Gold Mountain to the New Millennium*. Ed. Susie Lan Cassel. Walnut Creek, Calif.: Altamira Press, 2002. 106–21.

Lee, Rachel. *The Americas of Asian American Literature: Gendered Fictions of Nation and Transnation*. Princeton: Princeton University Press, 1999.

Lee, Robert G. *Orientals: Asian Americans in Popular Culture*. Philadelphia: Temple University Press, 1999.

Li, David Leiwei. *Imagining the Nation: Asian American Literature and Cultural Consent*. Stanford: Stanford University Press, 1998.

Li, Peter S. *Chinese in Canada*. 2nd ed. Toronto: Oxford University Press, 1998.

Libin, Mark. 'Lost in Translation: Hiromi Goto's *Chorus of Mushrooms*.' *Canadian Literature* 163 (Winter 1999): 121–40.

Lieu, Nhi T. 'Remembering "the Nation" through Pageantry: Femininity and the Politics of Vietnamese Womanhood in the *Hoa Hau Ao Dai* Contest.' *Frontiers: A Journal of Women's Studies* 21.1/2 (2000): 127–51.

Lim, Jaime An. 'Requiem for an Old Timer: B.N. Santos's *The Man Who (Thought He) Looked Like Robert Taylor.' Reading Bienvenido N. Santos.* Ed. Isagani R. Cruz and David Jonathan Bayot. Manila: De La Salle University Press, 1994. 262–75.

Lim, Shirley Geok-lin. *Among the White Moon Faces: An Asian-American Memoir of Homelands.* New York: Feminist Press, 1996.

– 'Asians in Anglo-American Feminism: Reciprocity and Resistance.' *Writing S.E./ Asia in English: Against the Grain.* London: Skoob Books, 1994. 31–44.

– *Crossing the Peninsula and Other Poems.* Kuala Lumpur: Heinemann Education Books, 1980.

– 'The English-Language Writer in Singapore (1940s–1980s).' *Writing S.E./ Asia in English: Against the Grain.* London: Skoob Books, 1994. 107–34.

– 'Immigration and Diaspora.' *An Interethnic Companion to Asian American Literature.* Ed. King-Kok Cheung. New York: Cambridge University Press, 1997.

– *Nationalism and Literature: English-Language Writing from the Philippines and Singapore.* Quezon City: New Day, 1983.

– 'Semiotics, Experience, and the Material Self: An Inquiry into the Subject of the Contemporary Asian Woman Writer.' *Women, Autobiography, Theory: A Reader.* Ed. Sidonie Smith and Julia Watson. Madison: University of Wisconsin Press, 1998. 441–52.

Lim, Shirley Geok-lin, and Amy Ling, ed. *Reading the Literatures of Asian America.* Philadelphia: Temple University Press, 1992.

Ling, Amy. *Between Worlds: Women Writers of Chinese Ancestry.* New York: Pergamon Press, 1990.

Ling, Jinqi. *Narrating Nationalisms: Ideology and Form in Asian American Literature.* New York: Oxford University Press, 1998.

Lowe, Lisa. *Critical Terrains: French and British Orientalisms.* Ithaca: Cornell University Press, 1991.

– 'Heterogeneity, Hybridity, Multiplicity: Marking Asian American Differences.' *Diaspora* 1.1 (Spring 1991): 24–44.

– *Immigrant Acts: On Asian American Cultural Politics.* Durham, N.C.: Duke University Press, 1996.

Ma, Sheng-mei. *The Deathly Embrace: Orientalism and Asian American Identity.* Minneapolis: University of Minnesota Press, 2000.

– *Immigrant Subjectivities in Asian American and Asian Diaspora Literatures.* Albany: State University of New York Press, 1998.

Manchester, William Raymond. *American Caesar: Douglas MacArthur, 1880–1964.* Boston: Little Brown, 1978.

Marchetti, Gina. *Romance and the 'Yellow Peril': Race, Sex, and Discursive Strategies in Hollywood Fiction.* Berkeley: University of California Press, 1993.

Maynard, Mary. '"Race," Gender and the Concept of "Difference" in Feminist Thought.' *Feminism and 'Race.'* Ed. Kum-Kum Bhavnani. Oxford: Oxford University Press, 2001. 121–33.

McClintock, Anne. *Imperial Leather: Race, Gender and Sexuality in the Colonial Contest.* London: Routledge, 1995.

Miki, Roy. 'Asiancy: Making Space for Asian Canadian Writing.' *Broken Entries: Race, Subjectivity, Writing.* Toronto: Mercury Press, 1998. 101–24.

Mills, Sara. *Discourse.* London: Routledge New Critical Idiom, 1997.

Mohanty, Satya P. *Literary Theory and the Claims of History: Postmodernism, Objectivity, Multicultural Politics.* Ithaca: Cornell University Press, 1997.

Morgan, Margery M. *The Shavian Playground: An Exploration of the Art of George Bernard Shaw.* London: Methuen, 1972.

Morrison, Toni. *Beloved.* New York: Penguin Plume, 1988.

– *The Bluest Eye.* New York: Plume, 1994.

Mukherjee, Arun P. 'Teaching Ethnic Minority Writing: A Report from the Classroom.' *Literary Pluralities.* Ed. Christl Verduyn. Peterborough, Ont.: Broadview Press, 1998. 162–71.

Mulvey, Laura. *Visual and Other Pleasures.* Bloomington: Indiana University Press, 1989.

Nadel, Alan. *Invisible Criticism: Ralph Ellison and the American Canon.* Iowa City: University of Iowa Press, 1988.

Naves, Elaine Kalman. 'An Ocean Made of Tears.' *Montreal Gazette.* 16 March 1996: Ii.

Ng, Maria N. 'Chop Suey Writing: Sui Sin Far, Wayson Choy, and Judy Fong Bates.' *Essays on Canadian Writing* 65 (Fall 1998): 171–86.

Nguyen, Viet Thanh. *Race and Resistance: Literature and Politics in Asian America.* New York: Oxford University Press, 2002.

Okihiro, Gary Y. 'Is Yellow Black or White?' *Asian Americans: Experiences and Perspectives.* Ed. Timothy P. Fong and Larry H. Shinagawa. Upper Saddle River, N.J.: Prentice-Hall, 2000. 63–78.

Oliver, Kelly. *Witnessing Beyond Recognition.* Minneapolis: University of Minnesota Press, 2001.

Omi, Michael, and Howard Winant. 'On the Theoretical Status of the Concept of Race.' *Asian American Studies: A Reader.* Ed. Jean Yu-wen Shen Wu and Min Song. New Brunswick, N.J.: Rutgers University Press, 2000. 199–208.

– *Racial Formation in the United States: From the 1960's to the 1980's.* New York: Routledge and Kegan Paul, 1986.

Ommundsen, Wenche, ed. *Bastard Moon: Essays on Chinese-Australian Writing.* Special Issue. *Otherland Literary Journal* 7 (2001).

Ong, Aihwa. *Flexible Citizenship: The Cultural Logics of Transnationality*. Durham, N.C.: Duke University Press, 1999.

Padolsky, Enoch. 'Ethnicity and Race: Canadian Minority Writing at a Cross-roads.' *Literary Pluralities*. Ed. Christl Verduyn. Peterborough, Ont.: Broadview Press, 1998. 19–36.

Palumbo-Liu, David. *Asian/American Historical Crossings of a Racial Frontier*. Stanford: Stanford University Press, 1999.

– 'The Minority Self as Other: Problematics of Representation in Asian-American Literature.' *Cultural Critique* 28 (Fall 1994): 75–102.

Parreñas, Rhacel Salazar. *Servants of Globalization: Women, Migration, and Domestic Work*. Stanford: Stanford University Press, 2001.

Phelan, Peggy. *Unmarked: The Politics of Performance*. London and New York: Routledge, 1993.

Philippine Women Centre of B.C. *Canada: The New Frontier for Filipino Mail-Order Brides*. Ottawa: Status of Women Policy Research, 2000.

Phillips, Gene D. *The Films of Tennessee Williams*. East Brunswick, N.J.: Associated University Presses, 1980.

Pomeroy, William J. *The Philippines: Colonialism, Collaboration, and Resistance*. New York: International Publishers, 1992.

Posadas, Barbara M. 'Crossed Boundaries in Interracial Chicago: Pilipino American Families since 1925.' *Amerasia Journal* 8.2 (1981): 31–52.

Pratt, Mary Louise. *Imperial Eyes: Travel Writing and Transculturation*. New York: Routledge, 1992.

Quigley, Ellen. 'Unveiling the Ghost: Denise Chong's Feminist Negotiations of Confucian Autobiography in *The Concubine's Children*.' *Essays on Canadian Writing* 63 (Spring 1998): 237–53.

Radcliffe, Ann. *The Mysteries of Udolpho*. Ed. Bonamy Dobrée. Oxford: World's Classics, 1980.

Realuyo, Bino. 'Bino Realuyo's Homepage.' 20 February 2001. http://www.geocities.com/realuyo/.

– 'A Conversation with Bino Realuyo.' *The Umbrella Country*. New York: Ballantine Books, 1999. 303–7.

– *The Umbrella Country*. New York: Ballantine Books, 1999.

Recto, Claro M. 'Our Lingering Colonial Complex.' Address Delivered before the Baguio Press Association, 1951. *Philippine Contemporary Literature in English and Filipino* (1962). 6th ed. Ed. Asuncion David-Maramba. Makati: Bookmark, 1993.

Rimonte, Nilda. 'Colonialism's Legacy: The Inferiorizing of the Filipino.' *Filipino Americans: Transformation and Identity*. Ed. Maria P.P. Root. Thousand Oaks, Calif.: Sage, 1997. 39–61.

Rose, Jacqueline. *Sexuality in the Field of Vision*. London and New York: Verso, 1986.

Rugg, Linda Haverty. *Picturing Ourselves: Photography & Autobiography*. Chicago: University of Chicago Press, 1997.

Said, Edward W. *Culture and Imperialism*. New York: Vintage Books, 1993.

– *Orientalism*. New York: Vintage, 1979; rpt with an Afterword, 1994.

Sakamoto, Kerri. *The Electrical Field*. Toronto: Vintage Canada, 1998.

San Juan, Epifanio, Jr. *Allegories of Resistance: The Philippines at the Threshold of the Twenty-First Century*. Quezon City: University of the Philippines Press, 1994.

– *Articulations of Power in Ethnic and Racial Studies in the United States*. Atlantic Highlands, N.J.: Humanities Press, 1992.

– *The Philippine Temptation: Dialectics of Philippines–U.S. Literary Relations*. Philadelphia: Temple University Press, 1996.

– 'Postcolonial Theory Versus Philippine Reality: The Challenge of Third World Resistance Culture to Global Capitalism.' *Journal of English Studies and Comparative Literature*. 1.1 (December 1996): 25–57.

Santos, Bienvenido N. *The Man Who (Thought He) Looked Like Robert Taylor*. Quezon City: New Day, 1983.

– 'Pilipino Old Timers: Fact and Fiction.' *Reading Bienvenido N. Santos*. Ed. Isagani R. Cruz and David Jonathan Bayot. Manila: De La Salle University Press, 1994. 24–34.

– *Scent of Apples*. Seattle: University of Washington Press, 1979.

Schatenstein, Elaine. 'Concubine's Granddaughter Relates Intriguing Family History.' *Montreal Gazette*. 14 May 1994: I:3.

Schaub, Thomas. 'Ellison's Mask and the Novel of Reality.' *New Essays on Invisible Man*. Ed. Robert O'Meally. New York: Cambridge University Press, 1988. 123–56.

Scott, Joan Wallach. 'The Evidence of Experience.' *The Historic Turn in the Human Sciences*. Ed. Terrence J. McDonald. Ann Arbor: University of Michigan Press, 1996. 379–406.

Seiler, Tamara Palmer. 'Multi-Vocality and National Literature: Towards a Post-Colonial and Multicultural Aesthetic.' *Literary Pluralities*. Ed. Christl Verduyn. Peterborough, Ont.: Broadview Press, 1998. 47–63.

Shankar, Lavina Dhingra, and Rajini Srikanth, eds. *A Part, Yet Apart: South Asians in Asian America*. Philadelphia: Temple University Press, 1998.

Shaw, George Bernard. *Saint Joan*. *Modern British Literature*. Ed. Frank Kermode and John Hollander. New York: Oxford University Press, 1973. 34–104.

Shohat, Ella, and Robert Stam. 'From the Imperial Family to the Transnational Imaginary: Media Spectatorship in the Age of Globalization.' *Global/Local:*

Cultural Production and the Transnational Imaginary. Ed. Rob Wilson and Wimal Dissanayake. Durham, N.C.: Duke University Press, 1996. 145–70.
– *Unthinking Eurocentrism: Multiculturalism and the Media*. London and New York: Routledge, 1994.
Siemerling, Winfried, ed. *Writing Ethnicity: Cross-Cultural Consciousness in Canadian and Québécois Literature*. Toronto: ECW Press, 1996.
Silverman, Kaja. *The Acoustic Mirror: The Female Voice in Psychoanalysis and Cinema*. Bloomington: Indiana University Press, 1988.
– 'Fragments of a Fashionable Discourse.' *Studies in Entertainment: Critical Approaches to Mass Culture*. Ed. Tania Modleski. Bloomington: Indiana University Press, 1986. 139–52.
– *The Subject of Semiotics*. New York: Oxford University Press, 1983.
– *The Threshold of the Visible World*. New York and London: Routledge, 1996.
Singh, Kirpal. 'An Interview with Shirley Geok-lin Lim.' *ARIEL: A Review of International English Literature* 30.4 (October 1999): 135–41.
Smith, Paul. *Discerning the Subject*. Minneapolis: University of Minnesota Press, 1988.
Smith, Shawn Michelle. 'Photographing the "American Negro": Nation, Race, and Photography at the Paris Exposition of 1900.' *With Other Eyes: Looking at Race and Gender in Visual Culture*. Ed. Lisa Bloom. Minneapolis: University of Minnesota Press, 1999. 58–87.
Smith, Sidonie. *A Poetics of Women's Autobiography: Marginality and the Fictions of Self-Representation*. Bloomington: Indiana University Press, 1987.
Sollors, Werner. *The Invention of Ethnicity*. New York: Oxford University Press, 1989.
Souris, Stephen. '"Only Two Kinds of Daughters": Inter-Monologue Dialogicity in *The Joy Luck Club*.' *MELUS* 19.2 (Summer 1994): 99–123.
Stallybrass, Peter, and Allon White. *The Politics and Poetics of Transgression*. Ithaca: Cornell University Press, 1986.
Stam, Robert. 'The Question of Realism.' *Film and Theory: An Anthology*. Ed. Robert Stam and Toby Miller. Oxford: Blackwell, 2000. 223–28.
Statistics Canada. 'Visible Minority Population, 1996 Census.' 4 July 2001. http://www.statcan.ca/english/Pgdb/People/Population/demo40b.htm.
Stewart, Susan. *On Longing: Narratives of the Miniature, the Gigantic, the Souvenir, the Collection*. Durham, N.C.: Duke University Press, 1993.
Strobel, Leny Mendoza. '"Born-Again Filipino": Filipino American Identity and Asian Panethnicity.' *Amerasia Journal* 22.2 (1996): 31–53.
Tadiar, Neferti Xina M. 'Sexual Economies in the Asia-Pacific Community.' *What's in a Rim? Critical Perspectives on the Pacific Region Idea*. Ed. Arif Dirlik. Lanham, Md.: Rowman and Littlefield, 1998. 219–48.

Tagg, John. *The Burden of Representation: Essays on Photographies and Histories.* Amherst: University of Massachusetts Press, 1988.

Takaki, Ronald. *Strangers from a Different Shore: A History of Asian Americans.* Boston: Little, Brown and Company, 1989.

Tan, Amy. *The Bonesetter's Daughter.* New York: Ballantine, 2001.

– *The Joy Luck Club.* New York: Ivy Books, 1989.

– *The Kitchen God's Wife.* New York: Ivy Books, 1991.

Thinkquest Team. 'The Philippines Under Martial Law.' *The Edsa Revolution Website.* 30 January 2001. http://library.thinkquest.org/15816/the beginning.article4.html.

Tolentino, Rolando B. 'Bodies, Letters, Catalogs: Filipinos in Transnational Space.' *Transnational Asia Pacific: Gender, Culture, and the Public Sphere.* Ed. Shirley Geok-lin Lim, Larry E. Smith, and Wimal Dissanayake. Urbana: University of Illiniois Press, 1999. 43–68.

Tomlinson, John. *Cultural Imperialism: A Critical Introduction.* Baltimore: Johns Hopkins University Press, 1991.

Trinh, Minh-ha T. 'Outside In Inside Out.' *Questions of Third Cinema.* Ed. Jim Pines and Paul Willemen. London: British Film Institute, 1989. 133–49.

TuSmith, Bonnie. *All My Relatives: Community in Contemporary Ethnic American Literatures.* Ann Arbor: University of Michigan Press, 1994.

Ty, Eleanor. *Empowering the Feminine: The Narratives of Mary Robinson, Jane West, and Amelia Opie, 1796–1812.* Toronto: University of Toronto Press, 1998.

– 'Exoticism Repositioned: Old and New World Pleasures in Wang's *Joy Luck Club* and Lee's *Eat Drink Man Woman*.' Vol. 11 *Literary Studies East and West: Changing Representation of Minorities East and West.* Honolulu: University of Hawaii, 1996. 59–74.

– 'A Filipino Prufrock in an Alien Land: Bienvenido Santos' *The Man Who (Thought He) Looked Like Robert Taylor*.' *Lit: Literature, Interpretation, Theory. Special Issue on Asian American Literature and Culture.* Part II. 12.3 (2001): 267–83.

– 'Struggling with the Powerful (M)Other: Identity and Sexuality in Kogawa's *Obasan* and Kincaid's *Lucy*.' *International Fiction Review* 20.2 (1993): 120–6.

– *Unsex'd Revolutionaries: Five Women Novelists of the 1790s.* Toronto: University of Toronto Press, 1993.

– 'Welcome to Dreamland: Power, Gender, and Post-Colonial Politics in *Miss Saigon*.' *Essays in Theatre* 13.1 (November 1994): 15–27.

Uchida, Aki. 'The Orientalization of Asian Women in America.' *Women's Studies International Forum* 21.2 (1998): 161–74.

University of Michigan, Museum of Zoology, Insect Division. 'Cicadas of
     Michigan.' 18 April 2001. http://insects.ummz.lsa.umich.edu/...chigan_
     cicadas/Michigan/Index.html.
U.S. Army Center for Military History. *A View of Our Past*. 14 January 2003.
     http://www.army.mil/cmh-pg/.
U.S. Census Bureau. 'Resident Population Estimates of the United States by
     Sex, Race, and Hispanic Origin: April 1, 1990 to July 1, 1999, with Short-
     Term Projections to November 1, 2000.' 2 January 2001, 4 July 2001. http://
     www.census.gov/population/estimates/nation/intfile3-1.txt.
Varadharajan, Asha. *Exotic Parodies: Subjectivity in Adorno, Said, and Spivak*.
     Minneapolis: University of Minnesota Press, 1995.
Verduyn, Christl, ed. *Literary Pluralities*. Peterborough: Broadview and *Journal
     of Canadian Studies*, 1998.
Walker, Alice. 'In Search of Our Mothers' Gardens.' *The Norton Anthology of
     Literature by Women*. Ed. Sandra Gilbert and Susan Gubar. New York:
     Norton, 1985. 2374–82.
Whitford, Margaret. *Luce Irigaray: Philosophy in the Feminine*. London and New
     York: Routledge, 1991.
Williams, Tennessee. *A Streetcar Named Desire*. *The Norton Introduction to
     Literature*. Shorter Seventh Edition. Ed. Jerome Beaty and J. Paul Hunter.
     New York: Norton, 1998. 1584–651.
Wolf, Margery. *Revolution Postponed: Women in Contemporary China*. Stanford:
     Stanford University Press, 1985.
Wong, Sau-ling Cynthia. 'Denationalization Reconsidered: Asian American
     Cultural Criticism at a Theoretical Crossroads.' *Amerasia Journal* 21.1–2
     (1995): 1–27.
  – 'Ethnicizing Gender: An Exploration of Sexuality as Sign in Chinese Immi-
     grant Literature.' *Reading the Literatures of Asian America*. Ed. Shirley Geok-
     lin Lim and Amy Ling. Philadelphia: Temple University Press, 1992. 111–29.
  – '"Sugar Sisterhood": Situating the Amy Tan Phenomenon.' *The Ethnic
     Canon: Histories, Institutions, and Interventions*. Minneapolis: University of
     Minnesota Press, 1995. 174–212.
  – *Reading Asian American Literature: From Necessity to Extravagance*. Princeton:
     Princeton University Press, 1993.
Wong, Sau-ling Cynthia, and Stephen H. Sumida. *A Resources Guide to Asian
     American Literature*. New York: Modern Language Association, 2001.
Woodside, Alexander. 'The Asia-Pacific Idea as a Mobilization Myth.' *What's
     in a Rim? Critical Perspectives on the Pacific Region Idea*. Ed. Arif Dirlik.
     Lanham, Md.: Rowman and Littlefield, 1998.
Woolf, Virginia. *To the Lighthouse*. Frogmore: Triad Panther, 1977.

– 'Women and Fiction.' *Prose Pieces: Essays and Stories.* Ed. Pat C. Hoy and
  Robert Diyanni. New York: Random House, 1988.
Wu, David Yen-ho. 'The Construction of Chinese and Non-Chinese Identities.'
  The Living Tree: The Changing Meaning of Being Chinese. Ed. Tu Wei-Ming.
  Stanford: Stanford University Press, 1994. 148–66.
Xing, Jun. *Asian America through the Lens: History, Representations and Identity.*
  Walnut Creek, Calif.: Altamira Press, 1998.
Xu, Ben. 'Memory and the Ethnic Self: Reading Amy Tan's *The Joy Luck Club.*'
  MELUS: Multi-Ethnic Literature of the United States 19.1 (Spring 1994): 3–18.
Yamamoto, Traise. *Masking Selves, Making Subjects: Japanese American Women,
  Identity, and the Body.* Berkeley: University of California Press, 1999.
Young, Robert J.C. *Colonial Desire: Hybridity in Theory, Culture and Race.* New
  York: Routledge, 1995.
Yuan-Yuan. 'Mothers' "China Narrative": Recollection and Translation in
  Amy Tan's *The Joy Luck Club* and *The Kitchen God's Wife.*' *The Chinese in
  America: A History from Gold Mountain to the New Millennium.* Ed. Susie Lan
  Cassel. Walnut Creek, Calif.: Altamira Press, 2002. 351–63.
Zackodnik, Teresa. 'Suggestive Voices from "the Storeroom of the Past":
  Photography in Denise Chong's *The Concubine's Children.*' *Essays on Cana-
  dian Writing* 72 (Winter 2000): 49–78.
Zwick, Jim. 'Militarism and Repression in the Philippines.' Reprinted from *The
  State as Terrorist: The Dynamics of Governmental Violence and Repression.* Ed.
  Michael Stohl and George A. Lopez. Westport, Conn.: Greenwood Press,
  1984. 30 January 2001. http://www.boondocksnet.com/sctexts/
  zwick84a.html.

Index

abjection, xii, 26, 111; abject figures, 38–9; splitting of abject qualities, xiv

Adachi, Ken, 15, 16, 17, 18, 20, 21, 22

African Americans: 5, 25; hypervisibility of, 24; parallels in racialization, 27

Ahmad, Aijaz, 199n5

Alaras, Consolacion, 201n9

Allen, Woody: *Manhattan*, 196n2

American dream, 65–6, 179

American goods, 148, 172, 174. *See also* United States

Anderson, Benedict, 43, 91

Ang, Ien, 70, 71, 72, 85

Asian Americans, 5; authors, 12, 185; bodies, 88; history of 13–19; identities, 81; literature, 30; men, 14–17, 160; relationship with other ethnic minorities, 63; theory, 30; women, 24, 159

Asian Canadians: actors, 78–9; authors, 12, 185; characteristics, 117; classification of, 7–8; development of literature, 24; experiences, 81, 122–3; history of, 13–19; identities, 121–2; theory, 30

Asians: fears of, 35, 56; markings on bodies, 4, 8, 11–12, 25, 28, 70, 186–7, 192n27; regulation of, 20; as scapegoats, 19; violence against, 14–16; women, 92

assimilation, 69, 165; women, 159

Austen, Jane, xi

autoethnography, 36, 43

Bakhtin, Mikhail: *Dialogic Imagination*, 76, 154, 156–7, 196n3; double-voiced discourse, 157; *Rabelais and His World*, 108. *See also* dialogic, heteroglossia

Bangladesh, immigrants from, 23

Bannerji, Himani, xiv, 6, 195n6

Banton, Michael, 190n10

Barthes, Roland, 39

Bataan, 200n2

Bates, Judy Fong, 199n9

Beauregard, Guy, 24, 153

Bell, Shannon, 34, 37, 194n4

Bergland, Betty, xiv